Everything on Earth

A DORLING KINDERSLEY BOOK

LONDON, NEW YORK, MUNICH,
MELBOURNE, AND DELHI

Written by Michael Allaby, Trevor
Day, Dr Frances Dipper, Ben Morgan
Senior Editors Carrie Love and
Caroline Stamps
Project Art Editor Rachael Grady
Design Team Jacqueline Gooden,
Tory Gordon-Harris, Elaine Hewson,
Marcus James, Claire Penny
Editorial Team Simon Holland,
Lucy Hurst, Fran Jones, Deborah Lock,
Lee Stacy, Zahavit Shalev, Lee Simmons
Category Publisher Mary Ling
Art Director Rachael Foster
Publishing Manager Bridget Giles
Jacket Design Natalie Godwin
Jacket Editor Mariza O'Keeffe
Production Editor Sean Daly
Production Controller Claire Pearson

Content first published in various titles of the
DK Guides series (Birds, Mammals, Oceans, Savage Earth,
and Weather) in the United Kingdom between 2000 and
2004 by Dorling Kindersley.
This edition © copyright Dorling Kindersley 2009.

Dorling Kindersley Limited
80 Strand, London WC2R ORL
A Penguin Company 8PS

2 4 6 8 10 9 7 5 3 1

Rap date 176800 - 08/09

A CIP catalogue record for this book
is available from the British Library

ISBN 9-7814-0534-909-3

Reproduced in Italy by GRB Editrice, Verona

Discover more at
www.dk.com

CONTENTS

EARTH

4 Earth
6 The Big Bang
8 All about Earth
10 Violent Past
12 The Atmosphere
14 Moving Continents
16 Volcanoes
18 Rivers of Fire
20 Emerging Islands
22 Making Mountains
24 Earthquakes
26 Shock Waves
28 Caves and Caverns
30 Buried Treasure
32 Icy Extremes
34 Glaciers
36 Deserts
38 Wildfires
40 Global Ecosystems
42 Savage Future
44 Earth Data

WEATHER

46 Weather
48 Restless Planet
50 The Weather Engine
52 Climate and Seasons
54 Clouds
56 Mist, Fog, and Dew
58 Rain
60 Light Shows
62 Solar Wonders
64 Snow
66 Hail
68 Storm Clouds
70 Lightning
72 Duststorms
74 El Niño
76 Tornadoes
78 Hurricanes
80 Floods
82 Hot and Dry
84 Weathering and Erosion
86 Volcanic Weather
88 Climate Change
90 Drowning World
92 Pollution
94 Weather Forecasting
96 Harnessing Weather
98 Weather Data

OCEANS

100 Oceans
102 One Ocean
104 The Big Blue
106 Ocean Motion
108 Creating Coasts
110 Sandy Shores
112 Rocky Shores
114 On the Edge
116 Coral Reefs
118 Reef Life
120 Forests and Meadows
122 Sunlit Waters
124 Submarine Landscapes
126 Midwater Mysteries
128 Deep Plains
130 Island Refuge
132 Frozen Seas
134 Marine Migrations
136 Perfect Balance
138 Partners and Parasites
140 Survival
142 The Killers
144 Going Down
146 Marine Archaeology
148 Tsunami
150 Harvest from the Sea
152 Impact on the Oceans
154 Remote Sensing
156 Fluid World
158 Tides of Change
160 Ocean Data

MAMMALS

162 Mammals
164 What is a Mammal?
166 Temperature Control
168 Reproduction
170 Growing Up
172 Primitive Primates
174 The Apes
176 Brain Power
178 On the Hoof
180 Cat Family
182 Social Lives
184 Small and Wily
186 Homes and Shelters
188 Endurance
190 Insect Eaters
192 On the Wing
194 Life in Water
196 Ocean Giants
198 Marsupials
200 Taming the Beast
202 Mammal Data

BIRDS

204 Birds
206 What is a Bird?
208 Built for Flight
210 Up and Away
212 Aerial Acrobats
214 Birds of Prey
216 Scavengers
218 Fisher Kings
220 Beside the Sea
222 Waders and Floaters
224 Bird Food
226 Birds in the Woods
228 Feathers and Finery
230 The Mating Game
232 Master Builders
234 Eggs
236 Family Life
238 Songbirds
240 Keep Away!
242 Epic Journeys
244 Flightless Birds
246 Strange But True
248 Bird Data

250 **GLOSSARY**
252 **INDEX**
255 **CREDITS AND ACKNOWLEDGEMENTS**

EARTH

SINCE ITS BIRTH SOME 4.5 BILLION YEARS ago, our planet has been shaped and moulded like a gigantic ball of putty. Although the rocks and mountains, the beaches and oceans around us look like they are stable, they are ever changing. Continents shift, sometimes resulting in violent earthquakes and volcanic eruptions. Mountains are born, and islands appear in the sea. Earth is a work in progress.

THE BIG BANG

To UNDERSTAND HOW OUR PLANET WAS CREATED, we have to look into space. The savage forces that batter, shake, and shape the Earth's surface today were set in motion billions of years ago and are still going strong. Beneath the surface, immense heat causes molten rock to circulate, moving giant sections of the crust, triggering earthquakes, and shooting out molten rock from volcanoes. The enormously high pressures and temperatures deep inside the Earth continue to generate heat through radioactive decay and chemical changes. The Sun, however, has much more power, and without its light and warmth, life here would not exist. But the Earth's story really begins with the biggest explosion the Universe has ever known – the one that created it.

SOMETHING FROM NOTHING

Most scientists now agree that everything we know – time, space, and all the matter in the Universe – started with the Big Bang. About 13.7 billion years ago, the Universe simply burst into existence from nothing. The bang was so violent that matter was created spontaneously out of energy. At the instant of creation, the Universe was infinitely hot and dense. In the next instant, it was 20,000 light years across. It continued to expand and created the galaxies, stars, and planets. About 4.6 billion years ago, our own Solar System came into being.

UNIQUE EARTH

Among the planets in the Solar System, Earth is unique. Seen from space, its swirling clouds and blue oceans show that it has plenty of liquid water. The Earth's gravity is strong enough to trap a protective atmosphere. It is also the right distance from the Sun to have habitable climates. Water and an atmosphere are two conditions vital for the evolution of life as we know it.

STAR MAKER

Inside its whirling clouds of cosmic dust, the spectacular Orion nebula gives birth to stars. Our Sun was created in the same way by the dust of the vast solar nebula, several billion years ago. When the solar nebula grew old, material was drawn into its centre, which became denser and hotter as it generated energy by nuclear fusion. In a gigantic nuclear explosion, the infant Sun was born, and began radiating the first sunshine in our Solar System.

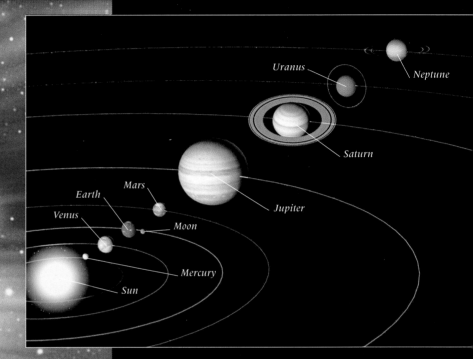

Uranus

Neptune

Saturn

Earth   *Mars*

Venus

Jupiter

Moon

Mercury

Sun

SOLAR SYSTEM

When our Solar System was forming, the early Sun probably lay at the centre of a disc-shaped cloud. Inside the cloud were liquids and gases, swirling around with dust and ice. Under the pull of gravity, dust particles clumped together to form rocks. Metal-rich rocks near the Sun came together to form the inner planets. In the cooler, outer regions, ice combined with rock and lighter gases to form the outer planets.

LIFE ELSEWHERE?

The conditions that allow complex life forms to flourish on Earth might be rare elsewhere in the Universe. Simple microbes, however, can survive in the most hostile places, and may exist on other planets or their moons. In 1996, a Martian meteorite found in Antarctica contained what at first appeared to be fossilized bacteria (*right*). Some scientists believe Mars may once have sustained simple, microbial life.

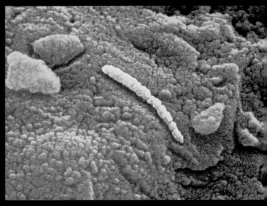

ALL ABOUT EARTH

PLANET EARTH – THE THIRD "ROCK" FROM THE SUN – is unique in many ways. It is the only planet scientists know that can support life – thanks to the water in its oceans and the oxygen in its atmosphere. Unlike Mercury, which is intensely hot, and Neptune, which is extremely cold, Earth sits at an ideal distance from the Sun. For its size, Earth is very heavy due to the large iron core at its centre. The churning motion of the liquid iron creates a powerful magnetic field that shields Earth from harmful particles streaming out of the Sun. Earth's atmosphere also screens out dangerous radiation from the Sun.

RESTLESS EARTH

The Earth is not a solid ball, but is made up of many different layers. On the surface is a thin shell of solid rock – the crust. This forms the continents and ocean floors. Heat carried upwards from the central core forces sections of the crust, called plates, to move. As this happens many of the Earth's natural features are created or changed.

This image shows the Earth's crust with the water drained away.

EARTH'S ATMOSPHERE

Water covers about 70 per cent of the Earth's surface. It keeps temperatures moderate and releases water vapour into the atmosphere. The mixture of water vapour and other gases wrapped around the Earth creates the atmosphere. Its swirling white clouds are constantly moving, blown round the planet by the wind.

From space, the continents appear dark green or brown, and the oceans appear blue. As most of the Middle East is free of clouds, the deserts of North Africa and the Arabian peninsula are visible.

A WATERY PLANET

Water on the Earth takes many different forms. It is found as a liquid (in rain, lakes, rivers, and oceans), as a gas (invisible water vapour), and solid (as ice). Water not only makes life on Earth possible, but also shapes the land. This photo shows a network of channels as the River Ganges enters the Bay of Bengal. The flat land has been built by river sediment deposited over thousands of years.

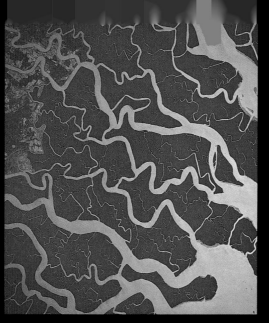

Ganges Delta seen from the Space Shuttle

MOUNTAIN RANGES

Great mountain ranges generally occur where two of Earth's plates have collided and one is forced up to form high peaks. Mt Everest in the Himalayas, seen here from the Space Shuttle, is the highest peak above sea level. However, Mauna Loa, a volcanic island in Hawaii, is Earth's tallest mountain, measured from its base on the ocean floor to its highest point.

Mt Everest lies on the border of China/Nepal.

Wildlife in Yosemite National Park, USA

TEEMING WITH LIFE

Life exists almost everywhere on Earth – from the highest mountains to the deepest underground caves. No one knows how many species of living things there are on Earth, but the total runs into millions. The first primitive forms of life probably appeared in the oceans about 3.8 billion years ago. Animals did not evolve until about 600 million years ago, while modern humans appeared only 100,000 years ago.

EARTHQUAKES AND VOLCANOES

The boundaries of Earth's plates can be dangerous places to live. Major earthquakes occur where plates collide or slide past each other. In cities such as San Francisco, large-scale earthquakes have produced more energy than an atomic bomb. Volcanoes erupt when molten rock escapes to the surface, exploding lava and ash over huge areas. Here Klyuchevskaya volcano in Russia belches a cloud of brown ash.

This view of Earth was taken from the Apollo 17 spacecraft on its journey to the Moon.

An erupting volcano, seen from the Space Shuttle

VIOLENT PAST

THE EARLY EARTH WAS A RED-HOT, MOLTEN HELL. Space debris from the collapsed solar nebula was flying in all directions, causing meteorites and comets to smash into the young planet's surface. These violent bombardments raised the Earth's temperature higher and higher. Then, not long after it was formed some 4.6 billion years ago, the Earth was struck by an object the size of Mars. The impact released a heat so intense that it melted the planet. Debris from the impact explosion splashed out into Space and gathered together to form the Moon. But the Earth did not remain searingly hot. It gradually cooled into a planet with a solid surface, oceans, continents, and an atmosphere. In fact, for more than three-quarters of its existence the Earth has sustained living organisms. Now approaching middle-age, the Earth has about five billion years left to bask in the life-giving heat of the Sun.

Atmosphere

Crust

Mantle

Outer core

Molten outer core

Solid inner core

EARTH'S TRANSFORMATION
More than four billion years ago, the Earth's molten rock began to separate into layers. Heavy, iron-rich material sank to the intensely hot core. Silicon-rich material gathered at the surface to form a crust. Molten rock became sandwiched between the core and crust to form the mantle. On the surface, granite-like rocks thickened the crust and formed the first continents.

BLASTS OF THE PAST
This is an artist's impression of the young Earth's violent landscape. Space debris and lava flows must have ravaged the brittle crust. As meteorites landed, they punched holes in the surface and plunged into the hot interior, sending up huge showers of molten rock. Gradually, the thin surface crust grew thicker. From time to time, slabs of cooled crust plunged back into the molten mantle below and were melted again.

DINO KILLER
For more than 100 million years, the Earth was ruled by dinosaurs. They became extinct quite suddenly about 65 million years ago. Their disappearance was probably caused by a massive meteorite or comet that collided with the Earth. The impact would have shrouded the world in a cloud of dust that blotted out the Sun for many months. In the freezing darkness, most of the world's plant and animal life died, including the dinosaurs. Some small, hibernating racoon-like mammals survived.

OCEANS

The water that filled the first oceans may have come from comets that collided with the Earth. A comet (*left*) is a giant snowball of ice and rock. Water also came from the steam given off by molten rock (magma) flowing onto the surface. The steam condensed in the atmosphere, formed clouds, and fell to Earth as rain, just as the steam from volcanoes does today.

THE SUN

Our Sun is an average-sized star similar to billions of others in the galaxy. Without its heat, Earth would be uninhabitable. Scientists calculate that the Sun has about five billion years of life left before it uses up its fuel supply of hydrogen. When it does, it will expand 100 times in size into a massive sphere called a red giant, and will destroy the Earth.

ATMOSPHERE

The Earth's early atmosphere was rich in volcano gases such as carbon dioxide. Today's atmosphere has little carbon dioxide, but contains oxygen. The change was caused by early life forms – tiny organisms that released oxygen as waste. These clumps (*left*) are made by microbes called cyanobacteria, which trap sunlight to make food. They are very similar to the early oxygen-making organisms.

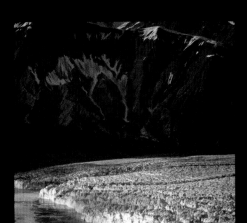

ICE AGES

Despite its fiery origins, much of the Earth has been covered in ice during its history. Ice spread from the poles towards the Equator when the climate cooled, and retreated as it warmed. This may have been caused by a slow wobble of the Earth's axis, which alters its distance from the Sun. Present-day glaciers (*left*) show us how the world must have looked during the ice ages.

THE ATMOSPHERE

S EEN FROM SPACE, EARTH IS SURROUNDED by a glowing blue
haze. This haze is the atmosphere – the blanket of air and
moisture, trapped by gravity, that covers our planet and makes
life possible. The atmosphere is surprisingly thin. If you could
drive straight up in a car, it would take less than 10 minutes to
pass through the bottom layer, or troposphere, where all the
weather takes place, and only about three hours to reach space.
Because of gravity, the troposphere is the most dense part of the
atmosphere, and contains 80 per cent of the air and nearly all
the moisture. Warmed by the Sun and stirred by Earth's
rotation, the troposphere is a continually swirling mass of cloud
and air. High above it, the thinning atmosphere gradually peters
out as the rarefied air fades into the vacuum of space.

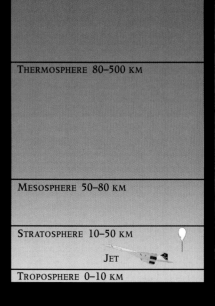

AURORA

SPACECRAFT

METEOR
TRAILS

AURORA

ATMOSPHERE LAYERS
Scientists divide the atmosphere into
distinct layers according to temperature.
The temperature drops as you go up
through the troposphere, but then starts
rising as you move through the next layer,
the stratosphere. The boundary between
these layers is called the tropopause. The
air at the tropopause is extremely cold
and dry, and there is almost no moisture
(and hence no weather) above it.

ABOVE THE CLOUDS
Clouds form in the troposphere. Only the
very biggest storm clouds grow tall enough
to poke through into the stratosphere.
Aeroplanes fly in the upper troposphere or
lower stratosphere so they often have to
pass through dense banks of cloud during
their climb to cruising height. As they
break through the layers of cloud they
give passengers breathtaking views
across the cloud tops.

THERMOSPHERE 80–500 KM

MESOSPHERE 50–80 KM

STRATOSPHERE 10–50 KM

JET

TROPOSPHERE 0–10 KM

Dry air sinks over the world's deserts.

Warm air rises at the equator until it hits the top of the troposphere and can rise no further.

The circulating air patterns are called "cells".

WESTERLIES

TRADE WINDS

DOLDRUMS

DOLDRUMS

TRADE WINDS

WESTERLIES

The area where the trade winds die out is known as the doldrums. Sailors used to fear being stranded there.

Very cold air sinks at the poles and flows outwards, creating winds called easterlies.

GLOBAL WINDS

The Sun's heat and the Earth's rotation combine to create global patterns of wind. Warmed by hot, tropical sunshine, air at the equator rises to the top of the troposphere and then spreads north and south, dumping most of its moisture as rain over the wet tropics. Further north and south, the now dry air sinks, creating desert conditions. After sinking, some of it flows back to the equator as the "trade winds" (red arrows), deflected west by the Earth's spin. The rest flows poleward as winds called "westerlies" (orange arrows) until it meets cold polar air (blue). Where the two air masses collide, the warmer air is forced up again and recirculated in the troposphere.

ATLANTIC CROSSING

The trade winds are so dependable that explorers once used them to reach the Americas. Italian explorer Christopher Columbus made his first transatlantic voyage in 1492 thanks to the trade winds, and returned by the westerlies.

JET-STREAM

In World War II aircrews flying across the North Pacific found that sometimes they travelled very fast on eastbound routes and much more slowly on westbound routes. Scientists worked out that there must be a very strong wind blowing from west to east right around the world. This is called the jet-stream, and there are two in each hemisphere, both at the top of the troposphere. Even today pilots hitch a ride in the jet-stream, using it to cut hours off the time it takes to fly from the USA to Europe.

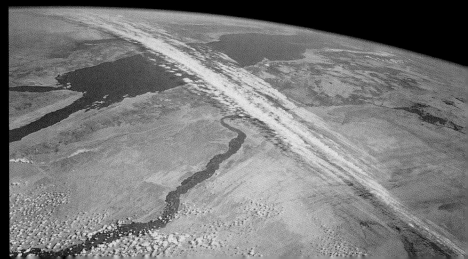

JET-STREAM CLOUDS
OVER THE RIVER

MOVING CONTINENTS

THE GROUND BENEATH OUR FEET IS NOT AS STEADY as we may think. In fact, the continents that make up most of the Earth's land surface are always on the move, shifted around by forces deep inside the Earth. This movement is known as continental drift. It takes place because the inside of the planet is hot and turbulent. The intense heat generated at the Earth's core is carried upwards where it disturbs the cool, rocky surface. This forces the plates of crust that make up the continents, called tectonic plates, to move. Each year the continents drift by about a centimetre (half an inch). Some are crunching together, some are splitting apart, others are grinding past each other. As this happens the Earth's features are created or changed. Violent earthquakes and volcanoes are dramatic reminders that the plates never stop moving.

TECTONIC PLATES
Each tectonic plate has a lower layer of solid rock and an upper layer called the crust. The plates ride upon Earth's slowly moving, mostly solid mantle. Where the crust is thin, the Earth's surface is low-lying and covered by seas and oceans. Continents form where the crust is thicker and stands higher. As the tectonic plates move, the continents are carried with them and the oceans change shape.

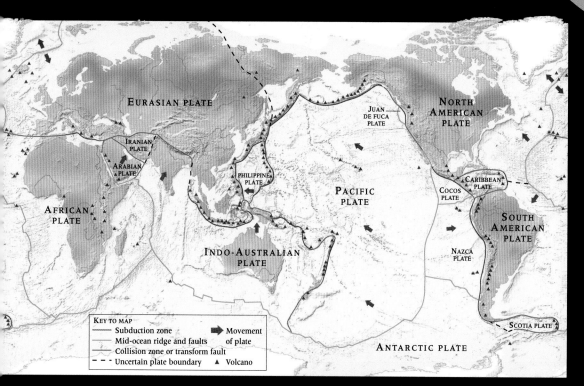

KEY TO MAP
— Subduction zone
— Mid-ocean ridge and faults
— Collision zone or transform fault
- - - Uncertain plate boundary
➡ Movement of plate
▲ Volcano

EURASIAN PLATE
IRANIAN PLATE
ARABIAN PLATE
AFRICAN PLATE
PHILIPPINE PLATE
INDO-AUSTRALIAN PLATE
JUAN DE FUCA PLATE
NORTH AMERICAN PLATE
PACIFIC PLATE
COCOS PLATE
CARIBBEAN PLATE
SOUTH AMERICAN PLATE
NAZCA PLATE
SCOTIA PLATE
ANTARCTIC PLATE

GLOBAL JIGSAW PUZZLE
The plates that form the Earth's surface fit together like a jigsaw puzzle. This map shows the boundaries of the Earth's plates and the directions in which the plates are drifting. The pieces slowly change shape as they move. Great mountain ranges have formed along the blue zones where plates are colliding. Lines of volcanoes are dotted along the red zones where one plate is sinking (subducting) below another, causing molten rock to erupt to the surface.

THE EVIDENCE
When the German scientist Alfred Wegener stated in 1915 that today's continents were once part of a single landmass, people ridiculed him. But Wegener was right. He argued that although ancient plant fossils, such as the *Glossopteris* fern (*right*) are found on widely separated continents, they could only have come from one original continent. Today, geologists agree with Wegener that the continents did indeed drift apart

Ocean trench forms where one plate sinks below another.

Spreading boundary, where two plates move apart.

Transform fault, where two plates slide past each other.

Continental crust

Subsiding plate

Volcano fed from subsiding plate.

Magma rising from the mantle.

Convergent boundary, where collided continental crust has uplifted mountains.

WHEN PLATES COLLIDE

The Andes Mountains of South America extend along the Pacific coast for about 8,900 km (5,530 miles). They began to form some 170 million years ago when the Nazca Plate collided with (and sank beneath) the South American plate. The foothills (*above*) show where a folding, or buckling, of the continental crust has occurred. Mountain-building in the Andes slowed down about 6 million years ago.

PLATE BOUNDARIES

The illustration above shows what happens at the boundaries that separate one plate from another. At spreading boundaries, plates are moving apart, and molten rock (magma) rises up to fill the gaps. Transform faults lie along boundaries where plates scrape past one another, generating earthquakes. Where convergent boundaries are found, plates are pushing together to create mountain ranges in a process of folding and uplifting.

WEST OF JAVA

This is Anak Krakatoa in Indonesia, a volcano that first erupted in 1927. It is one of a long string of volcanoes that lies along a boundary where the Indo-Australian plate is sliding below the Eurasian plate. The subsiding plate melts as it is forced downwards into the Earth's mantle, and squeezes magma to the surface to form volcanoes.

SPREADING RIDGES

The Mid-Atlantic Ridge is a spreading plate boundary that stretches from the Arctic to the Southern Ocean. Most of it lies beneath the ocean, but at Thingvellir in Iceland (*left*), it crosses over land. The boundary between the North American plate on the left and the Eurasian plate on the right is clearly visible. Where the plates have moved apart, the crust in between has collapsed, forming a steep-sided rift valley. The region is very active volcanically. In 1963, a huge underwater eruption occurred 130 km (80 miles) south of Thingvellir. Lava rose to fill the gap in the widening ridge, and cooled to form the new island of Surtsey (learn more on page 20).

15

VOLCANOES

THERE IS A THUNDEROUS EXPLOSION, the ground trembles, and the sky darkens. A volcano is erupting, firing red-hot boulders into the air and belching out clouds of ash and poisonous fumes. Volcanoes are vents or fissures in the Earth's crust that allow molten rock to rise up from the hot interior and spill onto the surface. An active volcano may erupt continuously, and over time may become a broad mountain with gentle slopes. Other volcanoes may lie dormant (sleeping) for most of the time. They erupt only at rare intervals but with explosions violent enough to destroy their own cones and a wide surrounding area. Many of the Earth's mountains were formerly volcanoes, but are now extinct. Today, there are more than 1,000 active volcanoes on land, and many more under the sea.

INSIDE AN EXPLODING VOLCANO

Within and beneath Earth's crust, rock can become so hot that it melts. This molten rock, called magma, can rise through a gap in the crust and become trapped in a magma chamber – a cavity beneath the volcano. As more magma enters, pressure builds up until the volcano's clogged vent is blasted open. The feeder pipe to the vent then acts like a gun barrel that shoots out lava, rocks, ash, and steam.

Cone is built up by successive layers of lava and ash over thousands of years.

Magma collects in the magma chamber and builds up pressure in the clogged vent.

ALL SHAPES AND SIZES

A volcano's shape depends on the thickness of its lava and the frequency and size of its eruptions. Dome volcanoes build up cones from the layers of lava and ash they produce. Fissure volcanoes are fairly flat, and trickle lava from big cracks in the ground. Caldera volcanoes, like this one (*left*) at Crater Lake, Oregon, USA, lie inside vast craters made by a previous, massive explosion that collapsed the original mountain.

HOTSPOT

Most volcanoes occur where the Earth's plates collide or move apart. But some, like the Hawaiian islands, arose in the middle of a plate because they were created by a "hot spot" in the Earth's mantle, which burned through the crust and formed a volcano. The volcano stops erupting as the moving plate carries it away from the hot spot, and a new volcano forms. The chain of islands grows as the plate moves.

Hawaii is formed from the world's tallest volcanic cone. It is a recent island that emerged from the sea within the last million years.

Oahu was created between two and three million years ago by the same hot spot that gave birth to Hawaii.

SLEEPING BEAUTY

The graceful slopes of Mount Fuji in Japan rise more than 3,500 m (12,000 ft) above the surrounding plain. Its perfect cone – built up from layers of lava and ash – is a favourite symbol in Japan. Some believe that gods live in the summit, which is always covered in snow. It last erupted in 1707 and has been dormant ever since.

VOLCANO BREATH

Scientists in Iceland wear gas masks to monitor the poisonous gases escaping from a fumarole – a small volcanic vent. These sites are sampled regularly. An increase of gases, or a change in their mixture, can give an early warning of an eruption.

VOLCANIC WONDERLAND

Over thousands of years, underground water heated by volcanic activity has trickled down the side of this famous plateau at Pamukkale, Turkey. The salts in the water have crystallized to create a magical landscape of "frozen" waterfalls, stalactites, and basins. People have come to bathe in its warm waters since ancient times

RIVERS OF FIRE

FLOWING LAVA GLOWS, SPITS, HISSES, and crackles, and
seems to have a life of its own. Lava is magma that
has erupted on to the surface. Hot spot volcanoes, such
as Kilauea on Hawaii, produce fiery rivers of bubbly, runny
lava. Its surface cools to a thick skin, which breaks as more
red-hot lava oozes forwards underneath. This lava poses little
danger to people as it rarely flows faster than a walking pace.
However, it can travel great distances and is almost impossible
to stop. Some explosive volcanoes, such as Mount St Helens,
Washington, USA, produce a very thick, pasty lava that looks like
ash. It moves at a snail's pace, but can be hundreds of metres deep.

STOPPING THE FLOW

Lava from Mount Etna, Italy (*right*),
is flowing towards the town of
Zafferana. Although slow moving,
lava is very destructive, burning
and burying everything in its path.
Concrete barriers, trenches, and
even explosives are used to divert
lava flows away from homes.

LAVA MEETS SEA

Tourists in Hawaii (*left*) are watching the intense glow of
hot lava turning sea water into steam. Underwater, the
runny lava cools to produce shapes like pillows. Continued
eruptions mean the island is always expanding into the sea.

PAHOEHOE FLOW

Two types of lava flow have Hawaiian names.
Pahoehoe, shown here, flows from a hot spot
vent and develops a skin that wrinkles into
rope-like coils. Aa spits or tumbles out of
the volcano and cools into crumbly,
lumpy shapes.

VOLCANOLOGY

Clad in a heat-
reflective suit, this
volcanologist can
collect samples of hot
lava – if he is quick.
Volcanoes are very
unpredictable. In 1991,
husband and wife team
Maurice and Katia Krafft
were killed by a sudden
ash flow on Mount
Unzen, Japan. The risks
volcanologists take to
predict eruptions have
saved many lives.

GALÁPAGOS ISLANDS

The Galápagos islands in
the Pacific Ocean are still
growing. They are fed by
lava from a hot spot in
the Earth's mantle.
Galápagos volcanoes
produce lava that flows
over wide areas and
becomes craggy when
cool. Rainfall disappears
down its cracks and soil
is slow to form, making
the islands rugged and
relatively barren.

THE LAVA OF LIFE

Volcanic eruptions do not always spell
bad news. The land around volcanoes,
like these green plains in Mexico, can be
made fertile by the occasional shower of
ash, which adds nutrients to the soil. But
too much ash or lava is a catastrophe for
the farmer. Thick lava flows can take
months to cool, and decades to weather
enough for plants to grow again.

EMERGING ISLANDS

THERE ARE MANY ISLANDS THROUGHOUT the world's oceans, but the greatest number occurs in areas where there is a lot of volcanic activity. Some islands take millions of years to form. Parts of continents sink slowly beneath the sea, leaving the tops of mountains exposed above the water. In contrast, volcanic islands can appear almost overnight – and can also disappear just as quickly. The volcanic island of Krakatoa, in Indonesia, literally blew apart in 1883 – but since then the island has been slowly building up again.

GOD OF FIRE

On 15 November 1963, the island of Surtsey suddenly came up from the sea south of Iceland. An underwater volcano had erupted from the mid-Atlantic ridge, which comes near to the surface in Iceland. Within a few days, the new island was 60 m (197 ft) high and more than 0.5 km (0.3 miles) long.

Surtsey is named after the Old Norse god of fire, Surtur. Seawater poured onto boiling lava as Surtsey was born, and huge clouds of steam and ash rose high into the air.

DRIFTING IN

A new island formed in the middle of the ocean will not remain barren and lifeless for long. The first creatures to arrive will be flying insects and birds. Drifting logs bring in crabs, snails, and even lizards. "Sea beans" from tropical trees can drift thousands of kilometres to Europe and will still sprout, despite such a long journey!

Coconuts will last for about four months in the sea. After that they start to rot.

CHANGING SHORES

In 1964, a huge earthquake shook the Pacific coast of Alaska. Buildings collapsed, landslides swept roads away, and huge waves battered the coast. Some parts of the coast were lifted up while others sank by several metres. Villages once safe from the sea were now flooded at each high tide, while others found that their boats became stranded well above the new seashore.

Land that was previously under the sea was pushed up by the earthquake to form a wide coastal platform.

Fernandina is the most recently formed of the Galápagos Islands and its volcano, called La Cumbre, is the most active in the entire region. Volcanic eruptions may occur on Fernandina as often as every few years.

FIRE AND WATER

Long after they have been formed, volcanic islands can change in shape and size. This photograph (left) shows lava pouring into the sea from a volcanic eruption on the Galápagos island of Fernandina, in 1995. Once it cools, new ground like this will become a home for many creatures – including humans. The Japanese volcanic island of Miyake-Jima, pictured below, is inhabited by 3,800 people.

The island of Miyake-Jima is dominated by a volcano called Mount Oyama, which is 820 m (2,700 ft) high. This 3-D image of the island was generated using data from a US Space Shuttle mission.

MAKING MOUNTAINS

THE EARTH'S SPECTACULAR MOUNTAIN RANGES are places of sheer, towering rock, raised up by the movements of tectonic plates. Some mountains are isolated volcanic peaks, built up by successive eruptions. Others are great blocks of rock thrust skywards as the Earth's crust cracks and splits. But most form where one tectonic plate collides with another, causing the crust to buckle and fold. Most of the great mountain ranges of the world, such as the Himalayas in Asia, and the Alps in Europe, were formed in this way, and lie in long chains close to plate boundaries. Mountain ranges have been created and destroyed many times in the Earth's 4.6-billion-year history. As soon as they are lifted up, erosion takes over and wears them away with wind, water, and ice. Mountains that are tall and rugged are usually still growing. Once there is no more uplift, erosion will smooth them down until only gentle hills remain.

Kauai

Niihau

A fault runs between a block mountain and a rift valley.

A rift valley forms where the ground has sunk between two faults.

A recumbent fold forms where rock is compressed on top of another fold.

A block mountain forms where the land has risen between two faults.

If the rocks cannot bend more, they break, forming a thrust fault.

As the rocks of the crust are compressed, they begin to fold.

PUSHING AND SPLITTING

Mountains are formed in three main ways. Fold mountains occur where plate collisions cause the Earth's crust to crumple and fold. Others are created by volcanic eruption. Elsewhere, the crust may fracture to produce cracks called faults. The land alongside the fault may rise or fall, creating block mountains, rift valleys, and cliffs. Moutain-making involves both stretching and compression. This model (*left*) shows the types of folding and fracturing seen in mountain ranges.

Everest's summit is pushed upwards at the rate of 4 mm (0.16 in) a year.

YOUNG AND TALL

Mount Everest in the Himalayas, Asia, is the highest point on Earth. In 1999, it was measured accurately at 8,850 m (29,035 ft) above sea level. It may still be rising from a collision that began 50 million years ago, when the Indian tectonic plate collided with Asia. In geological terms, the Himalayas are still very young. Weathering and erosion has sculpted the mountains into their present dramatic shapes, but has not yet begun to wear them down significantly.

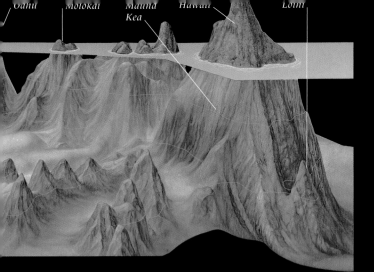

Oahu   Molokai   Mauna   Hawaii   Loihi
                  Kea

HAWAIIAN GIANTS

Towering above the sea floor are huge submerged
mountains. Some are volcanoes that will eventually
emerge above the surface. Measured from the sea
floor, the volcanic Mauna Kea is really the world's
tallest mountain. It rises to a height of 9,632 m
(31,601 ft), with its summit on the island of Hawaii.
Its volcanic neighbour, Loihi, is still below the water.

HIGHLAND EROSION

The two landmasses that created Britain were once separated
by the ancient Iapetus Ocean. England and Wales lay on one
continent and Scotland on another. About 420 million years
ago, the two continents collided with a force that slowly
formed the Scottish Highlands. Once as high as the Himalayas,
the Highlands have been eroded away with only hard granite
outcrops, such as Glen Coe (*above*), remaining.

ZIG-ZAG FOLDING

Rocks generally form in flat layers
called strata. However solid they may
seem to us, rocks stretch, buckle, and
fold when squeezed by movements in
the Earth's crust. On a large scale, this
happens along a mountain range. On
a smaller scale, strata sometimes fold
into zig-zag patterns, like these shale
strata in Cornwall, England, which
buckled more than 250 million
years ago.

*Sir Chris Bonington, who
reached Everest's summit
at the age of 51, has led
several expeditions up
Everest's toughest routes.*

EXTREME ENVIRONMENTS

The world's highest places can be very hostile
to human life. Climbers risk injury from
rockslides and avalanches, and may suffer
altitude sickness, snow blindness, and
frostbite. Technology, such as satellite
phones and breathing equipment, helps
to improve the safety of climbers.

EARTHQUAKES

FROM A GENTLE SHUDDER to terrifying and violent movements in the Earth, earthquakes literally rock the world. Earthquakes are tremors in the ground, created by the sudden movement of tectonic plates. Most plate boundaries slide past each other, but some get jammed together. The forces pushing the plates then build up until stress causes the rocks to distort. At the moment of rupture, the plates judder past each other and the rocks snap back to their original shapes like springs. This releases a stored energy in the form of seismic waves – the vibrations that cause an earthquake. Most 'quakes are very minor, but others flatten whole cities.

CALIFORNIA'S FAULT

Although tremors can occur anywhere, they are more frequent in earthquake zones. These zones lie near the sliding edges of the tectonic plates, called fault lines. This picture shows the famous San Andreas fault in California. It runs for 1,207 km (750 miles), passing close to the cities of San Francisco and Los Angeles, and causes constant tremors.

TURKISH TREMORS

In August 1999, a devastating earthquake hit the city of Ada Pazari on the western coast of Turkey. More than 3,000 people died when some of the city's poorly built apartment blocks collapsed in the tremor. Survivors are seen here walking on what were once the roofs of their homes. The disaster showed how important it is to build secure structures in earthquake zones.

Inadequately built structures collapsed quickly when the earthquake struck.

Some people survived for a week buried under rubble. Rescuers listened for their tapping sounds.

A 'quake that causes objects to fall measures V on the Mercalli scale.

Damaged buildings and general panic measure IX on the Mercalli scale.

The point at which an earthquake occurs is called the focus.

SCALES OF DESTRUCTION

This model shows the effect of an earthquake as it is measured by the Mercalli scale. A swinging lightbulb measures III; total devastation measures XII. The famous Richter scale tells us the strength of an earthquake. It takes readings from a machine called a seismometer, which measures the force of a tremor. The strongest tremor ever recorded measured 8.9, in Chile, in 1960.

RAGING INFERNO

Raging fires are a major hazard after an earthquake strikes. Fires break out when tremors damage electrical equipment and gas pipes. In Kobe, Japan (*right*), fire spread quickly through the city's wooden buildings when firefighters ran out of water. San Francisco was devastated by earthquakes in 1906 and 1991. In both disasters, fire caused huge damage.

Children are taught to duck under desks.

UNSTABLE COUNTRY

Regular safety drills are held in the schools, homes, and workplaces of Japan. Because it lies close to a junction of three tectonic plate margins, Japan experiences hundreds of earthquakes a year. Tremors of various force are recorded every day.

Within seconds, parts of the city were buried beneath tons of rubble.

Many of the city's residents were left homeless by the disaster.

EARTHQUAKES ARE IMPOSSIBLE TO PREVENT, but they can sometimes be predicted. Scientists use seismographs to detect certain vibrations in the ground called foreshocks. These are minor tremors produced by deep rocks fracturing shortly before an earthquake. In 1975, scientists detected clear foreshocks in China's Haicheng province. Buildings were evacuated before the 'quake struck and few people died. Animals may be sensitive to foreshocks too, and their behaviour can signal approaching earthquakes. Hours before a 'quake flattened Kobe, Japan, in 1995, sealions at the zoo began leaping out of the water and behaving erratically. The main earthquake shock is always followed by smaller ones – aftershocks – caused by the rocks on either side of a fault settling into new positions. Aftershocks cause additional damage and pose a threat to rescuers.

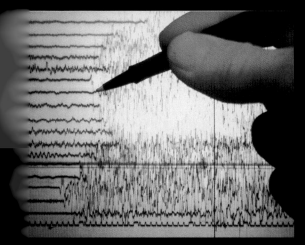

SHOCKING DISPLAY

A scientist points to earthquake shock waves recorded by a modern seismograph. The greater the wave, the wider the zigzagging movement on the seismograph's display. Various horizontal lines across the display record the different frequencies (vibrations) of a shock wave. Seismographs can record the seismic waves from earthquakes thousands of kilometres away.

SHOCK PROOF

The Transamerica Building in San Francisco, USA, is designed to withstand earthquakes. It is built on pads made of rubber and steel and has reinforced concrete walls. These absorb tremors and resist sideways shaking.

THE BIG ONE

On 18 April 1906, massive shock waves along the San Andreas fault destroyed two thirds of San Francisco. The disaster showed that steel-framed buildings, such as the City Hall tower (*above*), were more likely to remain standing and were safer than brick. Today, the city has one of the strictest building codes in the world.

JAPANESE WAVES

When the earthquake struck Kobe, shock waves caused the ground to roll and undulate, like waves in the sea. Soft earth "liquefied" as it moved and the city's raised freeway collapsed, even though it had been strengthened before the 'quake. Destruction like this is caused by surface waves – earthquake vibrations that travel at ground level. Scientists divide surface waves into two types. Love waves move from side to side, and Raleigh waves move up and down, like the sea.

PERSON DETECTOR

When buildings collapse during an earthquake, people are buried alive. Rescuers have a race against time to find survivors. Sensitive equipment, such as this trapped person detector, is used to listen for noises. It can distinguish between background noise and human movement, and can even pick out a human heartbeat.

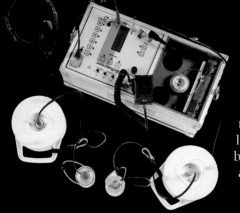

CHINESE DRAGONS

The Chinese mathematician and astronomer Chang Heng designed this bronze seismoscope in about AD 130. Shock waves make the pendulum inside it swing, releasing a ball from a dragon's mouth. The direction of the earthquake source is shown by whichever toad catches a ball!

DANGEROUS WORK

An earthquake in Mexico, in 1985, toppled many tall buildings. This specially trained dog was used to sniff for survivors in the rubble. Aftershocks can make damaged structures even more unstable and too dangerous for rescuers. But sniffer dogs can tread lightly over the wreckage to locate trapped survivors.

CAVES AND CAVERNS

FOR MANY PEOPLE, THE DARKNESS OF DRIPPING CAVES hides the threat of
the unknown. But an underground place can also be a safe refuge, and
for thousands of years, humans made their homes in caves. The action of
lava, ice, and waves can form a cave, but the most spectacular results occur
where limestone is eroded by rainwater. This can produce vast caverns full
of strange rock formations. When water absorbs carbon dioxide from the
air or soil, it becomes slightly acidic and dissolves limestone, which is
porous and erodes more easily than harder rocks such as granite. The
process is very gradual. It can take 100,000 years for flowing water
to carve a cave only 3 m (10 ft) deep. But the bigger the cave
becomes, the more rapidly it is eroded, until eventually the
water leaves a system of tunnels and caverns.

VANISHING STREAMS

Where streams disappear
through gaps in the ground,
they may erode the rock to
form great shafts called
swallow-holes. At Gaping Gill
Cave in Yorkshire, England, a
stream falls 110 m (361 ft)
through a swallow-hole in the
roof of a vast limestone cavern.
This unbroken waterfall, and
the cavern below it, are the
largest of their kind in Britain.
Gaping Gill is part of a system
of caves that extends for more
than 60 km (37 miles).

CHINESE KARST

The Guilin Hills in southwest China are fine
examples of a limestone scenery called karst.
Heavy rain, high humidity, and rich plant
growth combine to produce plenty of acidic
surface water. The acid's erosion of the
limestone, in a process called carbonation,
has sculpted a dramatic landscape. These
porous, stony hills lack streams, because
all water permeates the rock to create
honeycombs of caves and caverns.

CAVE FORMATIONS

Dripping water has created these
beautiful, multicoloured cave
formations in Nevada, USA.
Water percolating through the
limestone has dissolved calcium
carbonate and different coloured
minerals, such as iron, to form
long, icicle-shaped deposits called
stalactites, which hang from the
ceiling. Where water drips from
the stalactite, some carbonate falls
to the floor and builds up a candle-
like pinnacle called a stalagmite. It
can take several thousand years for a
stalagmite to grow just 2.5 cm (1 in).

CAVE BATS

These endangered ghost bats roost near the entrances of caves in Australia. They emerge at night to hunt insects and small animals. Like most other cave-dwelling animals, these bats use senses other than sight to locate their food. By emitting high-pitched squeaks, and listening like radar to the returning echoes, the bats can build up a "sound picture" of their surroundings.

COLLAPSE!

People sometimes build on karst landscapes with disastrous results. Limestone caverns may form just a few metres below the surface, and heavy rain can cause a cavern's ceiling to collapse. This happened in Winterpark, Florida, USA, in 1981, when a house and six parked cars plunged into a previously unknown cavern. The hole reached 200 m (656 ft) across and 50 m (164 ft) deep.

CAVE HOME

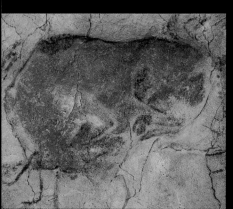

This painting of a crouching bison, with its head between its front hooves, is at least 15,000 years old. Discovered in 1869 by a hunter entering Altamira Cave, northern Spain, it is one of dozens of vivid animal images on the walls and ceilings of the cave. The paintings depict the hunting life of the cave dwellers.

BURIED TREASURE

BENEATH THE EARTH'S SURFACE IS A treasure trove of materials that is constantly being rearranged, sifted, and sorted by geological processes. People have found many uses for these materials, from building roads, to using them as fuel or to decorate jewellery. But it is only when the Earth deposits materials in bulk, and in an accessible place, that they are worth mining. For example, the oceans probably contain about 10 million tonnes of the mineral gold, but it is too thinly spread to be worth extracting. Gold is one of the most treasured of the Earth's many minerals. Unless they can be recycled, the supply of many minerals will eventually become exhausted, as underground reserves are used up.

ANCIENT PLANT ENERGY

During a period 280–345 million years ago, primitive land plants the size of modern trees thrived in vast swamps. When their remains were buried without decaying, heat and pressure gradually converted them to coal, creating many of the coal seams we mine today. Burning coal releases the sunlight energy captured by these ancient plants.

BLACK GOLD

Coal is a valuable fuel. People have been mining it since the Middle Ages. At first, many mines were open-cast, and exposed coal could simply be dug from the land's surface. Nowadays, most coal is mined from seams hundred of metres below ground, although in some places, such as here in southern Chile (*above*), coal is even salvaged from the sea.

FROM PLANKTON TO FUEL

Oil and natural gas are derived from marine plankton that have died and fallen to the sea floor. Over millions of years, as sediment accumulates on top, heat and pressure gradually transform plankton remains into petroleum oil. If the process continues, oil becomes gas. Many oil and gas deposits on land are becoming depleted, so prospectors have turned their attention to deposits beneath the sea floor, for example, in the North Sea (*left*).

GRAVEL PIT

We use sediment deposits dug from the ground to build towns, cities, and roads, and to help grow our food. For example, sand and limestone are used to make concrete, and potash is mined for fertilizer. Many sediment deposits were once beaches and river channels that became buried. They have since been uplifted, or exposed by erosion.

MINE POLLUTION

Some naturally occurring metals are valuable because they are scarce and desirable. Many, such as copper, tin, tungsten, lead, and aluminium, are found in combination with elements within metal-rich ores. Others, such as gold, silver, and platinum, exist on their own as native elements. Mining for metals can cause pollution. Metals leaching from this huge copper mine in Utah, USA (*below*), have made the local ground water unfit to drink.

ROCK TRANSFORMATION

Marble, the metamorphic rock used to make this statue, forms when the sedimentary rock limestone is subjected to heat and pressure. Rocks are created and transformed within the rock cycle. As rock material is eroded, buried, squeezed, or heated it can change from igneous to sedimentary to metamorphic rock. Rock that melts back inside the Earth completes the rock cycle.

UNCUT DIAMOND

KOH-I-NOOR DIAMOND

ROUGH AND SMOOTH

Gems are highly prized crystals. Some – such as topaz – form inside igneous rock. Diamonds are carbon crystals formed at great heat and pressure. Most gems, such as sapphires, opals, and rubies, are created by

UNCUT TOPAZ

POLISHED TOPAZ

metamorphic or igneous processes. Many gems look dull and unexciting when dug from the ground, but professional gem-cutters transform them into lustrous polished objects.

31

ICY EXTREMES

THE PLACES MOST HOSTILE TO HUMAN LIFE ARE FOUND at the ends of the Earth. Polar ice caps cover the Arctic at the North Pole, and Antarctica at the South Pole, keeping them icy all year round. Yet the two regions differ in an important respect. The Arctic is a frozen ocean bordered by continents, but Antarctica is a continent surrounded by the Southern Ocean. The Sun's rays strike the poles at a shallow angle. Because the Earth's axis of rotation is tilted, the Arctic is plunged from total darkness during the winter to constant daylight during the summer, as the North Pole moves nearer to or away from the Sun. But despite the low temperatures, polar regions are teeming with wildlife that has adapted to the intense cold. Seals and whales thrive in the freezing waters, protected by thick blubber. Bears are a common sight on Arctic ice, as birds are in Antarctica.

CARIBOU TRAIL
These North American caribou, or reindeer, migrate northwards in the summer to graze on the grasses, shrubs, and mosses uncovered by the melting ice of the Arctic tundra. Unlike other deer, caribou migrate in large herds, and both males and females have antlers.

ARCTIC OCEAN
All year round, more than half of the Arctic Ocean is covered in sea ice to a depth of at least 3 m (10 ft). In summer, some of the ice melts and breaks up to create ice floes like those shown here. For centuries, explorers believed that the Arctic ice lay over a vast continent. In 1958, a nuclear submarine sailed right under the ice cap and proved that this was untrue.

ARCTIC POLAR BEAR
The largest predators in the Arctic roam across the ice floes hunting seals, their favourite food. Polar bears are well adapted to Arctic life. Layers of blubber keep them warm, creamy white fur provides camouflage when hunting, and hollow hairs provide buoyancy in the water. Polar bears have non-slip soles to grip the ice, and partially webbed feet. They can swim for many hours in the freezing sea.

ICEBERG, DEAD AHEAD!

Icebergs are giant chunks of floating ice that break away, or calve, from ice sheets or glaciers. Most of their mass lies hidden below sea level. This berg, newly broken away from the Antarctic ice shelf, is flat-topped. Storm waves have not yet eroded it into sharp pinnacles. Antarctic icebergs can be enormous. The biggest ever recorded had a sea area larger than Belgium.

ANTARCTIC PENGUINS

These young Emperor penguins, with their mothers, are several months old. In autumn, adults gather on Antarctica to pair and mate. The female lays a single egg that she passes to the male. Throughout the Antarctic winter, when temperatures can plummet to –50°C (–58°F), the male incubates the egg on his feet, which nestle under a warm flap of skin. The female returns when the egg hatches, and takes over parenting duties.

STUDYING ANTARCTICA

This scientist is slicing an ice core drilled from the Antarctic ice cap. The core is a time capsule containing trapped air from thousands of years ago. Analysis will reveal what the Earth's atmosphere was once like. It tells scientists how naturally occurring greenhouse gases may have caused global warming in the past. The information may help us to predict what might happen in the future.

GLACIERS

A T THE NORTH AND SOUTH POLES, and in high mountain regions, immense glaciers are shaping the landscape. Glaciers are titanic rivers of snow and ice. They move slowly and are easily deflected, but their sheer weight and size give them enormous strength. As glaciers creep forwards, they dislodge and carry away gravel and boulders that scratch and grind the rocks beneath. Wide valleys are carved, great bowls are gouged in the mountainside, and entire hills are sliced away in a glacier's relentless advance. During the last Ice Age, northern glaciers and ice-sheets extended across much of Europe and North America. However, over the past 10,000 years, many glaciers have shrunk or become shorter because they are melting faster than they are replenished with snow.

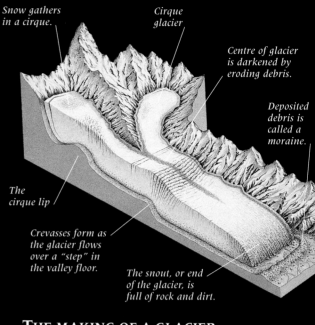

Snow gathers in a cirque.

Cirque glacier

Centre of glacier is darkened by eroding debris.

Deposited debris is called a moraine.

The cirque lip

Crevasses form as the glacier flows over a "step" in the valley floor.

The snout, or end of the glacier, is full of rock and dirt.

THE MAKING OF A GLACIER

An Alpine valley glacier (*above*) forms when snow gathers in high-altitude basins, called cirques. Further snowfall feeds the glacier, until its ice becomes thick and compacted. Slowly, it begins to move under the pressure of its own weight, and grinds against the valley sides, collecting rocks as it goes. When it reaches lower ground the glacier melts and deposits rocky debris.

FRANZ JOSEF GLACIER

This glacier in New Zealand's Southern Alps is probably the world's fastest. It often reaches speeds of 7 m (23 ft) a day during summer. Giant cracks, or crevasses, are clearly visible where the brittle surface has fractured. This happens where the glacier rises over a bump or is deflected around a bend. Crevasses are treacherous. Often many metres deep, they can swallow an unwary walker.

NORWEGIAN FJORD

This Norwegian fjord was carved by glaciers about two million years ago, during the last Ice Age. Fjords are long, deep-sea inlets gouged out by glaciers. Most formed in existing V-shaped river valleys, which were made U-shaped by the glacier's erosion. Some are as deep as 1,000 m (3,280 ft). A fjord's mouth is sometimes shallower, where the glacier began to float in the sea and its erosive power was reduced. When the ice melted, the sea level rose, and flooded the fjords.

GLACIER MARKS

Wherever they go, glaciers leave their tell-tale marks. We know that many landscapes in today's temperate regions were carved by glaciers, because exposed rocks have been polished flat by moving ice. In areas such as Scotland's Highlands, deep grooves, called striations, have been scoured into the valley sides by the passing rocks embedded in a long-vanished glacier.

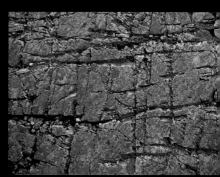

SLIP, SLIDING AWAY

At Gilkey Glacier, Alaska, USA, three glaciers meet. Rock scraped away from the valley sides darkens the glaciers' edges, and reveals movement. A glacier flows fastest in its central section. The outer edges move more slowly, held back by friction with the valley sides. Glaciers speed up in summer because their undersides melt, making them slide along more easily.

THE HUBBARD GLACIER

In 1986, the enormous Hubbard Glacier in Alaska suddenly speeded up. It normally travels at 5 cm (2 in) a day, but for one month it sped along at 45 m (148 ft) a day, and blocked off the Russell Fjord in Yakutat Bay. Seals, sea lions, and porpoises became trapped in a seawater lake behind the ice. The lake gradually became brackish as melt water entered from the glacier. The animals finally escaped when the glacier retreated.

DESERTS

AMONG THE MOST DESOLATE PLACES ON EARTH are the deserts. About 15 per cent of our planet's land surface is covered in true desert, and this ratio is gradually increasing. Some deserts are hot and dry all year round, others are dry with intensely cold winters. The cold lands of the Arctic and Antarctic are also deserts. What they have in common is a lack of water. A desert is an area that receives less than 25 cm (10 in) of rain in an average year, though years may go by when no rain falls at all. The air over a desert may be very dry or cold, or both, so any surface water quickly evaporates or freezes. Even hot deserts can be bitterly cold at night. Clear skies trap little heat and by morning there may be dew on the ground – a vital source of moisture for plants and animals that live in the desert.

RAIN-FREE ZONE

A typical year in Chile's Atacama Desert means no rainfall at all. In 1971, parts of the Atacama received rain for the first time in 400 years. Cold ocean currents off South America cool the wind as it blows onto land. Any moisture turns to fog at the coast, so very little reaches the desert. This makes the Atacama one of the driest places on Earth.

PRICKLY GIANT

The saguaro cactus of the southwestern USA, is marvellously adapted to desert life. This plant takes 200 years to grow to a height of 15 m (49 ft). Its roots reach out 18 m (59 ft) in search of water, which it can store in its thick, cork-covered stem. Instead of leaves, cactuses have sharp spines. These reduce water loss through evaporation, and deter grazing animals.

DUNE SEA

When people think of deserts, they imagine dunes – hills of loose sand blown by the wind. In fact, only about 20 per cent of the world's deserts are sandy. Most are wildernesses of rock and stone. Where a desert is mainly sand – such as here, in the Namib Desert of southwest Africa – the wind creates large drifts and dunes, some of which can be 500 m (1,640 ft) tall. Sand is blown up the shallow side of a dune and tumbles down the steep side. Grain by grain, the dune drifts, like a slow-moving wave on a great dune sea.

SAND-CARVED WONDERS

These flat-topped rock formations in Monument Valley, Arizona, USA, are called buttes. They are made of hard sandstone left behind after the softer shale surrounding them was washed away by flash floods. Wind, extreme temperatures, and flooding shape the desert landscape. Blowing dust sandblasts the rocks, carving out strange shapes, while the sudden cold at nightfall causes them to crack and split. The rare flash floods cut deep gorges and channels.

BADLANDS

Badlands are barren, dry, and hilly. Their terrain is inhospitable, and difficult to walk upon. French explorers dubbed them "bad lands to cross," hence the name. These regions have a desert-like appearance, but receive more rain than most true deserts. Often, badlands are made by people. Poor farming practices can remove the vegetation that binds soil together. Flash floods then wash the loosened soil away, turning fertile land into a dry wasteland. This process is known as desertification. These badlands in Alberta, Canada, formed naturally when flash floods carved drainage channels in the soft clay and rocks.

TRAPPING MOISTURE

Although deserts are expanding in some places, they are disappearing in others. Here, in Israel's Dead Sea region, farmers are irrigating watermelon plants with piped water. The plants are protected by plastic sheeting, which reduces water evaporation. By drip-feeding water to individual plants, farmers can cultivate barren land and make it bloom.

37

WILDFIRES

FIRST THERE IS A SMELL OF SMOKE AND A DISTANT ROAR. Then flames burst suddenly from the top of a tree, and then from another and another. Once the treetops start burning, a forest fire advances literally by leaps and bounds, creating a white-hot inferno of intense heat and clouds of dense, smothering smoke. Burning embers are carried high above the forest and fall randomly, igniting trees ahead of the main blaze. Air rushes in to replace the hot air carried upwards, causing gales and fire-storms that suck even more fuel into the flames. Extinguishing a fire that has taken hold in this way is almost impossible. Wildfires occur naturally – all it takes is hot, dry weather, parched vegetation, and a lightning strike. Occasionally, however, they are started by people, either accidentally or on purpose. Grassland and scrub are often fired deliberately to encourage new plant growth in the ashes.

RAGING FURNACE

Australia suffers from about 15,000 bushfires each year. The bush landscape of trees, shrubs, and grass becomes tinder-dry in the hot, arid Australian climate and is readily ignited by the smallest spark. The worst fires for years broke out in many places simultaneously on 16 February 1983. Driven by strong winds, this "Ash Wednesday" fire spread at terrifying speed, racing through forests and grasslands as fast as a person can run. It was so hot in places that trees literally burst into flames ahead of the advancing fire. The fires claimed 72 lives and left 8,500 people homeless.

OUT OF THE ASHES

Ashes are rich in nutrients, and plants, such as these saw banksia in the Australian bush, soon start to emerge after a fire dies. Some plants actually depend on fire to remove their competitors. Bottle-brush trees in Australia and the jack pine and lodgepole pine in North America do not release their seeds unless there has been a fire, so that the seeds can germinate in the ashes. Other trees burn readily, but then sprout up again from their roots or seeds. Redwood trees survive by having thick, spongy bark that will not burn.

MASS DESTRUCTION

The history of the devastating fires in Indonesia in 1997 began with El Niño, a periodic natural phenomenon causing changes in weather and wind patterns across the Pacific Ocean. A severe drought gripped Indonesia, and when farmers and plantation owners carried out seasonal burning of the dry vegetation, the fires grew out of control. They continued to rage into 1998, casting a pall of smoke right across Southeast Asia. Schools and offices had to close, and on 26 September 1997 an airliner flew into the smoke and crashed, killing all 234 people on board. Eventually the burning rampage was halted when seasonal rains quenched the fires.

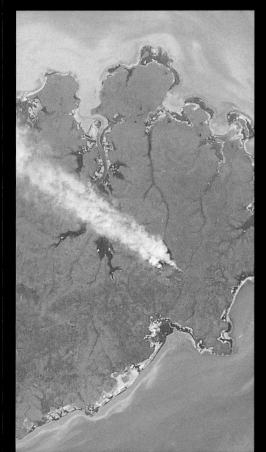

CALIFORNIA BURNING

Wildfires pose a terrifying threat to urban areas. In late 1993 wildfires scorched large areas of southern California, killing three people and forcing 25,000 from their homes. Flames, driven by winds gusting up to 113 kmh (70 mph), burnt timber and brush that had accumulated over six years of drought. Many homes were destroyed before the fire was brought under control on the outskirts of Los Angeles.

GLOBAL ECOSYSTEMS

O N LAND, CLIMATE AND SOIL INFLUENCE which plants grow where. In turn, the plants determine which animals thrive locally. In this way, biomes – great global ecosystems – become established. There are about ten biomes. Travelling from the poles to the Equator, biomes change as the climate changes from ice-covered expanses in polar regions to the hot deserts of the tropics. Human activities can change biomes. Temperate grasslands, for example, form naturally in mild climates where there is insufficient water to support the lush growth of trees. But in Europe and North America, thousands of years of tree cutting and animal grazing have replaced many forests with grasslands. Further change has occurred where grassland has been turned into vast fields for cereal crops.

TROPICAL RAINFOREST
Lush, tropical rainforest (*above*) develops where strong sunlight and high rainfall combine with warm temperatures all year round. Various communities of plants and animals live in different layers of the rainforest, from ground level to tree tops. Rainforests contain the greatest diversity of organisms of any biome on land – at least two million species.

SAVANNAH
Savannah develops in tropical areas where rainfall is highly seasonal. Typically, savannahs are grasslands scattered with small trees or shrubs. The savannahs of East Africa are famous for their spectacular big mammals, from giraffes and antelope, to lions and elephants. About 12,000 years ago, large areas of North America supported savannahs containing big cats, elephants, and giant ground sloths. These were hunted to extinction and the landscape has since been tamed for agriculture.

BOREAL FOREST

Boreal forest, or taiga, grows in cold temperate regions of the northern hemisphere. Here, a lack of rainfall and long cool seasons, produce conifers – spruces, pines, and firs – and broadleaved evergreens rather than deciduous trees (those that seasonally shed their leaves). Some boreal forests remain prime targets for extracting softwood timber for furniture and packaging, and pulpwood for making paper. Boreal forests, like tropical rainforests, are recognized as important "lungs of the Earth". They remove atmospheric carbon dioxide and replace it with oxygen.

TUNDRA

Tundra forms in regions of the Arctic where winters are too long and too cold (below -10°C (14°F) for at least half the year) to support the growth of trees. The short, ice-free summers encourage a growth of grasses, mosses, lichens, and dwarf shrubs. During the summer, caribou (reindeer) graze in the area, and migrating birds arrive to nest, and feed upon the vegetation and dense populations of flies and mosquitoes.

TEMPERATE FOREST

Deciduous broadleaved forests are typical of temperate regions, where the climate is humid but winters are cold. Most of the trees stop growing and lose their leaves in winter. Beeches (*right*), oaks, hickories, and maples dominate this woodland, while birch, hazel, and sycamore grow closer to the rich soil. This forest is home to animals such as deer and foxes.

SCRUBLAND

This shrub-covered landscape is found in Mediterranean-type climates, with cool, wet winters, and hot, dry summers. This landscape is called chaparral in North America, mallee in Australia, fynbos in South Africa, and mattoral in Chile. Trees are small, and horny shrubs and aromatic herb plants predominate. Aromatic oils can spontaneously burst into flame in high summer, starting fires

SAVAGE FUTURE

WHAT DOES THE FUTURE HOLD FOR US? Is a natural disaster looming on the horizon? Or will something created by human actions be our undoing? Major geological hazards affecting millions of people could be unleashed within the next century. The possibilities include a super-volcanic eruption in Yellowstone Park, USA, a landslide in the Canary Islands sending a megatsunami across the Atlantic, and a giant earthquake crippling Tokyo, Japan. But top of the list of near-future hazards are those caused by global warming – sea level rise, flooding, and extreme weather. Where natural disasters are concerned, it pays to plan for the future and to minimize damage to the environment, but expect the unexpected...

COOLER OR WARMER?

Ironically, global warming may also cool the Earth. If polar ice continues to melt, fresh water would gather in the surface waters of polar seas. This would alter the way ocean currents move and may stop warm currents, such as the Gulf Stream, bringing mild weather to northwest Europe, causing it to become much colder.

DRIED UP EARTH

As the Earth warms, some areas, such as parts of California, USA (*above*), will become hotter and drier, making it even harder for life to exist. Extensive over-grazing by animals on the edge of desert areas will lead to increased desertification, as plant cover is reduced and there is less soil to retain water. The destruction of habitats such as these could cause the loss of many plants and animals, altering the balance of nature with unknown effects.

UNDER WATER

The best guess for the next two centuries is that the world will become warmer. Rising temperatures make seawater expand and polar ice melt, raising sea levels by about 1 m (3 ft 3 in) in the next 200 years, devastating low-lying tropical islands and countries. A warming climate is also likely to make weather more extreme, meaning there could be more storms and severe floods, such as this one in Kenya (*right*).

DEFORESTATION

Since 1945, more than 40 per cent of the world's tropical rainforest has been destroyed, and more is being lost every year. Here (*left*), a section of the Amazon rainforest is being cleared. After trees are removed, the fragile topsoil is often washed away so trees cannot regrow. Forests play a vital role in replenishing the atmosphere's oxygen and absorbing carbon dioxide. This important role is threatened because we are removing forest faster than we are replacing it.

OVER-FISHING

Technology today enables fishermen to find and catch entire shoals of fish. By the 1990s, 13 of the world's 17 major fisheries were being fished to the limit or were over-fished. In the early 1990s, Canada restricted access to cod fisheries in the northeast Atlantic because harvesting had dramatically reduced fish populations. In 2001, North Sea cod fishing was also halted. Over-fishing and over-hunting have devastated animal populations. Many will never recover.

COMBATING BACTERIA

Disease-causing bacteria, such as staphylococci (*left*) that cause pneumonia and blood poisoning, are becoming resistant to the antibiotics used to control them. Unless medical advances keep ahead, fighting bacterial diseases could return us to the days before antibiotics, when common diseases like tuberculosis (TB) killed millions of people.

STAPHYLOCOCCI BACTERIA

GAIA

According to the Gaia hypothesis of British scientist James Lovelock, the Earth and its lifeforms function as if they were a single living organism, regulating their own global climate. This would mean that the Earth naturally changes its environment to maintain the right conditions for life. Even if humans make the Earth unfit for most lifeforms by polluting it and degrading its resources, the Earth would find a way of surviving – without humans if necessary.

EARTH DATA

EARTH RECORDS

Biggest volcanic eruption About 74,000 years ago Mount Toba in Sumatra erupted. The volcano's crater left a hole 100 km (62 miles) long by 60 km (37 miles) wide.

Worst floods In 1931, a 30-m (98-ft) rise in China's Yangtze River caused floods and famine. About 3.5 million people died.

Highest earthquake death toll In 1556, earthquakes in China killed about 800,000 people.

Worst drought Between 1876 and 1879 about 10 million people starved to death during a drought in northern China.

Worst hailstorm In 1888, grapefruit-sized hailstones pummelled the district of Moradabad in India, killing 246.

Worst series of avalanches During World War I,

soldiers fighting in the European Alps used explosives to set off avalanches that would engulf enemy troops. At least 40,000 died.

Most severe tornado outbreak The Tri-state Tornado cluster crossed three central US states in March 1925, killing 689 people.

Highest tsunami On 9 July 1958, a landslide generated a tsunami that reached 524 m (1,720 ft) high in Alaska, USA.

Worst lightning strike In December 1963, lightning struck a jet aircraft over Maryland, USA, killing 81 people.

Worst avalanche and landslide In 1970, a collapse of ice and rock on Peru's Huascarán Mountain killed more than 20,000 people.

Worst cyclone In 1970, a cyclone in the Bay of

Bengal killed about 500,000 people in Bangladesh.

Strongest storm winds The northwest Pacific's Typhoon Tip maintained winds of 305 kph (190 mph) on 12 October, 1979.

Hottest place The highest recorded temperature on Earth's surface was in the town of El Azizia in Libya in 1922. The thermometer reached 58°C (136°F).

Largest recorded earthquake This occurred in Chile in May 1960. It measured 9.5 on the Richter Scale.

Longest mountain range The Mid-Ocean Ridge extends 64,374 km (40,000 miles) from the Arctic Ocean to the Atlantic Ocean, around Africa, Asia, and Australia, and under the Pacific Ocean to the west coast of North America.

EARTH FACTS

- The Earth averages a distance of 149,600,000 km (92,960,000 miles) from the Sun.
- The Earth is not exactly round, but bulges slightly at the Equator, where it measures 40,075 km (24,900 miles) around. The diameter of the Earth is 12,715 km (7,900 miles) at the Poles, and 43 km (27 miles) more than this at the Equator.
- The temperature at the centre of the Earth is believed to be about 5,000°C (9,000°F) and the pressure about 3.5 million atmospheres.
- The Earth weighs about 5,976 billion billion tonnes (6,574 billion billion US tons).
- At its equator, Earth rotates at a speed equivalent

to 1,600 km/h (1,000 mph).
- Earth's crust ranges from 25 to 70 km (16 – 45 miles).
- Earth's atmosphere, a layer of gases, extends about 700 km (430 miles).
- Earth orbits the Sun at a speed of about 108,000 kph (67,000 mph).
- Water covers 70 per cent of Earth's surface. Of this, 97 per cent is saltwater and 3 per cent freshwater.
- Scientists estimate that there are 500,000 detectable earthquakes in the world each year, of which just 100 cause damage.

EARTHQUAKE CATEGORIES

Mercalli scale	Description	Effects	Richter scale
I	Instrumental	Recorded by instruments but not felt.	Less than 4.3
II	Feeble	Felt by people on upper floors.	
III	Minor	Indoors, feels like a heavy truck passing by; hanging objects swing.	
IV	Moderate	Outdoors, felt by walkers; indoors, crockery rattles.	4.3–4.8
V	Slightly strong	Sleepers awake; doors swing.	
VI	Strong	Windows break; hanging pictures fall; walking difficult.	4.8–6.1
VII	Very strong	Plaster and tiles fall; standing difficult large church bells ring.	
VIII	Destructive	Chimneys fall; car steering affected.	6.1–6.9
IX	Ruinous	General panic; some buildings collapse.	
X	Disastrous	Many buildings destroyed.	6.9–7.3
XI	Very disastrous	Most buildings and bridges collapse; railway tracks bend; roads break up.	7.3–8.1
XII	Catastrophic	Total destruction; ground waves seen; vision distorted.	8.1–8.9

VOLCANIC EXPLOSIVITY INDEX (VEI)

Volcanic explosivity index (VEI)	Description	Height of eruption column km (miles)	Eruption rate tonnes/second
0	Effusive	Below 0.1 (0.06)	0.1–1
1	Gentle	0.1–1 (0.06–0.6)	1–10
2	Explosive	1–5 (0.6–3)	10–100
3	Severe	3–15 (2–9)	100–1,000
4	Violent	10–25 (6–15)	1,000–10,000
5	Cataclysmic	25+ (15+)	10,000–100,000
6	Paroxysmal	25+ (15+)	100,000–1,000,000
7	Colossal	25+ (15+)	1,000,000–10,000,000
8	Terrific	25+ (15+)	More than 10,000,000

EARTH TIMELINE

13 billion years ago Big Bang creates the Universe.

5 billion years ago The solar system begins to form.

4.6 billion years ago Earth begins to form as a ball of molten rock.

4.5 billion years ago Earth is hit by Mars-sized body.

4 billion years ago Earth has cooled and Earth's core, mantle, and crust have formed.

3.5 billion years ago Earliest known life forms are preserved in rock.

2.9 billion years ago Earliest photosynthetic microbes appear (they trap sunlight to make food, and release oxygen).

2.5 billion years ago Oxygen levels rise in the atmosphere.

c.2 billion years ago Early supercontinent forms.

700 million years ago Earliest many-celled life forms are preserved in rock.

570 million years ago Early supercontinent breaks up; many-celled marine animals become abundant and diverse.

500 million years ago Early fish are preserved as fossils.

450 million years ago Caledonian mountain-building begins in what will become Scotland, Norway, and the eastern United States.

350 million years ago Tree-like ferns, clubmosses, and horsetails have appeared. Their remains will form major coal deposits. Early reptiles have appeared.

320 million years ago The first flying insects appear.

290 million years ago New supercontinent Pangaea forms.

225 million years ago Supercontinent Pangaea begins to break up to form Laurasia and Gondwanaland.

140 million years ago Early flowering plants have appeared.

65 million years ago Dinosaurs become extinct probably as a result of a meteorite impact, and the climate change that followed.

55 million years ago Indian subcontinent collides with Asia.

c.3 million years ago Stone tools are being used by human-like beings.

c.2 million years ago Most recent major Ice Age begins.

c.15,000 years ago Current interglacial period begins.

c.1850 Atmospheric carbon dioxide levels begin to rise noticeably as a result of air pollution.

1990s Hottest decade on record.

ANCIENT MYTHOLOGY

Flat Earth Many ancient cultures believed the Earth to be flat. The idea of Earth as spherical appeared around 300 BCE in ancient Greece, but was slow to take hold.

Gaea or Mother Earth The ancient Greeks worship this goddess as a representation of Earth. They believed that she created the Universe.

Yggdrasil In Norse mythology, Earth was represented as a gigantic tree (Yggdrasil). The tree's branches supported the Universe.

Pangu An early myth tells how the Universe was egg shaped. It broke to reveal a giant called Pangu who had two elements: Yin and Yang. Yin was destined to become Earth, Yang to form the sky.

KNOWLEDGE

1500s Nicolaus Copernicus was the first person to argue that the planets orbited the Sun and that Earth spins on its axis. At the time, people believed that Earth was at the centre of the Universe.

1800s Scottish scientist James Hutton, published *Theory of the Earth* in 1785–88

1900s German meteorologist and geophysicist Alfred Wegener proposed that continents were once joined in a supercontinent, Pangaea. His ideas were strengthened by the work of Canadian geophysicist John Tuzo Wilson.

1935 American seismologist Charles Richter devised the scale for measuring earthquakes.

1956 American physicist Claire Patterson provides first accurate estimate of Earth's age, by comparing measurements from meteorites and Earth minerals.

EARTH WEBSITES

www.dsc.discovery.com/
Discovery Channel's planet Earth site.

www.crustal.ucsb.edu/ics/understanding/
Understanding Earthquakes educational site.

http://earthquake.usgs.gov/
USGS Earthquake Hazards Program provides details of latest earthquakes, and lots of earthquake facts.

www.ess.washington.edu/tsunami/index.html
Hosted by the University of Washington, this site provides lots of information about tsunamis.

http://volcano.und.nodak.edu/
Catch up on the latest volcanic rumblings at Volcano World.

http://solarsystem.nasa.gov/planets/profile.cfm?Object=Earth
NASA site, packed with facts about Earth.

BACKGROUND SHOWS AMMONITE FOSSILS

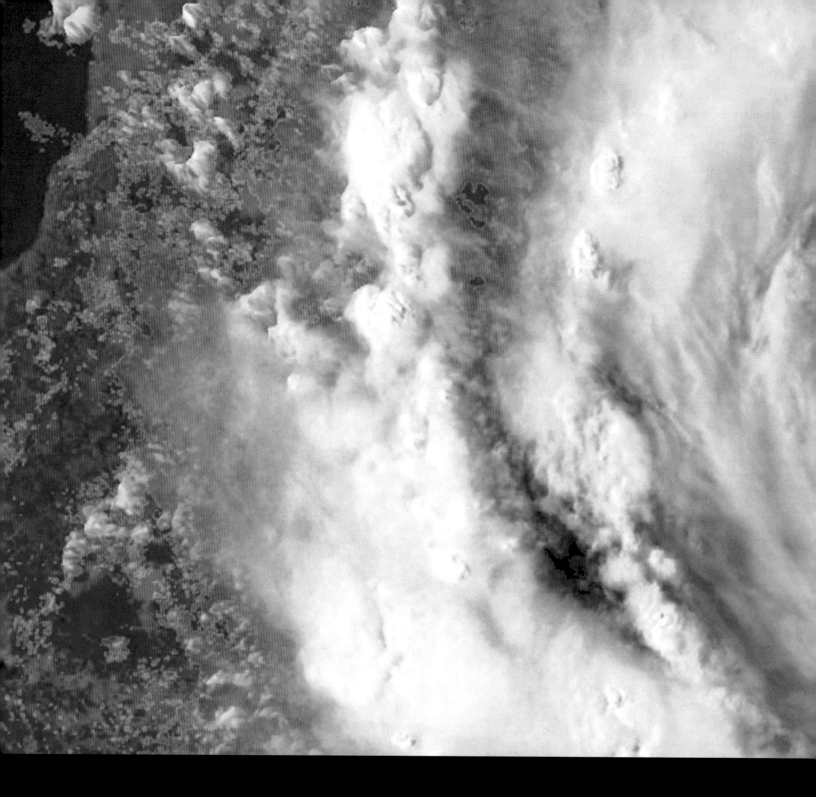

WEATHER

EARTH'S WEATHER IS AN EXTRAORDINARY
and powerful force that controls conditions
on the planet's surface. We can predict the
weather, but we cannot control it. From savage
hurricanes and tornadoes to blistering
droughts, from driving hail and freezing snow
to the dramatic effects of El Niño, the weather
has an ever-present and on-going influence on
our lives, sometimes good and sometimes bad.

RESTLESS PLANET

PEOPLE DEPEND ON THE WEATHER in countless ways. Farmers depend on rain to water their crops, sailors count on strong winds to fill their sails, and holidaymakers take sunshine for granted. Yet Earth's weather is anything but dependable. Our planet's atmosphere is in constant turmoil, a chaotic brew of gas and water kept in motion by the Sun's energy. Sometimes this energy is unleashed with sudden and unexpected savagery – tornadoes can send cars flying through the air, and category-5 hurricanes can turn cities into a wasteland of rubble. Thanks to meteorologists, our ability to predict where chaos might strike next is better than ever, yet weather remains the most deadly natural force at work on our planet.

BLUE PLANET

Water covers three quarters of Earth's surface. Warmed by the Sun, it evaporates and fills the air with invisible vapour. This turns into cloud as it cools, and then falls back to Earth as rain or snow. Without this continual recycling of water through the air, life on land would not be possible. But as well as giving life, water is responsible for the most deadly weather, from hurricanes to killer hail.

FUELLING THE WEATHER

Weather happens because the Sun warms Earth unevenly. Tropical countries receive more heat than the poles, and this imbalance makes the air and clouds in Earth's atmosphere move around constantly. The Sun itself has "weather". Gigantic storms erupt from its surface, hurling scalding gases into space. When these gases collide with Earth they cause the fabulous auroras, or northern and southern lights.

SAVAGE EARTH

The most savage weather happens in storm clouds. A small storm can kill with a well-aimed bolt of lightning; larger storms have more exotic weapons at their disposal. "Supercell" clouds bombard the land with giant hail and spawn tornadoes – ferocious whirlwinds that suck up anything in their path. Over water these turn into towering waterspouts, like this one in Florida. But top prize for savage weather goes to hurricanes, which kill hundreds every year.

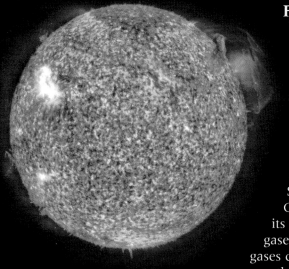

MONSOON FLOODS IN CALCUTTA, INDIA

TOO MUCH OF A GOOD THING

Without rain, everyone on Earth would starve. Rain is vital for raising crops, especially the one crop on which half the world's people depend for their staple food – rice. Rice grows in submerged fields, so it can be cultivated only in countries that receive lots of rain. In India and Nepal the monsoon rains make it possible to grow rice in the wet summer, while in equatorial countries rice can be grown all year round. But where heavy rain is a regular occurrence, so are floods. Floods cause more damage, destroy more homes, and kill more people than any other kind of bad weather.

Paddies are fields that farmers deliberately flood to grow rice. Seedlings are sown in mud, then once the crop has ripened, the field is drained and the rice is picked.

RICE PADDY IN CHINA

PARCHED EARTH

Even in wet countries, rain sometimes fails to fall for long periods. The result is a drought, and this is just as deadly as too much rain. Once-fertile soil turns to dust and blows away in choking duststorms, stripping the land of nutrients. In other places the ground bakes solid and splits as it shrinks. A very severe drought can kill millions if it causes a famine.

LIFE IN THE FREEZER

Earth is a planet of extremes. While deserts roast under the tropical Sun, polar regions shiver under a permanent layer of ice. Freezing weather brings its own hazards, such as avalanches, ice storms, and lethal cold snaps. Yet it can also produce weird and wonderful clouds, as well as spectacular "icebows" – rainbows made of ice crystals.

Seen from space, Earth is covered by continually swirling cloud.

49

THE WEATHER ENGINE

THE AIR AND WATER THAT COVER EARTH work together like a gigantic engine driven by the Sun's heat. The Sun warms Earth unevenly, heating equatorial regions more than the poles. Air and water then spread this heat out, carrying the warmth to the poles via ocean currents and global winds. The constant mixing action, stirred by the planet's rotation, also brings cold air and water back to the equator, where they are reheated. We experience the working of the weather engine as wind, rain, snow, mist, or fog. Underlying all these weather types are a handful of simple, physical principles that govern how air and water mix together and react to heat.

FLOATING ON AIR

When air warms up it expands and becomes lighter, making it rise. This process, called convection, keeps hot-air balloons afloat. A burner keeps the air inside the balloon warmer, and hence lighter, than the air outside, so the balloon rises.

Air is continually circulating between the cold, upper regions and warmer, lower regions of our atmosphere. As warm air rises, it cools. The resulting cold air is heavier than warm air, so it then sinks towards the ground.

When you breathe out on a cold day, water vapour in your breath condenses into liquid droplets. Fog and clouds form in the same way.

INVISIBLE WATER

When water heats up it evaporates – it turns into an invisible gas, or vapour, that mixes with the air. The amount of water vapour that air can hold depends on its temperature. Warm air can hold a lot of water vapour, but cold air holds little. When warm air cools down, its water vapour starts turning back into liquid water, and this process is called condensation. Condensation causes car windows to steam up and breath to become misty on a cold day. The same process also causes fog to form on cold nights, and clouds to form when warm air rises and cools down.

The burner beneath a hot-air balloon heats the air inside. This makes the air warmer and lighter, so it rises, taking the balloon with it.

HIGH PRESSURE

Although air is extremely light, it is not weightless. The weight of all the air in the atmosphere squashing down on us is called air pressure. When the air above us is relatively cold, it slowly sinks and compresses the air below, causing higher pressure. Although high pressure is caused by cold air, it brings fine, sunny weather. This is because the sinking air stops clouds from forming, creating clear blue skies.

HIGH PRESSURE

High pressure is caused by sinking cold air. Earth's rotation makes the air circle around the high-pressure centre as it sinks. It flows clockwise in the northern hemisphere and anticlockwise in the southern.

LOW PRESSURE

When warm air rises from the ground, it creates an area of low pressure below. Low pressure usually means bad weather. As the rising air cools down its water vapour turns into clouds, which may produce rain, snow, or storms. At the same time, air flows in at ground level to replace the rising warm air, creating windy weather. The weather is much more changeable during periods of low pressure.

LOW PRESSURE

Low pressure is caused by rising warm air. It circulates anticlockwise in the northern hemisphere and clockwise in the southern. At the top, air flows outwards and is carried away.

FRONTAL SYSTEMS

When a mass of cold air from the poles collides with warm air from the tropics, the two do not mix together well and a boundary called a front develops between them. Because the cold air is heavier it slides under the warm air, forcing it upwards and producing clouds. If the air on one side of the front moves faster, a wave may form along the front. This produces an area of low pressure called a depression, and the air moves in a curve around it. Depressions produce swirls of cloud that show clearly on satellite pictures.

DEPRESSING WEATHER
The swirling air in a depression contains a cold front as well as a warm front. The cold front usually moves faster than the warm front and can overtake it, lifting all the warm air from the ground. When this has happened, the fronts are described as occluded.

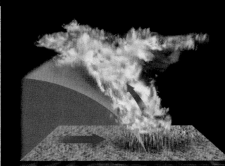

COLD FRONT

Cold air lies behind a cold front. The front slopes more steeply than a warm front, making the warm air rise rapidly. This often produces towering clouds, showers, and thunderstorms.

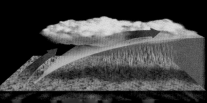

Warm air lies behind a warm front. Its slope is very shallow so the warm air rises gently, producing sheets of cloud and rain or drizzle.

CLIMATE AND SEASONS

IF YOU TOOK A JOURNEY from the north pole to the equator, you would discover that there are different patterns of weather around the world. At the north pole the Sun is always low in the sky (except in winter, when it never rises) and the weather is very cold and clear. As you travel south the Sun gets higher and the weather warmer. At the equator the Sun is directly overhead at midday and the weather is hot and humid. The warm air absorbs a lot of moisture from the oceans, which means frequent rain. Weather also depends on the time of year. Towards the poles there are warm and cold seasons, while nearer the equator it is warm all year but there may be wet and dry seasons.

Although the poles have many hours of daylight in summer, the Sun's rays are weak because they fall on land obliquely, like a torch beam held at an angle. As a result, the climate is always cold.

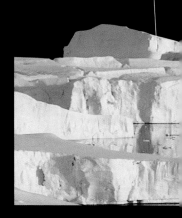

Surface ocean currents are shown here in blue (cold water) and red (warm water). As well as these surface currents, there is a very deep, cold current called the Atlantic conveyor, which takes 1,000 years to circulate from Greenland to Australia and back.

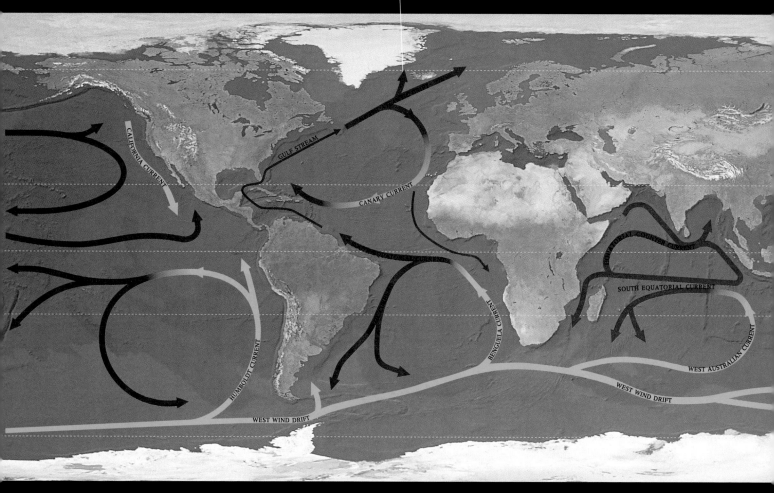

CALIFORNIA CURRENT

GULF STREAM

CANARY CURRENT

EQUATORIAL COUNTER CURRENT

SOUTH EQUATORIAL CURRENT

BENGUELA CURRENT

HUMBOLDT CURRENT

WEST AUSTRALIAN CURRENT

WEST WIND DRIFT

WEST WIND DRIFT

WEATHER AND THE SEA

Oceans have an enormous influence on the weather. Water acts as a heat store, absorbing the Sun's warmth near the equator and carrying it towards the poles in ocean currents, which are driven by the wind. For instance, the Gulf Stream, which carries warm water from the Caribbean to western Europe, makes British winters very mild. The warm, moist air associated with the Gulf Stream increases rainfall, so British summers are often overcast. In each ocean the currents form a giant circle, with cold water generally flowing along the western coasts of continents and warm water along the eastern coasts.

CLIMATE

The pattern of weather that a country experiences through the year is known as its climate. The coldest climates are found at the poles, the driest in deserts, and the wettest near the equator, where tropical rainforests flourish in constantly warm and rainy weather. Europe and North America have a temperate climate, with distinct warm and cold seasons. A country's climate depends not just on how far it is from the equator, but also on how close it is to the sea. Central Asia has a very dry climate because it is very far from the sea.

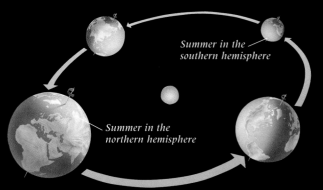

Summer in the southern hemisphere

Summer in the northern hemisphere

SUNNY SIDE UP

Earth spins on a tilted axis as it orbits the Sun. Because of this, first one pole is turned towards the Sun and then the other, and this is what causes seasons. In June the northern hemisphere gets the most sunlight, bringing summer weather to Europe, Asia, and North America. In December it is summer in the southern hemisphere. The equator always receives plenty of sunlight, so it stays hot and sunny all year round.

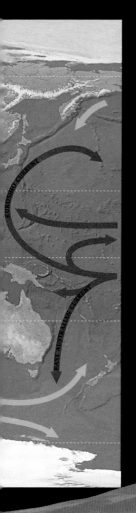

Temperate climates like that in Europe have mild weather and hot and cold seasons.

Equatorial climates like that in the Amazon rainforest are warm all year round and receive a lot of rain.

Deserts occur wherever rainfall is very low. They may be hot, such as the Sahara, or cold, such as the Gobi.

SPRING

SUMMER

AUTUMN

WINTER

CLOUDS

HOW COULD YOU DAYDREAM WITHOUT CLOUDS? As you watch their cotton-wool shapes sail across the sky you might wonder what it feels like to fly through one in a hot-air balloon or fall through one with a parachute. In fact, clouds are just like fog – grey and damp inside. Despite the endless variety of shapes, all clouds are made of the same ingredients, water droplets and ice crystals. These are so tiny that they float in the air like dust. Cloud droplets are smaller than specks of flour; it would take four of them to cover the width of a human hair. It is only when the water droplets or ice crystals crash together that they grow large enough to start falling to Earth as rain or snow.

Some cumulus clouds mushroom up to 10 km (6 miles) into the sky.

When air absorbs heat from the ground it expands and gets lighter, which makes it rise (convection). It then cools and its water vapour condenses into droplets.

HOW CLOUDS FORM

Clouds form when warm air rises and then cools down until it reaches the dewpoint temperature. This is the temperature at which the invisible water vapour in air starts condensing into liquid droplets. Warm air is forced to rise by one of three processes: by simple convection; by meeting a physical obstacle such as high ground; or by encountering a mass of cold air (a front), which forces the lighter, warmer air upwards.

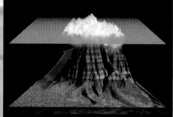

When moving air encounters hills or mountains it is forced upwards. The rising air cools and clouds form at the dewpoint.

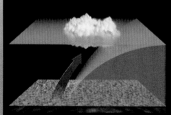

When a mass of cold air and a mass of warm air collide, the warm air is forced to rise above the denser cold air. Clouds form as the warm air cools.

CLOUD TYPES

Although clouds vary enormously from day to day, they can all be identified as one of 10 basic types. Clouds were first classified by the English meteorologist Luke Howard in 1803. His system divided them into clouds that are wispy and hair-like (cirrus), piled and lumpy (cumulus), layered sheets (stratus), or low and grey (nimbus). Each of these types has a number of variations.

CLOUD TYPES

CIRRUS ABOVE 5,000 m (16,500 ft)

Clouds that are whipped into wisps by steady, high-altitude winds. They are often referred to as "mares' tails".

CIRROCUMULUS ABOVE 5,000 m (16,500 ft)

Waves or dappled ripples of cloud high in the sky that are made of tiny ice crystals. Sometimes these clouds form a distinctive, scaly pattern called a "mackerel sky".

ALTOCUMULUS 2,000–5,000 m (6,500–16,500 ft).

Mid-level, layered or rolling cloud with a ridged structure. Separate stripes of cloud are often clearly visible.

CUMULONIMBUS 600–20,000 m (2,000–65,000 ft)

Heaped cloud with a low base that mushrooms to a massive height, especially in the tropics. Beneath them the sky looks dark. They bring heavy showers and thunderstorms.

CUMULUS 600–1,200 m (2,000–4,000 ft)

Fat, fluffy clouds with a flattish base and tops like cauliflowers. Scattered, fair-weather clouds like these are often seen in summer, but they can pack together to form bigger masses.

STRATOCUMULUS 600–1,800 m (2,000–6,000 ft)

Low-level, grey or white, soft-looking cloud. It forms rounded masses, rolls, or other shapes that may join together in one dense, drizzle-producing layer.

WEIRD AND WONDERFUL CLOUDS

IT'S NOT WHAT YOU THINK

Many a reported UFO has turned out to be a lenticular, or lens-shaped, cloud. As air is forced up and down over a mountain range it develops a pattern of waves. Vapour may condense in the peaks of each wave, forming smooth, rounded clouds that remain stationary and "hovering" for hours.

TRAIL-BLAZERS

Aircraft flying at high altitude can produce clouds called vapour trails. Water vapour emitted from the exhaust of missiles and aircraft as they climb through the atmosphere turns into ice crystals, forming a temporary trail. The lower part of the trail shown above is red because the light has been scattered by dust particles in the air. Winds will gradually disperse the trail.

PAINTED SKY

Iridescence occurs when light from the Sun or Moon passes through tiny water droplets or ice crystals in a cloud and is bent into a display of delicate colours. The range of colour depends on the size of the droplets and the angle of the Sun or Moon above the cloud. In this case, the Sun is above the cloud, just outside the photograph.

MIST, FOG, AND DEW

EVER WONDERED WHAT it would feel like to walk through a cloud? Without realizing it you have probably already done so, as mist and fog are actually types of cloud that have formed near the ground. On clear evenings when the ground cools rapidly, fog can sometimes blanket the ground in a dense layer up to waist height. Walking through it is a strange experience – your feet disappear in the swirling fog, yet the sky is clear above you. Mist, fog, clouds, and dew are all formed when it is cold enough for water vapour in the air to condense into tiny water droplets.

DEW ON A SPIDER'S WEB

MORNING DEW
In the morning after a cold, cloudless night, the ground – or any outdoor surface – is often covered with millions of gleaming droplets of water, or dew. Dew forms when low-lying water vapour condenses onto cold surfaces. Scientists call the temperature at which water vapour condenses into droplets the "dewpoint".

RESTRICTED VIEWING

The most common type of fog is called radiation fog. On clear nights, when there is no blanket of cloud to trap heat over the land, the ground radiates heat into space and cools down. Because the ground gets very cold, low-lying air also cools. If this air is humid and cools to the dewpoint, its moisture will turn into droplets, producing fog.

MISTY DAWNS

Wooded valleys are often shrouded in veils of mist at dawn, when colder temperatures higher up the valley slopes cause water vapour from the trees to condense and become low cloud. Mist is made from tiny droplets. It is less dense than fog so does not seriously affect visibility. As the Sun warms the ground, the mist gradually evaporates, heralding a clear day.

FOG WRAPPED

Fog soon disperses when the Sun comes up and warms the air. Sometimes the Sun's rays pass right through the fog and warm the ground below. Heat from the ground makes the bottom of the fog evaporate, clearing the air below and leaving a thin layer hovering over the ground. This is called fog stratus.

FOG STRATUS IN THE FRENCH ALPS

IN THE CLOUDS

One of the most famous fog-draped sites is the Golden Gate Bridge, which spans the San Francisco Bay in the USA. For long parts of the day throughout most of August the bridge is blanketed in fog. The fog is caused by the California Current, a current of cold water that runs south through the Pacific from the Arctic Ocean. When cold air rolls in from the California Current it mingles with warm summer air surrounding the bay. The water vapour in the warm air condenses, creating a dense sea fog that is often slow to clear.

RAIN

WE ARE SURROUNDED BY WATER. Three quarters of our planet is covered by it, and the atmosphere is constantly moving and recycling it. Every day more than 300 billion tonnes of water falls on land as rain. If you tried to drink this much water it would take 10 million years to get through it at a rate of a litre a second. This colossal volume of water does not fall evenly across the continents. Most rain falls in the tropics, where it sustains the world's rich tropical rainforests. On the island of Kauai in Hawaii, for instance, it rains on about 350 days a year. In contrast, the world's deserts are starved of rain. The driest place on Earth is the town of Arica in Chile's Atacama desert, which receives a minuscule 0.1 mm (0.004 in) of rain each year.

In a cloud, water vapour condenses into tiny droplets and ice crystals. These will merge and grow until they are heavy enough to fall.

BURSTING OUT ALL OVER

A big cumulonimbus storm cloud can produce a heavy rainstorm, causing enough rain to swamp a large city in ankle-deep water. As the cloud dies, the rain may become even heavier. The cloud starts to die when its downward air currents overwhelm the upcurrents. Then the cloud releases all its water at once in a cloudburst.

HOW BIG IS A RAINDROP?

Drops come in many different sizes. The smallest is a mist droplet, which is so tiny and light that it just floats in the air. Mist droplets are similar to those that make clouds. Inside a cloud, droplets merge together, like the drops on a wet window, until some are round and heavy enough to fall. A drizzle drop is made from the smallest and lightest drop that will fall. More than 3,000 cloud droplets have to join together to make one drizzle drop. The largest drop, a raindrop, is made of almost 2 million cloud droplets.

RAINING FROGS

"It's raining cats and dogs" is just an expression, but other animals, such as fish and frogs, have been known to fall from the sky during storms. These small creatures can be sucked up from ponds or lakes by tornadoes and carried some distance, before falling to the ground later with the rain.

LIFE FORCE

In many parts of the world almost all the rain falls in one season. Rain pours down on the grassy plains of East Africa in summer, but during the rest of the year dry weather turns plants brown, and the grass disappears. The parched earth cracks, and the trees seem to die. Vast herds of zebra and wildebeest migrate west in search of water. However, when the rains arrive, the grass revives, seeds germinate, and the animals return.

The East African landscape is parched, but the plants are not dead, just dormant and waiting for the summer rain to help them grow again.

When the rain returns, seeds germinate, the grass revives, and the trees grow leaves. The plants must produce new seeds before the rain stops and the ground becomes too dry.

LIGHT SHOWS

THE SKY IS LIKE A VAST STAGE that produces spectacular light shows. The spotlight illuminating this stage is the Sun, which bathes our planet with a brilliant white light. This white light is really a mixture of different colours. When sunlight hits the atmosphere, the colours are scattered in different directions by air, dust, water droplets, or ice crystals – sometimes with dazzling effects. Perhaps the most stunning light show is a rainbow, a vast circle of colour produced by sunlight falling on rain. Rainbows are not real objects, just tricks of the light.

The sky below a rainbow is often brighter than above it because the raindrops here reflect more light.

SEEING A RAINBOW

The best time to see a rainbow is in the morning or late afternoon, when the Sun is out, but rain is falling in the distance. If you stand with your back to the Sun and look towards the rain, you have a good chance of seeing a rainbow. The lower the Sun is, the wider the bow. You can create your own rainbow with a garden sprinkler on a sunny day – stand with your back to the Sun and look through the mist. If you are lucky enough to see a rainbow from a plane you won't see a bow but a whole circle of colours.

WHY DIFFERENT COLOURS?

We see rainbows because sunlight splits into seven different colours as it passes through raindrops. As light enters a raindrop it bends. The different colours bend by different amounts, which makes them separate. The colours are reflected off the rear surface of the raindrop, then they bend again and separate further when they leave the droplet. Red always appears at the top of a rainbow, followed by orange, yellow, green, blue, indigo, and violet.

THE SUN

You see a rainbow when sunlight is reflected at an angle of 40–42°. Violet light is reflected at 40°, red at 42°, and the other colours fall in between.

The larger the raindrops, the brighter and sharper the colours will appear.

Sometimes a second, fainter bow accompanies a rainbow. It is always a little higher in the sky than the main bow, and the colours appear in reverse order, with red at the bottom. The second bow is caused by light being reflected twice on the rear surface of each water droplet. Some sunlight is lost with each reflection, so the second bow is not as bright as the main one.

ICEBOW

In frozen polar regions, where clouds are made of very tiny ice crystals, you can sometimes see bright white icebows spreading across the horizon. Icebows are produced when sunlight is bent and reflected by the ice crystals. The crystals' small size means that the light rays have no room to spread apart into different colours. Instead, the colours remain close together and the light you see is bright white.

FOGBOW

On a foggy day, if you stand with your back to a low-lying Sun, you can sometimes see a fogbow. Fog consists of tiny water droplets that can bend and reflect light in the same way that raindrops do to produce a rainbow. However, the difference is that a fogbow, like an icebow, appears white. This is because fog droplets are too small to bend light enough for the colours to separate.

SOLAR CORONA

A solar corona is a series of blurry, coloured rings that appear around the Sun. For one to occur, the Sun has to be veiled by a thin layer of cloud. Before the sunlight reaches your eye it passes through droplets in the cloud. In much the same way that raindrops bend sunlight to produce a rainbow, cloud droplets bend and separate sunlight to make a solar corona.

LUNAR CORONA

Sometimes at night the only hint that there are clouds overhead is the appearance of a large bright disc surrounding the Moon. This disc is known as a lunar corona. It occurs when sunlight reflected off the Moon passes through tiny water droplets or ice crystals in thin cloud. The droplets or ice crystals diffuse, or spread out, the white light.

SOLAR WONDERS

RAINBOWS AND ICEBOWS are not the only magical light effects that the Sun and sky can conjure up. Brilliant colours and eerie phenomena – from wavy, green curtains that brighten the whole sky to ghostly apparitions with glowing haloes – can be witnessed if you are in the right place at the right time. This might mean travelling to Alaska, standing atop a very high mountain, or taking a trip in a space shuttle, but if you are lucky enough to see one of these dazzling displays – and don't blink because some of them last only a few seconds – you'll remember it for ever.

CURTAINS OF LIGHT

Auroras (also called the northern and southern lights) are like huge, green curtains, often tinged with pink and blue. They wave gently in the skies above the Arctic and Antarctic regions, and can be as bright as moonlight. They are caused by the "solar wind" – an invisible stream of electrically charged particles hurled into space by storms on the Sun. The solar wind flies through space at up to 3 million kph (2 million mph). When the particles are about 64,000 km (40,000 miles) from Earth, they are caught in the Earth's magnetic field. The magnetic field carries the particles around the Earth and draws some of them down towards the north and south magnetic poles. High above the poles, the charged particles slam into the atmosphere and collide with air molecules, which absorb the electrical energy and instantly release it as light. The oxygen molecules in air emit a greenish-white light; nitrogen molecules produce pink and blue light.

COSMIC SHOW
The best way to see the aurora is to fly through it in a space shuttle. Seen from space, the aurora forms spectacular dancing curtains of light high above the sky. It seems to radiate into space, but actually the opposite is happening. The solar wind collides first with air molecules in the thinnest, highest part of the atmosphere and works its way down.

HERALDING GOOD WEATHER?

At the beginning and end of cloudy days, rays of sunshine can often be seen pouring out from behind clouds. These are known as crepuscular rays (crepuscular means twilight). The glowing rays are caused by sunlight shining through gaps in the clouds and illuminating dust particles and water droplets in the lower atmosphere. People used to think that crepuscular rays meant the Sun was drawing up water in order to bring fine weather. Unfortunately, such light effects are not reliable predictors of weather.

SCARY SPECTRE

If you are in the right place between the Sun and a cloud, you might see your shadow cast on to the cloud. This rare sight, called a brocken spectre, is seen most often from planes and mountain tops. The spectre may appear huge and terrifying because it usually looks much further away than it really is. Sometimes a colourful glowing ring, or glory, surrounds it. If the spectre is the shadow of a person, the glory appears around the head like a halo.

GREEN FLASH

Occasionally, when the Sun is just about to disappear at sunset, it turns bright green. This "green flash" happens because light from the setting Sun is split by the atmosphere into different colours. Just before sunset, red disappears below the horizon and other colours are scattered or absorbed, until only green is visible.

SUN PILLARS

A vertical shaft of light can appear above the Sun (and occasionally below it) when sunlight is reflected from the undersides of tiny ice crystals falling slowly through the air. These "Sun pillars" are best seen just after dawn or before sunset, when they pick up the rich, orange-red hue of the setting or rising Sun.

SUNDOG

Also called a mock Sun, a sundog is a bright spot of light that appears in the sky to one side of the Sun. This strange phenomenon is caused by falling crystals of ice that bend the Sun's light, creating the illusion of a second Sun. Sometimes there are two sundogs, one on either side of the Sun, and these may be joined by a bow of light called a winter rainbow. Sundogs are often coloured, with red on the side nearest the Sun and a white tail on the opposite side. A similar effect can occur at night, producing "mock Moons".

SNOW

SNOW CAN TRANSFORM THE WORLD into a winter wonderland, but it can also be deadly. In the afternoon of 23 February 1999, a slab of snow some 170,000 tonnes in weight broke away from a mountain slope in Austria and started careering towards the village of Galtür. Within less than a minute a gigantic avalanche slammed into Galtür and demolished everything in its path. More than 30 people died, crushed under a torrent of snow and rubble 10 m (33 ft) deep. Snow can also create "white-outs", blinding clouds of snow that reduce visibility to centimetres, causing drivers to veer off roads and walkers to get hopelessly lost in subzero conditions.

Snowflakes come in an amazing variety of shapes, but they usually have six sides. No one has ever found two the same.

SNOWFLAKES

Snow forms when tiny ice crystals in clouds stick together and form snowflakes. When these grow large enough, they fall out of the bottom of the cloud as snow and land on the ground in a jumble, trapping air between them. In fact, snow is mostly air. The largest snowflakes ever seen were at Montana, USA, in January 1887. They measured 38 cm (15 in) wide and 20 cm (8 in) thick. Outside the tropics, most rain starts as snow, but it usually melts before it reaches the ground.

AVALANCHES

Avalanches happen when heavy snow builds up in unstable layers on a mountain. The slightest vibration can set one off – even someone shouting. First the snow slides downhill, but soon it starts tumbling, growing into a terrifying, roaring wall of snow that moves faster than a speeding car. Big avalanches gather up huge clods of earth and boulders, and create a hurricane-force wind ahead of the snow. The wind alone can uproot trees and tear roofs off houses. Avalanches are extremely dangerous – anyone caught in the path of one has just a 5% chance of survival.

BLIZZARDS

A blizzard is a fierce wind that drives falling snow or whips it up from the ground. Severe blizzards hit North America every winter. One of the worst ever was in 1888, when snow piled up to 9 m (30 ft) deep in New York City and 400 people died. In January 1996 heavy snow produced drifts 6 m (20 ft) deep in the city, and people had to cross Times Square on skis to get to work.

BLIZZARD IN TIMES SQUARE, NEW YORK

POWDER CRAZY

For winter sports enthusiasts, nothing beats the exhilaration of speeding downhill through fresh powder, the "driest" form of snow. Skiers even fly by helicopter to find powder and say skiing on it is like floating on a cushion of air. Snowboarders carve up powder into huge clouds, leaving a wavy track behind them. The snow is so soft that falling into it is like falling on a mattress.

Ski-rack on car

SNOWED IN

Because snow is mostly air, it is very bulky and does not take long to bury objects, like this car in Germany. Snowfalls are heaviest when the air temperature hovers around freezing; if the weather is too cold, air cannot hold enough moisture to produce rain or snow. As a result, the north and south poles receive very little snow, and Antarctica is one of the world's driest deserts. Tamarack, on the slopes of Mount Whitney in California, has the heaviest snowfall in North America. In January 1911 it received an incredible 10 m (33 ft) of snow in a month – almost enough to bury houses.

HAIL

IMAGINE STANDING IN THE MIDDLE of a Nebraskan cornfield at the end of a hot, still summer's day. You look up and notice a great, amorphous cloud obscuring the Sun and casting a shadow across the field. All of a sudden, something thuds painfully on your head. Soon, lumps of ice are falling all around you, pelting the crops with terrible force and falling so thickly that you can hardly see ahead. Hurtling at 160 kph (100 mph), the hailstones are as big as golf balls – big enough to flatten the corn, to bruise, even to kill. This is exactly what happened in Coffeyville, Kansas, USA, on 3 September 1970, when a violent hail-storm caused immense destruction to crops and property.

OUT ON THE PLAINS
Hail forms inside big storm clouds (cumulonimbus), where the temperature is often below freezing and air currents are very strong. Hail-storms occur everywhere, but they are most frequent and violent across the plains of central USA. This photograph, taken in the desert of Nevada, shows a cumulonimbus cloud with a hail-storm clearly visible below it.

This windscreen has been smashed by a huge hailstone.

HAIL HAVOC
Giant hail causes havoc on the roads, smashing windscreens, denting car roofs, and badly injuring anyone caught in the open. This picture of a violent hail-storm near Shamrock, Texas, USA, was taken from the car of a tornado-chaser, risking massive damage to his car. The cumulonimbus clouds that produce the biggest hail-storms can also trigger tornadoes.

HOW HAIL FORMS

Hailstones form when ice crystals are blown around in the violent and freezing updraughts (air currents) of a storm cloud. When the updraughts weaken, or the hail becomes too heavy to be supported by the updraught, the hailstones fall to the ground.

Violent updraughts keep hail airborne.

Warm air is drawn into the cloud.

Layers of ice

CROSS-SECTION OF A GIANT HAILSTONE

Large hailstones tend to have irregular shapes.

ACTUAL SIZE

LAYER AFTER LAYER

As a small hailstone circulates in a cloud, it is coated with frost as it is carried up to the top of the cloud and then layered with clear ice as it drops into warmer air. This happens repeatedly, coating the hailstone with layers and increasing its size. The more turbulent the cloud, the larger the hailstone becomes.

RECORD BREAKER

Very occasionally, hailstones grow to gigantic proportions, like this one, the largest authenticated hailstone in the world. Weighing 0.77 kg (1 lb 11 oz), it fell on Coffeyville on 3 September 1970. An even bigger hailstone, weighing 1.02 kg (2 lb 4 oz) is said to have fallen in Bangladesh on 14 April 1986 during a hail-storm that killed 92 people. But the worst reported hail-storm occurred in India on 30 April 1888. Hailstones the size of grapefruits killed 246 people, some of whom were completely buried by the hail.

STORM CLOUDS

THE TOWERING CLOUDS that herald a thunderstorm are magnificent to look at, with their thunderous grey bases, topped by billowing columns of cloud. Storms result from the violent mixing of air, water vapour, water droplets, and ice crystals inside cumulonimbus, the biggest clouds on Earth. A single cumulonimbus releases as much energy as the explosion of a nuclear bomb. As well as producing thunder and lightning, storm clouds bring heavy rain or snow, and strong winds that can increase in sudden, unpredictable gusts.

MAMMA FROM HEAVEN
These spectacular clouds are called mammatus ("mamma" is Latin for breast). They form from down-currents of air in the underside of a storm cloud's anvil. When they appear it is wise to find shelter, as they signify that a severe storm with gales and torrential rain is close, and there is a serious risk of tornadoes.

BIRTH OF A STORM CLOUD
Storm clouds develop as warm, moist air rises and cools, causing its water vapour to condense into droplets. Condensation releases heat, which makes the air rise further and the cloud grow taller. A storm cloud may keep growing until it reaches the top of the troposphere. Here, the air temperature levels out and the cloud can rise no further. For about an hour the cloud releases heavy rain, snow, or even hail, until it runs out of moisture and starts to disappear.

Cool air sinks.

Warm, moist air rises.

The anvil shape is normally a useful indicator of the way a storm is heading, as the tail end tends to spread out in the direction of the upper winds.

TROPICAL MENACE
Cumulonimbus clouds are most common in the hot, moist air of the tropics, such as here, above Zaire. Air inside these turbulent giants rises and sinks in currents travelling 50 kph (30 mph) or more. The strong up-currents can create clouds over 11 km (7 miles) tall – high enough to reach into the stratosphere and show up clearly from space. The top, made from ice crystals, is swept into a huge anvil shape by the wind.

Storm clouds can be visible up to 320 km (200 miles) away, particularly in low-lying terrain, such as here in Arizona, USA. Aircraft pilots steer clear of these clouds as they can be extremely dangerous. If caught in the middle of one, fierce winds can throw an aircraft upwards and then downwards with enough force to make the pilot lose control.

LIGHTNING

YOU KNOW IT IS COMING. The sky darkens. Cats and dogs start acting strangely. Then the storm is directly overhead, a magnificent but terrifying spectacle of blinding light, deafening noise, and pouring rain. A summer thunderstorm releases as much energy as the explosion of 12,000 tonnes of dynamite, and much of this energy is released in the form of lightning. Lightning heats the air to about 30,000°C (54,000°F) – five times hotter than the surface of the Sun – and it kills 100 people and starts 10,000 fires every year in the USA. As you read this, about 2,000 thunderstorms are in progress around the world, producing some 100 lightning flashes every second, or more than 8 million a day.

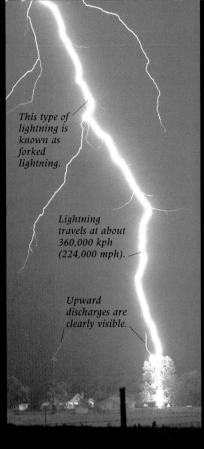

This type of lightning is known as forked lightning.

Lightning travels at about 360,000 kph (224,000 mph).

Upward discharges are clearly visible.

HOW LIGHTNING FORMS

Inside a cumulonimbus storm cloud, violent air currents cause ice crystals to crash into each other, generating static electricity. The bottom of the storm cloud becomes negatively charged, while the ground and the cloud top are positive. These charges build up until electricity starts leaping between them, at first between different parts of the cloud, and then from the cloud to the ground.

POWER SURGE

This incredible photograph of a lightning bolt striking a tree has captured a very rare sight – two upward lightning discharges, which occur only in the area of a downward stroke. Cloud-to-ground lightning occurs when a downward lightning stroke is met by an upward stroke from the ground. The split-second collision triggers a massive surge of electricity, which heats the air so fast that it explodes, causing the sound of thunder.

GREAT BALLS OF FIRE

Ball lightning is a mysterious, unexplained phenomenon. It appears from nowhere during thundery weather as a globe of light between the size of a golf ball and a beach ball. Glowing with a dim, yellowish light and lasting just seconds, it floats in the air not far from the ground, and bounces around in random directions.

This fulgurite was dug up by someone who saw lightning strike the ground in Avra Valley, Arizona, USA.

TURNED TO STONE

Lightning strikes the ground with so much energy that it heats the soil to about 1,800 °C (3,300 °F) in less than a 100,000th of a second. When lightning tunnels into dry, sandy soil, the heat fuses the soil into the shape of the electricity's path. These curious formations are called fulgurites.

Light travels faster than sound, so you can tell how far away a storm is by counting the time between seeing the lightning and hearing the thunder. A gap of 3 seconds means the storm is 1 km away (5 seconds means 1 mile).

CLOUD-TO-CLOUD LIGHTNING

As well as flashing from a cloud to the ground, lightning also sparks between regions of positive and negative charge inside clouds, between clouds, and between clouds and the air. This lightning flash between clouds is clearly visible in the night sky above Arizona, USA. Each flash lasts about one fifth of a second and can be up to 5 km (3 miles) long. If the lightning flash is obscured by cloud, it appears to make the cloud glow and is called sheet lightning.

DUSTSTORMS

THE FIRST SIGN THAT A DUSTSTORM is on the way is the hot, dry wind that tears through the streets, flicking grit into the air and stinging your eyes. Next comes the towering wall of dust – so tall that it reaches the sky and merges into the clouds. When the wall of dust engulfs the town, it blots out the Sun and casts an eerie yellow light across everything. People cover their faces with scarves and rush indoors, but there is no escape. Shutting windows and doors may help, but the fine dust gets everywhere. It gets into food and drink, into people's eyes, ears, and mouths. It even works its way between the pages of books. Outside, the suffocating cloud of dust reduces visibility to metres, making it almost impossible to find your way around.

DUST BOWL

In the 1930s the North American Midwest suffered a devastating drought that turned millions of acres of farmland into a parched desert called the Dust Bowl. Once-fertile soil turned to dust and was blown off the ground by strong winds, forming choking clouds that killed ducks and geese in midair. The dust settled on ships 480 km (300 miles) out to sea and it covered the President's desk in the White House as fast as it was cleared. One cloud of dust was 5 km (3 miles) high and covered an area from Canada to Texas and from Montana to Ohio.

THE VIEW FROM SPACE

This picture, taken from a space shuttle, shows a monster duststorm sweeping across the Sahara in Africa. Small white clouds have formed at the storm's leading edge, where the warm, dust-laden air is rising and cooling. Storms like this can lift dust so high that the winds carry it all the way from Africa to America.

DUST-DEVIL

Dust-devils are twisting columns of sand and dust up to 2 km (1.2 miles) tall, with winds strong enough to knock down flimsy buildings. They develop over areas of ground that are hotter than than their surroundings. Hot air rises rapidly over the ground, and the surrounding air rushes in at ground level, spiralling upwards and lifting dust as it approaches the centre

A cold front meets a body of warm air and pushes under it.

The rising warm air carries airborne dust and sand to a great height.

The air is turbulent and windy under the rising warm air. The winds pick up dust and sand, blowing them into clouds.

SAHARA DOCTOR

The harmattan is a hot, dry wind that crosses the Sahara, absorbing heat from the scorching sand. It can split wood, harden leather, and bake farmland solid. Sometimes it lifts dust clouds high in the sky and then drops the dust, letting it settle everywhere. Despite this, people call the harmattan "the doctor", as it brings relief from humid, clammy weather.

HOW A DUSTSTORM FORMS

Deserts are often windy, and a light breeze will lift dust and blow it about. Sand grains are heavier than dust and it takes a stronger wind to lift them. Really violent sandstorms and duststorms happen only when cold air pushes beneath warm air. The warm air rises and the surrounding air rushes in to replace it. This produces winds that blow dust and sand off the ground. The rising warm air carries the cloud of debris to a great height.

EL NIÑO

JANUARY IS ORDINARILY DRY IN PERU, but 1998 was no ordinary year. Time and again, violent storms battered the coast, bringing torrential downpours even to places where it had hardly rained in years. Floods drove 22,000 people from their homes and mudslides engulfed whole villages, burying 300 people alive. And it was not just Peru that was suffering freak weather. Thousands of kilometres north, storms raged in Florida and California, causing floods, landslides, and tornadoes; meanwhile, Australia and Papua New Guinea were in the grip of a drought during what should have been the rainy season. The cause of all these events was El Niño – an ocean current that throws global weather systems into chaos.

THE BOY-CHILD

Every 5 to 7 years the prevailing winds temporarily change direction over the Pacific, driving warm water east towards South America. The warm sea makes the air more humid, causing heavy rain and violent storms. At the same time, countries in the west Pacific, deprived of the warm ocean current, have very dry weather. El Niño is Spanish for boy-child. The name refers to the baby Jesus because the strange weather usually begins at Christmas.

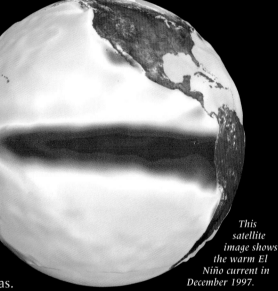

This satellite image shows the warm El Niño current in December 1997.

FRENZIED OCEAN

The coast of California is normally bathed by cool ocean currents running south from the Arctic, but during El Niño years the waters off California are much warmer. The result is a succession of massive storms that thrash the coast with giant waves, furious winds, and driving rain. The onslaught was particularly bad during the 1982 El Niño, when whole beaches were swept away. The 1997 El Niño triggered a Pacific hurricane that ploughed across the Baja peninsula and dumped 150 mm (6 in) of rain on the deserts of southern California and Nevada.

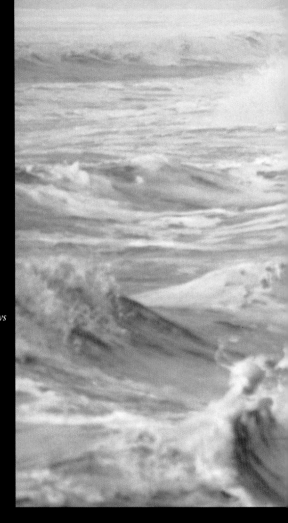

FREAK FLOODS

Water rose to roof level in the city of Eldorado, Brazil, after the rain-swollen River Ribeira burst its banks in 1997. Most of the inhabitants were driven from their homes. The 1997–98 El Niño also caused floods in the US states of Washington, Idaho, Nevada, Oregon, and California, making at least 125,000 people homeless. Of the 30 or so El Niños that occurred in the 20th century, this was the most violent. It was also the most expensive in history, causing an estimated $20 billion worth of damage

MUDSLIDE!

When prolonged heavy rain soaks into the ground, the earth turns into a soupy sludge. On steep, treeless slopes this waterlogged mass of mud may succumb to gravity and start slipping downhill, carrying everything with it – including roads and houses. Mudslides can shift thousands of tonnes of earth in seconds and carry enough force to smash through anything in their path. The mudslides caused by the 1997–98 El Niño in South America were all the worse because of widespread deforestation in the region.

TORNADOES

FROM THE WIZARD OF OZ to The Simpsons, tornadoes have played their part in myths and stories. But the terrifying power of a tornado is no legend – this is the most violent concentration of energy that the atmosphere can produce. A tornado can suck up a house and spit it out in splinters, or lift a whole train from the tracks. Tornadoes are best known for terrorizing the plains of North America, but they are common worldwide, although many go unseen. The UK has about 60 every year.

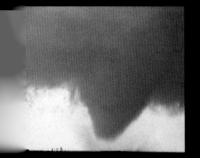

A funnel descends ominously from the base of a supercell cloud.

At touchdown the funnel becomes a tornado and starts sucking up debris.

A TORNADO IS BORN

Tornadoes form inside huge storm clouds called supercells. These are fuelled by warm air, which is drawn in at the base of the cloud and rises upwards in powerful air currents. Just as water sinking through a plughole starts rotating, so these warm updraughts start spinning. If the spin becomes sufficiently intense, the rotating air extends below the cloud base as a "funnel". The moment this touches the ground it becomes a fully-fledged tornado.

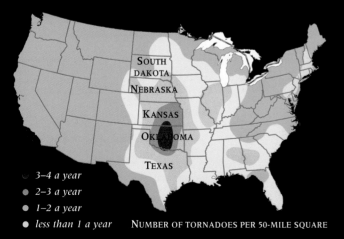

SOUTH DAKOTA
NEBRASKA
KANSAS
OKLAHOMA
TEXAS

○ 3–4 a year
● 2–3 a year
● 1–2 a year
● less than 1 a year   NUMBER OF TORNADOES PER 50-MILE SQUARE

TORNADO ALLEY

Tornadoes are more common in the United States than anywhere else in the world. Nebraska, Kansas, Oklahoma, Texas, and South Dakota, are known as Tornado Alley, where tornadoes strike regularly in

SIGHTS, SOUNDS, AND SMELLS

As a tornado approaches, the wind roars louder and louder until it is as deafening as a jumbo jet taking off. Then comes the crashing sound of debris smashing into buildings with immense force. Scraps of wood and metal are flung through the air like missiles. There can also be freak effects, such as cutlery embedded in tree trunks, or houses lifted from their foundations, turned through 90 degrees, and put back down again. As well as the noise there is a strong stench of sulphur, like rotting food, and sometimes a choking, acrid smell produced by lightning in the funnel.

SPAGHETTI TORNADO

At its base, a tornado may measure just 100 m (330 ft) across, while others spread up to 1.5 km (1 mile) wide. Tornadoes roam erratically but always remain attached to the storm cloud. This one has wandered further than most and is about to lift clear of the ground and disappear.

TORNADO SOUP

The wider a tornado is at its base, the more destructive it is. A giant like this one is capable of generating winds of over 400 kph (250 mph) because air accelerates as it is drawn into the spinning vortex. The further the air has to travel to the centre, the faster it gets.

WET 'N' WILD

A tornado over water is called a waterspout. Although it looks like a spout of water being sucked upwards, a waterspout is mostly cloud. Even so, it can whip up a huge amount of spray. This one off the coast of Spain killed six people as it dumped tonnes of water onto a pier.

HURRICANES

DOORS WERE FIRMLY SHUT, windows boarded up, everyone was indoors. A journalist telephoned his report to the mainland: "It's flinging shipping containers about like toys" – then the line went dead. It was 19 November 1999 and Hurricane Lenny was crossing the Caribbean island of St Martin, where it blew away beaches, flooded hotels, ripped off roofs, and washed away roads. Yet even Lenny was rated only category four on the five-point hurricane scale. Fortunately, the worst hurricanes – category fives – are very rare. But all hurricanes are huge and terrifying. They are the biggest, most violent, and most destructive storms our planet is capable of producing.

DOUBLE TROUBLE

This satellite picture shows two hurricanes in September 1999: Hurricane Floyd petering out over New York, and newly formed Hurricane Gert gathering force in the Atlantic. Also known as typhoons or tropical cyclones, hurricanes form over warm, tropical seas in late summer. There are about 40 worldwide each year. Most drift west, bending away from the equator as they move, carried by prevailing winds.

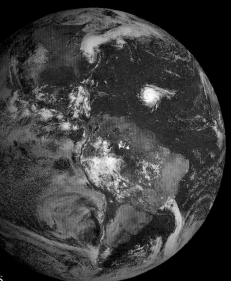

WHAT IS A HURRICANE?

Hurricane Fran, which swerved past Florida in September 1996, was a typical hurricane. Hurricanes form from small storms over tropical oceans. Fed by humid air rising from the warm ocean, and set spinning by the Earth's rotation, they grow into a monstrous, swirling mass of cloud as they drift westwards. The most dangerous part of a hurricane is near the centre, where the wind is so ferocious that it can flatten houses. But most of the damage inflicted by hurricanes is due to floods resulting from torrential rain and gigantic waves that breach the coast.

TRACKING FRAN

Thanks to weather satellites, scientists can track hurricanes and try to predict where they might make landfall. Hurricane Fran started life near the coast of Africa and drifted west into the Caribbean, growing in strength as she approached Florida. Then she veered north, eventually making landfall in North Carolina. When hurricanes pass over land they are no longer fed by heat from the ocean, and they soon lose force

07/9/96
06/9/96
05/9/96
05/9/96

WHERE HURRICANES HAPPEN

04/9/96
03/9/96 02/9/96
01/9/96
31/8/96
30/8/96
29/8/96

WIND SPEED

0–63 KPH
64–119 KPH
120–154 KPH

155–179 KPH
MORE THAN 179 KPH

A hurricane's most deadly winds occur in the eye wall, a circular wall of cloud surrounding a central hole called the eye. Wind speeds can reach more than 240 kph (150 mph) in the eye wall. But when the eye passes directly overhead, the sky clears and the wind drops to a gentle breeze.

LANDFALL

If a hurricane hits land, it leaves behind a trail of complete destruction, demolishing homes in its path. This house was hit by a hurricane in Louisiana, USA, which left a huge trail of carnage. With adequate warning, many people will leave the path of a hurricane well before it hits land.

FLOODS

Floods kill far more people and damage more property than any other natural phenomenon. Flash floods are the most terrifying because they are so sudden and violent. A flash flood sends a roaring wall of water surging down a river valley with enough force to sweep away trees and houses and even send giant boulders rolling downhill. But the most destructive floods are those that spread out as far as you can see in every direction, turning dry land into a gigantic lake and leaving thousands of people marooned and helpless.

THE GREAT FLOOD

The Mississippi has burst its banks many times, but the flood of 1993 was perhaps the worst. After months of rain in summer, the Mississippi and Missouri Rivers overwhelmed flood defences and inundated more than 80,000 sq km (31,000 sq miles) of low-lying land. The floods killed 50 people, left 70,000 homeless, and caused damage estimated at $12 billion.

Satellite image of the 1993 Mississippi flood, showing flooded areas in red

HURRICANE FLOODS

Hurricane Mitch struck Honduras in October 1998. A total of 896 mm (35 inches) of rain fell over five days, most of it in the space of just 41 hours. The rain caused floods and mudslides that killed around 11,000 people – the highest death toll from a hurricane in 200 years. Some people were buried alive under the mud, others were washed out to sea and drowned. Roads and bridges were destroyed, hampering relief efforts, and sewage mixed with water, spreading disease.

The Mississippi flood submerged thousands of homes. Many people had to wait on roofs or in treetops until boats came to rescue them.

Monsoon rains have
turned this stream in
Goa, India, into a
raging torrent, fed by
a gigantic waterfall.

Northeast
winds in
winter

Southwest
winds in
summer

THE DELUGE

Summer in India is the
monsoon season. Winds
from the southwest
bring towering clouds
that drench the country
with rain, sometimes
for weeks on end. The
rains refresh parched
land, but can cause
catastrophic floods. In
1997 more than 950
people were killed by
monsoon floods in India,
and more than 250,000
were driven from their
homes in Bangladesh.

MUDDY WATERS

When floodwater rushes
down a valley it can
carve out so much soil
that it becomes a torrent
of mud. If the water
flows into buildings, the
mud settles and can fill
a house up to the roof;
it then dries and sets
like concrete. Although
muddy floods cause
great damage, they also
bring life by spreading
nutrients on farmland.

81

HOT AND DRY

IT SEEMS CRIMINAL TO STAY INDOORS when the Sun is shining and the sky is blue. We usually think of hot weather as something to enjoy, but if scorching temperatures strike unexpectedly, or last for longer than usual, the effects can be disastrous. A heat wave can destroy crops, empty reservoirs, buckle roads, and create the perfect conditions for raging wildfires. And hot weather can kill. The human body copes with heat by producing sweat, which cools down the skin as it evaporates. But if the weather is too hot or the air too humid for sweat to evaporate, this cooling mechanism is taxed beyond its limits. The result is heatstroke, which can lead swiftly to dizziness, collapse, coma, and death.

DEADLY SUMMER

A heat wave sends many people crowding on beaches to soak up the Sun, but others stay in the shade or switch on the air conditioning – a luxury that can save lives. The death-rate in cities rises sharply when daytime temperatures exceed 35°C (95°F), especially if it stays very warm at night. First to succumb are usually the very young and the very old, but heatstroke can affect anyone. In July 1996 unusually fierce heat waves in the USA claimed 1,000 lives.

MIRAGE MAKER

Extreme heat can produce tricks of the light known as mirages. This truck looks as though it is driving through shallow water, but it is just an illusion. Air close to the ground is much hotter than the air a little higher, and light is bent as it passes across the boundary between the two temperatures. This creates a shimmering reflection that looks like water.

DUNE-BUSTING

Prolonged hot and dry weather can make deserts spread into bordering areas, burying farms and towns under giant sand dunes as they advance. Schemes like this one in Niger, where millet has been planted in a sand dune, can help to stop the desert in its tracks. The roots of the plants help to bind the sand together to give it some stability, and the leaves act as windbreaks, preventing the surface sand and soil from blowing away.

CATFISH IN A DRYING RIVER, TANZANIA

BURIED ALIVE

In many tropical countries there is a dry season every year, and nature must adapt to cope with the harsh changes this brings. River dwellers, especially, have ingenious means of survival. Some catfish can gulp air, allowing them to struggle through shallow mud to reach permanent waterways. Lungfish and other catfish have an even more dramatic survival strategy. As their rivers dry up they bury themselves in mud, leaving a tiny airhole through which they can breathe. The mud then bakes hard and their hearts slow down. They remain trapped underground until the rains return and free them again.

These two elands died during a drought in Africa, probably as a result of starvation.

DROUGHT

When hot weather outstays its welcome, depriving the land of life-giving rain, it causes drought. A drought can last for months or even years, with catastrophic results. First plants die and crops fail, then animals begin to starve. When food runs out, people begin to starve too. Africa's Sahel region (the area south of the Sahara) suffered a drought that lasted from the 1960s right up until 1980. More than 100,000 people died in the resulting famine, along with 4 million cattle.

WEATHERING AND EROSION

T HE FOOTPRINTS LEFT BY ASTRONAUTS on the surface of the Moon in 1969 are still there today. The Moon, without an atmosphere, lacks weather. Footprints left in the Earth's dust are covered or swept away within days or even hours. This is because weather constantly shapes our planet's surface. Even solid rock does not last forever. When exposed, it becomes weathered. Assault by physical, chemical, and biological processes breaks it down, eventually turning even the hardest granite to soft clay. Erosion is the wearing down and removal of rock in the form of sediment. This can be rapid or gradual, depending on the type of rock.

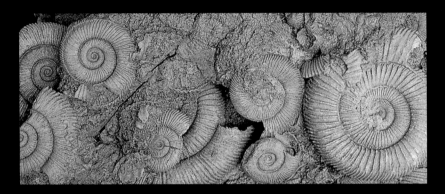

AMMONITE GRAVEYARD

These are the fossilized remains of ammonites – sea creatures related to squid and cuttlefish. They died and were smothered in sediment some 65 million years ago. Their shells and the sediment surrounding them eventually turned to rock. Weathering and erosion have now uncovered these fossils in their ancient graves.

HOODOOS

In Goblin Valley, Utah, USA, strange pedestals of rock, called hoodoos (*right*), are shaped by wind, water, and temperature change. A sharp drop in temperature at night causes the rock surface to splinter. During the day, sand-blasting winds carve out eerie shapes. Where the rock is resistant, a bulging head or belly forms. Where the rock succumbs more easily to erosion, a waist or neck develops.

ACID RAIN

This limestone sculpture has been disfigured by acid rain. The natural, weak acidity of rainwater has been strengthened by pollution. Traffic fumes and factory smoke contain oxides of sulphur and nitrogen. These react with air and rainwater to make sulphuric and nitric acids. When the acids fall in rain, they dissolve limestone, and damage trees and lake life.

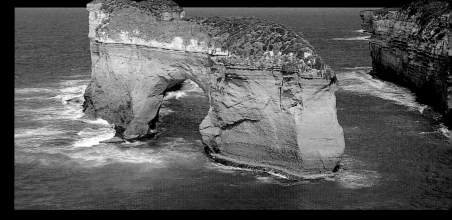

SEA EROSION

This naturally carved sandstone arch in Western Victoria, Australia, demonstrates the immense power of wind, waves, and currents to cut through solid rock. Waves wear away coastal rocks by pounding them with water, hurling stones at them, and forcing air into cracks so hard that the rocks burst apart. When the arch eventually collapses, it may leave behind spectacular tall pillars of rock called stacks.

NIAGARA FALLS

Waterfalls occur where there is an abrupt change in land level during a river's journey from source to sea. Flowing water will erode any soft rocks at the waterfall's edge or in the plunge pool at its base. Where harder rocks remain, creating rocky outcrops, steep rapids may appear. The Niagara Falls, on the USA's border with Canada, flow over hard limestone, which overlays a softer sandstone. The Falls are eroding the rock at the rate of 1 m (3 ft 3 in) a year. So far, the Falls have cut back the rock by 11 km (7 miles).

PLANT ATTACK

Plants speed up the weathering process by penetrating cracks in rocks. As this tree grows, its roots thicken and reach deeper into the rocky ground. Slowly, the roots widen the cracks and the rocks split further. Animals add to the process by burrowing through the cracks, and mosses dissolve the rocks' surfaces with plant acids.

GRAND CANYON

The majestic Grand Canyon in Arizona, USA, was carved by the Colorado River over a period of 20 million years. The river has eroded its way down to rock that is two billion years old. Wind, frost, rain, and tumbling streams have all shaped the canyon's sides. The rocks in various layers respond in different ways to the forces of erosion. Hard sandstones produce cliffs, soft shales form slopes. This creates the canyon's rich mix of shape and texture.

VOLCANIC WEATHER

I N 1815, WITH A ROAR THAT COULD BE HEARD hundreds of kilometres away, Mount Tambora in Indonesia exploded. The eruption – the most violent on record – obliterated the top third of the mountain and blasted some 145 cubic kilometres (35 cubic miles) of rock, dust, and ash into the sky, producing a cloud of debris so gigantic that it injected material into the stratosphere. Volcanic eruptions such as Tambora can have profound effects on weather across the planet. As well as triggering catastrophic tidal waves and landslides, they can launch so much dust into the upper atmosphere that skies darken around the world, robbing the ground of life-giving sunlight. People called 1816 "the year with no summer". While parts of the USA and Canada had frost and snow through summer, cold and miserable weather in western Europe caused crop failures and famine.

MOUNT ST HELENS

In the spring of 1980 the northern flank of Mount St Helens in the USA began to bulge ominously as pressure welled deep inside the volcano. On 18 May the inevitable happened. The northern slope collapsed, releasing a jet of superheated gas that blasted rock and ash sideways out of the mountain, flattening 10 million trees and producing a colossal cloud of debris. Next came the vertical eruption, which smashed the summit and threw ash and gas 19 km (12 miles) high. Carried by high winds, the ash from Mount St Helens encircled the entire planet, producing hazy skies, stunning red sunsets, and a brief drop in temperature worldwide.

The eruption of Mount St Helens blew the top 400 m (1,300 ft) off the mountain and lifted half a cubic km (0.1 cubic mile) of debris into the atmosphere.

MOUNT PINATUBO

When Mount Pinatubo exploded in the Philippines in 1991, a torrent of scalding ash incinerated the surrounding land for kilometres. Clouds of debris 40 km (25 miles) high blackened the sky and covered huge areas with ash, turning everything grey. Rain turned the ash into mud, causing mudslides that destroyed thousands of people's homes. Pinatubo's eruption was the most violent of the 20th century and killed nearly 800 people.

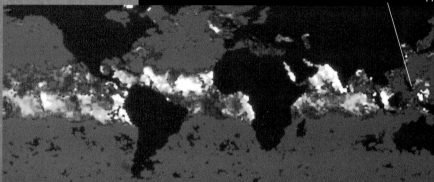

The Philippin

SATELLITE PICTURE
OF VOLCANIC CLOUD
FROM PINATUBO

GLOBAL COOLING

As well as belching out clouds of ash and molten rock, Pinatubo belched out a mass of volcanic dust and gas into the stratosphere. More than 15 million tonnes of sulphur dioxide formed clouds of tiny sulphuric acid droplets, which spread around the world and lingered in the air for over 18 months. The droplets blocked out sunlight, making temperatures around the world about 0.5°C (0.9°F) lower than usual.

VOLCANIC SUNSETS

Volcanoes can produce amazing sunsets. Tiny particles of volcanic ash scatter all of the colours in sunlight except red and orange, which pass through. The effect is greatest when the Sun is low in the sky and light has to pass through a lot of dusty air. Volcanic sunsets continue until all the dust has settled. They were seen around the world for months after Mount St Helens's eruption.

CLIMATE CHANGE

THE 1990S WERE THE NORTHERN HEMISPHERE'S warmest decade on record. Most scientists now believe that the Earth's climate is rapidly warming and that humans are to blame. Some of the Sun's heat bounces off the Earth, and travels out through the atmosphere in the form of infrared radiation. Certain gases, such as carbon dioxide, absorb infrared radiation and trap heat in the atmosphere. This occurs naturally and is called the greenhouse effect. But burning fossil fuels to provide power for homes, industry, and cars produces extra carbon dioxide. This accelerates the greenhouse effect and overheats the planet. Other polluting gases are responsible for thinning the atmosphere's ozone layer, which shields us from harmful ultraviolet radiation.

HOLE IN THE OZONE

The ozone layer protects the Earth's living organisms from the Sun's harmful ultraviolet radiation. The deep blue area on this computer-generated view of the Earth in 2000 (*right*), indicates a gigantic hole in the ozone layer above Antarctica. Gases called CFCs (chlorofluorocarbons), which are used in refrigerators and aerosol sprays, have risen into the atmosphere and destroyed ozone. Many countries have now banned the use of CFCs, and the hole may now be getting smaller.

APOLLO BUTTERFLIES FROM THE EUROPEAN ALPINE MEADOWS FACE EXTINCTION

ADAPT OR DIE

When climate changes abruptly, animals and plants that cannot withstand or adapt to the new conditions must leave or face extinction. The Apollo butterfly has adapted to the cool climates of mountains. If global warming makes its habitat too warm, it will have nowhere left to go.

HOT AND CHOKED

On a sunny day, many big cities are covered in a choking brown smog (*left*). Smog is produced when gases from vehicle exhausts react with sunlight. The result is a thick haze that contains carbon monoxide and other harmful gases. Governments meet regularly to decide what can be done to reduce greenhouse gas emissions, but it seems to be too little too late to prevent global warming.

ICE RIFT

Since the mid-1990s, giant cracks have been appearing in parts of Antarctica's Larsen Ice Shelf, (*right*) and massive ice chunks have been floating away. This may be because more polar ice is melting. In sub-Antarctica, some penguin populations are declining as sea ice reduces because they have to swim further to find fish to eat.

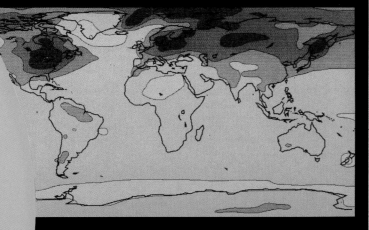

GLOBAL WARMING

If carbon dioxide and other greenhouse gases continue to pour into the atmosphere unchecked, the world may warm rapidly. This computer forecast (*above*) shows how much temperatures may increase by 2010 compared with temperatures in 1950. The red areas indicate a predicted increase of 4–5°C (7.2–9°F). Moderate rises are shown in orange. The pale areas indicate no change. Weather will probably become more unpredictable and extreme – with heavier rain in some places, and droughts in others.

Unbleached coral containing algae

WATER TOO WARM

In 1998, whole coral reefs in the Indian Ocean turned white and died when water temperatures rose just 1–2°C (1.8–3.6°F) above normal. Reef-building corals are animals containing tiny algae that make food for the corals. If the waters become too warm, the corals eject the algae and die. A strong El Niño, perhaps enhanced by global warming, caused the temperature rise.

Bleached coral without algae

CLOSE-UP OF DAMAGED CORAL, INDIAN OCEAN

DROWNING WORLD

IF THE EARTH CONTINUES TO WARM, more polar ice will melt and sea levels will rise. This could be a catastrophe for people living in low-lying coastal areas. But rising sea levels are nothing new. Land and sea have always had their ups and downs. During glacial times, rain froze and stayed on land instead of running into the sea, so sea levels were low. But when, like now, we are living in a milder period (interglacial), ice melts and sea levels rise. Since the beginning of the last major thaw, about 18,000 years ago, sea levels have risen by an incredible 120 m (394 ft). During the next 100 years, the Earth's surface may warm by 3°C (5.4°F), due to an enhanced greenhouse effect, causing sea levels to rise by at least 0.5 m (1 ft 7 in) – enough to affect the lives of millions of people.

LOST CITY OF ATLANTIS

In about 370 BC, the Greek philosopher Plato described a civilization called Atlantis, which sank beneath the waves because the gods were angry. In fact, the legend may be based on the ancient Minoan civilization in the Mediterranean Sea, which was probably devastated by volcanoes and earthquakes in about 1450 BC.

SINKING VENICE

During very high tides in St Mark's Square, Venice, Italy (*left*), visitors tread carefully along temporary walkways and wear rubber boots. The city's leading attraction is its canals, where boats replace cars. Venice was built in medieval times on wooden piles sunk into the marshy ground. It is sinking by about 1 cm (0.4 in) each decade, and its buildings flood several times a year. At the same time, the Adriatic Sea, which flows through Venice, is set to rise by 2.5 cm (1 in) by 2010.

TROPICAL THREAT

Rising seas threaten small tropical islands. Many lie only 1–2 m (3–6 ft) above sea level, and could vanish beneath the waves within the next few centuries if global warming trends continue. The losses could be catastrophic. Low-lying island states, such as the Maldives in the Indian Ocean, are highly populated and harbour rare and exotic wildlife. In the Florida Keys, USA (*right*), small islands are of historical and wildlife interest. Their disappearence will threaten the local tourist industry.

BUILDING A SEA WALL

As sea levels rise, low-lying developed countries, such as the Netherlands, are spending huge amounts of money building sea defences. In 1953 a high tide, coupled with a storm surge, overwhelmed the Netherlands' coast. It killed about 1,800 people and destroyed 43,000 homes. The same surge also caused Britain's worst peace-time natural disaster, claiming 300 lives.

PROTEST PRESSURE

At the 1992 Earth Summit in Brazil, environmental groups helped to pressure world leaders into signing the UN Convention on Climate Change. But progress in cutting greenhouse gas emissions has been slow.

Developed countries, such as the USA, still produce a large portion of the world's greenhouse gases. Despite this, the developed countries are less likely to be affected by climate change – and rising sea levels – than poor countries in tropical regions. Large areas of Bangladesh are less than 2 m (6 ft) above sea level and millions of people there are affected by floods caused by cyclone surges.

FLORIDA KEYS

Florida's coastline is threatened by erosion, rising sea levels, and storm surges. This map shows what would happen if the sea were to rise by 7.5 m (25 ft). Vast areas of the state would be swamped, including the city of Miami. Such an event is unlikely in the next few hundred years, but even a 1 m (3 ft) sea level rise would cover many of Florida's beaches and endanger wildlife.

POLLUTION

FOR FOUR DAYS IN DECEMBER 1952 a lethal concoction of fog mixed with smoke and soot from thousands of coal fires and steam trains engulfed London. Visibility was reduced to a few metres, streetlights came on in the middle of the day, and buses crawled at barely walking pace. People choked and spluttered as they walked, finding it difficult to breathe, and 4,000 people died, poisoned by the air. This kind of thick, toxic smog was once common in industrial cities. Since then, global concern has led to the introduction of laws to clean up urban air, but vehicle exhaust and industrial waste are still polluting the atmosphere and having a dramatic effect on life on Earth.

ACID RAIN

This conifer forest is suffering from the effects of acid rain. Acid rain occurs when sulphur and nitrogen oxides, released by factories and cars, interact with sunlight and water vapour in the clouds to form sulphuric and nitric acids. The airborne acid contaminates water supplies, takes vital nutrients from soil, and damages forests and crops. It can also kill fish and other freshwater animals in lakes and rivers. The problem is particularly bad in North America and northwest Europe.

OZONE HOLE

About 25–50 km (15–30 miles) up in the Earth's atmosphere is a thin layer of the gas ozone. The ozone layer protects life on Earth from harmful ultraviolet radiation from the Sun. In the 1980s, scientists discovered that a hole develops in the ozone layer over Antarctica each spring. They traced the cause to chemicals released by aerosol can propellants, fridges, and air conditioners. The combination of cold weather and bright sunlight causes these chemicals to destroy ozone.

POLLUTION IN MEXICO

Mexico City suffers from extreme photochemical smog. This forms when gases from vehicle exhausts react in strong sunlight, producing substances that reduce visibility and make the air difficult to breathe. Mexico City's smog is particularly bad because the town is surrounded by a ring of mountains that trap the polluted air.

GLOBAL WARMING

By the year 2025 there will be more than a billion cars on the roads, each belching out carbon dioxide and other exhaust fumes. Scientists fear that the rising level of carbon dioxide in the atmosphere is trapping the Sun's heat and causing a gradual warming of the world's climates (global warming). The effect of this may not just be hotter weather, but more extreme weather – increased rain and storms in some areas, and drier weather in others. It might even alter ocean currents. If the Gulf Stream changed course, for instance, northwest Europe would get much colder.

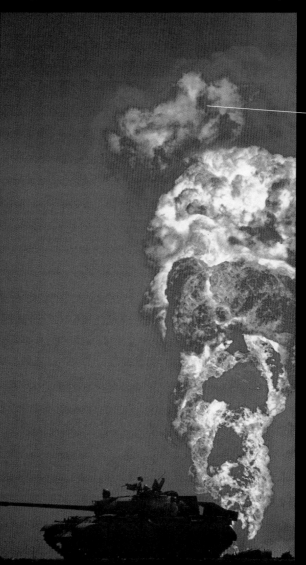

A billowing tower of fire and smoke from a burning oil well in Kuwait

GULF WAR FIRES

In 1990, during the Gulf War between United Nations forces and Iraq, oil refineries and storage depots at the northern end of the Persian Gulf were set on fire. They belched out so much black smoke that it was seen clearly by orbiting satellites and cast a shadow over the Earth's surface. The smoke soon cleared and, alarming though the spectacle was, it had no lasting effect on the weather.

The extent of the ozone hole over Antartica in October (spring) 1995

WEATHER FORECASTING

THE TV FORECASTER WHO TELLS US what the weather will be like is backed by teams of meteorologists (weather scientists), instruments located all over the world and above it, and some of the biggest and most powerful computers in existence. The first weather forecasts were issued in 1869 in the USA. They were compiled from observations sent by telegraph to a central office and calculations made with pen and paper. Today there is a global network of observing stations on land and at sea, satellites maintaining a constant watch over every part of the Earth, and radio and e-mail for the instant transmission of information.

WEATHER STATIONS

There are some 10,000 surface weather stations around the world like this one in Idaho, USA. Most are on land, but some are on moored ships in the middle of the sea. Weather stations send reports to a forecasting centre four times a day, giving details of cloud type, wind speed, temperature, pressure, and so on.

The GOES satellites orbit at a height of 36,000 km (23,000 miles).

THERE SHE GOES

Weather satellites orbit Earth taking pictures, monitoring the temperature, and even measuring the height of waves. The USA's weather satellites are called GOES (geostationary operational environmental satellites). They orbit at the same speed as Earth rotates, so they always stay over the same point. Other satellites are in polar orbits, which take them over the north and south poles alternately.

WEATHER BALLOON

At many weather stations, weather balloons are released each day at noon and midnight Greenwich Mean Time. They rise about 20–30 km (12–19 miles), then burst. The balloon's drift shows wind speed and direction. Beneath it, on a long cable, is a package of instruments that measure temperature, pressure, and humidity, and radio their readings to the ground station. When the balloon bursts, the instruments descend on a parachute.

NUMBER-CRUNCHING

The data from weather stations and satellites is fed into powerful supercomputers. These perform millions of calculations as they predict how the weather will change. Supercomputers are a massive improvement over pen and paper, but the weather is so complicated that it cannot be accurately predicted for more than a few days ahead.

SPIES IN THE SKY

This is North America as it appeared to one of the GOES satellites on 10 February 2000. The swirling cloud masses are areas where it may be stormy or rainy; where the land or coastline is clear, such as over Florida, the weather is fine. GOES satellites transmit their data to ground stations every 30 minutes. The pictures are uploaded onto the Internet, allowing anyone in the world to get an updated view of the continent's weather.

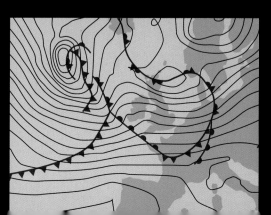

WEATHER MAPS

Forecasts are shown on special maps. Black lines on a weather map join places with the same air pressure; black circles show where pressure is high or low. Blue triangles are cold fronts, red semicircles are warm fronts, and a mixture of triangles and semicircles is an occluded front.

The Quickscat satellite measures wind speeds.

RESEARCH

Scientists also use weather satellites to study how Earth's climate and weather work. This satellite image shows wind patterns over the Pacific Ocean. By studying such patterns, meteorologists hope to improve forecasts of hurricane and iceberg movements, and so give ships and coastal inhabitants better warning of approaching danger.

Harnessing Weather

Every day the sun floods earth with 20 times more energy than is used by all the world's people in a year. Much of this energy is absorbed and released by the atmosphere. A rain shower, for instance, releases as much energy as New York City's streetlights use in a night. If scientists could somehow tap into this tremendous source of power, they could solve humanity's energy needs forever. Think of the coal, oil, gas, and nuclear fuel we would save if we could harness weather instead. Unfortunately, achieving this dream has proved far from easy.

SOLAR POWER

The problem with trying to capture the Sun's energy is that it is spread over a vast area. To get round this, solar power stations use thousands of wide mirrors to collect and concentrate as much sunlight as possible. This solar power station in California's Mojave Desert is part of a vast network that uses a total of 650,000 solar mirrors. The desert climate is ideal for solar power, but in other parts of the world cloudy skies make solar power less effective.

WIND FARM

These windmills belong to a wind farm in California that turns the wind's energy into electricity. The windmills must be far apart so that they do not steal wind from each other, and it takes around 3,000 of them to generate as much power as a coal power station. Wind farms only work in exposed places such as hilltops or coasts. Although they do not cause pollution, some people think they spoil the natural look of such wild places.

WIND GAMES

Wind may not drive the wheels of industry, but it provides endless fun. These spectacular kites at a kite fair could not fly without wind to lift them. Windsurfing, sailing, and land-yachting all depend on the wind, and hot-air balloonists and hang-gliders need the wind to carry them. Even surfers and body-boarders need wind because it is the wind that creates waves.

SUNNY DELIGHT

Bowl-shaped solar mirrors are called heliostats. They focus sunlight onto a central target, which gets very hot. Heliostats are expensive to build, work only in places with guaranteed sunshine, and yet they generate very little energy. In sunny countries many people have solar collectors on their roofs to heat water for showers and laundry. These are like trays containing pipes running back and forth. The collectors are black to absorb heat, and the heat warms water in the pipes. The pipes pass through a water tank indoors and warm the water.

Each of these computer-controlled mirrors tracks the Sun across the sky and reflects its heat onto tubes filled with oil. The heated oil is then used to boil water and make steam, and the steam drives a machine called a turbine to generate electricity.

FLOUR POWER

Sunshine and rain are vital for growing the crops that we depend on, such as this wheat, ripening on a North American farm. But crops can also be used to produce alternatives to petrol, and this is perhaps the most efficient way to use solar energy. In some countries, sugar extracted from maize, sugar beet, or potatoes is converted into alcohol by fermentation. The alcohol is then used as a fuel in specially adapted cars. Fast-growing plants like willow can also be used to fuel power stations.

Beaufort Scale

Force	Wind speed (mph)	Description	Effects
0	0.1 or less	Calm	Air feels still; smoke rises vertically.
1	1–3	Light air	Wind vanes and flags do not move, but rising smoke drifts.
2	4–7	Light breeze	Drifting smoke indicates the wind direction.
3	8–12	Gentle breeze	Leaves rustle, small twigs move, and lightweight flags stir gently.
4	13–18	Moderate breeze	Loose leaves and pieces of paper blow around.
5	19–24	Fresh breeze	Small trees that are in full leaf sway.
6	25–31	Strong breeze	Difficult to use an umbrella.
7	32–38	Moderate gale	The wind exerts strong pressure on people walking into it.
8	39–46	Fresh gale	Small twigs torn from trees.
9	47–54	Strong gale	Chimneys blown down; slates and tiles torn from roofs.
10	55–63	Whole gale	Trees broken or uprooted.
11	64–75	Storm	Trees uprooted and blown some distance, cars overturned.
12	above 75	Hurricane	Devastation widespread, buildings destroyed, and many trees uprooted.

HURRICANE CATEGORIES: THE SAFFIR/SIMPSON SCALE

Category	Wind speed (mph)	Damage
1	74–95	Trees and shrubs lose leaves and twigs; unanchored mobile homes damaged.
2	96–110	Small trees blown down, major damage to exposed mobile homes, chimneys and tiles blown from roofs.
3	111–130	Leaves stripped from trees, big trees blown down, mobile homes destroyed, small buildings damaged structurally.
4	131–155	Extensive damage to windows, roofs, and doors; mobile homes completely demolished; floods up to 10 km (6 miles) inland.
5	Above 155	All buildings severely damaged, small buildings destroyed.

THE FUJITA SCALE

Number	Wind speed (mph)	Effects
F0	40–72	Light damage. Branches broken from trees.
F1	73–112	Moderate damage. Trees snap, windows break, some roof damage.
F2	113–157	Considerable damage. Large trees uprooted, flimsy buildings destroyed.
F3	158–206	Severe damage. Trees flattened, cars overturned, walls demolished.
F4	207–260	Devastating damage. Frame houses demolished.
F5	261–318	Incredible damage. Cars moved more than 90 m (300 ft), steel-reinforced buildings badly damaged.

MAP OF WEATHER RECORDS

1. Coldest place
Vostok Station, Antarctica. On 21 July 1983 the temperature was measured as −89.2ºC (−128.6ºF).

2. Hottest place
El Azizia, Libya. On 13 September 1922 the temperature reached 57.8ºC (136ºF).

3. Greatest extremes
Verkhoyansk, Siberia. The lowest recorded temperature is −68ºC (−90ºF), the highest is 37ºC (98ºF).

4. Heaviest snowstorm
Mount Shasta Ski Bowl, California, USA. One storm, lasting from 13 to 19 December 1955, delivered 480 cm (189 in) of snow.

5. Snowiest day
Bessans, France. 173 cm (68 in) of snow fell in 19 hours on 5–6 April 1969.

6. Snowiest place
Mount Baker, Washington State, USA, received 29 m (95 ft) of snow in the winter of 1998–99.

7. Biggest hailstone
The largest authenticated hailstone fell at Coffeyville, Kansas, USA, on 3 September 1970 and measured 14.4 cm (5.7 in) wide and 0.77 kg (1 lb 11 oz) in weight. There are also reports of hailstones 1 kg (2 lb 4 oz) in weight (as heavy as a bag of sugar) falling at Gopalganj in Bangladesh on 14 April 1986.

8. Rainiest place
Lloro, Colombia, is estimated to have received an average 1,330 cm (524 in) of rain a year for 29 years.

9. Rainiest day
On 15–16 March 1952, 187 cm (74 in) of rain fell on the island of Reunion in the Indian Ocean.

10. Wettest year
Between August 1860 and July 1861 Cherrapunji, India, received approximately 26 m (86 ft) of rain.

11. Driest place
Arica in Chile's Atacama Desert had an average of less than 0.75 mm (0.03 in) of rain a year over 59 years.

12. Longest drought
Southwestern North America suffered a 59-year drought from 1246 to 1305. It was most intense between 1276 and 1299.

13. Strongest recorded wind gust
372 kph (231 mph) at Mount Washington, New Hampshire, USA, on 12 April 1934. The winds in tornadoes can be even faster.

14. Strongest sustained wind
About 322 kph (200 mph), when the Labor Day Storm struck the Florida Keys, USA, on 2 September 1935.

15. Fiercest hurricane
Typhoon Tip, in the northwest Pacific on 12 October 1979, had sustained winds of 305 kph (190 mph).

16. Lowest air pressure
Pressure in the eye of Typhoon Tip was 870 millibars.

17. Highest air pressure
A pressure of 1,083.8 millibars was recorded at Agata, Siberia, Russia, on 31 December 1968.

18. Most severe tornado outbreak
In March 1925 a series of possibly seven tornadoes (the Tri-state Tornado) crossed Missouri, Illinois, and Indiana, covering 703 km (437 miles) and killing 689 people.

19. Worst American hurricane
At Galveston, Texas, on 8 September 1900, a hurricane killed 6,000 people, injured more than 5,000, and destroyed half the town's buildings.

20. Worst cyclone
In November 1970 a cyclone moved from the Bay of Bengal across Bangladesh, causing floods that killed about half a million people.

1697 In October a castle exploded in the town of Athlone, Ireland, when lightning set fire to a store room containing 260 barrels of gunpowder.

1876–9 Between 9 and 13 million people starved to death in northern China as a result of one of the worst droughts in history.

1879 The Tay Bridge in Scotland was struck by two tornadoes simultaneously on 28 December. The bridge was destroyed and the evening mail train from Edinburgh to Dundee fell into the river. Between 75 and 90 people were killed.

1887 The Yellow River in China burst its banks and flooded about 26,000 sq km (10,000 sq miles) in September and October. Between 900,000 and 2.5 million people died.

1888 A hailstorm pummelled the town of Moradabad in India with hailstones the size of grapefruits, killing 246 people and over 1,000 sheep and goats.

1925 The "Tri-state Tornado" – the worst tornado disaster in US history – ploughed through the states of Missouri, Illinois, and Indiana, leaving a trail of devastation 1.5 km (0.9 miles) wide and killing 689 people. The Tri-state Tornado was probably a series of up to seven separate tornadoes. The death toll was unusually high because the tornadoes passed through a string of mining villages and farms, moving so swiftly that they caught people unawares.

1930s The North American Midwest had almost no rain for five years, turning thousands of square kilometres of farmland into a desert called the Dust Bowl. Hot winds whipped up the parched soil, causing choking duststorms. Around 5,000 people died as a result of heatstroke and breathing problems.

1931 The Yangtze River, China, rose 30 m (97 ft) following a period of heavy rain. About 3.7 million people died, some in the floods but most in the famine that followed.

1962 In January a huge block of ice broke off a glacier on Mount Huascaran in Peru. It fell a kilometre and then crashed into a snowfield, triggering a massive avalanche and mudslide that destroyed a town and six villages. Approximately 4,000 people were killed.

1963 In December a bolt of lightning struck the wing of a Boeing 707 aircraft over Maryland, USA, and set light to the fuel tank. The plane exploded in midair, killing 81 people.

1970 Half a million people died in Bangladesh in November when a tropical cyclone produced a gigantic wave that flooded the Ganges Delta.

1974 Cyclone Tracy destroyed 90 per cent of the city of Darwin, Australia, on Christmas Day. More than 50 people died.

1976 Hurricane Liza struck La Paz, Mexico, on 1 October. Heavy rain destroyed a dam, releasing a wall of water that killed at least 630 people in a shanty town downstream.

1977 A cyclone and storm surge washed away 21 villages and damaged 44 more in Andhra Pradesh, India, on 19 November. An estimated 20,000 people died and more than 2 million were made homeless.

1977 A cyclone killed at least 1,500 people and destroyed more than 500,000 buildings in Sri Lanka and southern India on 23 November.

1980 A heat wave lasting more than a month hit a vast area of the USA in the summer. In Texas, temperatures exceeded 38°C (100°F) almost every day. The scorching weather started forest fires, withered crops, buckled roads, and dried up reservoirs. The official death toll was 1,265.

1982 Monsoon floods in Orissa, India, in September killed at least 1,000 people and left 5 million marooned on roofs and high ground.

1983 Searing summer temperatures triggered hundreds of forest fires in southern Australia in February. The fires raged out of control, sending burning shreds of vegetation into the air that spread the blaze. Fire engulfed the mainly wood-built town of Macedon, killed more than 70 people, and damaged thousands of acres of land.

1984 Giant hailstones pelted the town of Munich, Germany, for just 20 minutes on 12 July, causing an incredible $1 billion worth of damage and injuring more than 400 people. The hail punched holes in roofs, smashed car windows, flattened greenhouses and wrecked more than 150 aircraft at the city's airport.

1985 A cyclone and storm surge struck islands off Bangladesh on 25 May, killing an estimated 2,540 people, but possibly as many as 11,000.

1988 Monsoon floods inundated 75 per cent of Bangladesh in late August and September, killing more than 2,000 people and leaving at least 30 million homeless.

1988 Hurricane Gilbert killed at least 260 people in the Caribbean and the Gulf of Mexico between 12 and 17 September, and generated nearly 40 tornadoes in Texas.

1991 A cyclone killed at least 131,000 people on coastal islands off Bangladesh on 30 April.

1992 Blizzards caused avalanches that killed 201 people in Turkey in February.

1992 Hurricane Andrew struck the Bahamas, Florida, and Louisiana in August, killing 65 people, destroying 25,000 homes, and almost completely demolishing the towns of Homestead and Florida City, Florida. It was the most costly hurricane in US history, with damage estimated at $20 billion.

1993 A blizzard from 12 to 15 March killed at least 238 people in the eastern United States, 4 in Canada, and 3 in Cuba.

1993 Mudslides killed 400 people and destroyed 1,000 homes in Honduras from 31 October to 2 November.

1995 A mudslide destroyed a village in Afghanistan on 27 March, killing 354 people.

1996 A tornado in Bangladesh destroyed 80 villages in less than half an hour on 13 May, killing more than 440 people and injuring more than 32,000.

1997 An avalanche buried at least 100 people in northern Afghanistan on 26 March. The victims had been walking along a road to catch a bus.

1997 Lightning killed 19 people and injured 6 in Andhra Pradesh, India, on 11 September.

1998 Tornadoes in Florida killed at least 42 people, injured more than 260, and left hundreds homeless on 23 February.

1998 A mudslide caused by heavy rain swamped the town of Sarno, Italy, in early May, killing at least 135 people. The "black tide" of mud swept away trees and cars, blocked roads, and destroyed houses, making 2,000 people homeless.

1998 A heat wave killed at least 2,500 people in India in May and early June.

1998 The Yangtze River, China, flooded from June to August. The floods affected an estimated 230 million people and 3,656 people died.

1998 A tsunami (tidal wave) struck Papua New Guinea on 17 July, killing at least 2,500 people.

1998 Floods along the River Nile in Sudan in September and October destroyed more than 120,000 homes, leaving at least 200,000 people homeless. At least 88 people died.

1998 Hurricane Mitch devastated Central America in October, producing winds up to 240 kph (150 mph) and causing widespread flooding and mudslides. More than 1.5 million people were made homeless, at least 8,600 people were killed, and 12,000 were unaccounted for.

1999 At least 10,000 were killed in Venezuela by floods and mudslides caused by torrential rains in December. The government proclaimed it the country's worst natural disaster of the century.

2000 Tornadoes swept through Georgia, USA, shortly after midnight on 14 February, killing 18 people and injuring about 100.

2000 In February, freak torrential rain in southern Africa caused the worst floods for 50 years in Mozambique. More than a million people were forced to leave their homes. Cyclone Eline hit the coast of Mozambique on 22 February, producing winds up to 257 kph (160 mph) and compounding the country's problems.

WEATHER WEBSITES

http://www.hurricanehunters.com

Hurricane Hunters – see photos taken from flights through the eyes of hurricanes

http://rsd.gsfc.nasa.gov/rsd/images

Catalogue of satellite pictures of hurricanes

http://weather.yahoo.com

Weather forecasts for anywhere in the world

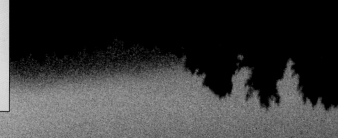

OCEANS

OCEANS MAKE UP 70 PER CENT OF THE surface area of our planet. They cover Earth's deepest valleys and highest mountains, and they teem with life. Their depths remain largely unexplored but the secrets that have been uncovered are plentiful. From underwater meadows and forests to small fish that climb trees and bus-sized whale sharks, oceans are enchanting.

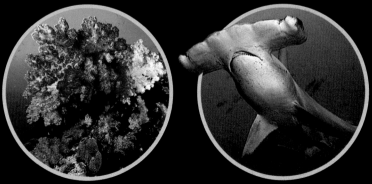

ONE OCEAN

PHOTOGRAPHS OF THE EARTH, TAKEN FROM SPACE, clearly show the shape and position of its continents and oceans. If we had similar photographs from millions of years ago, they would show that the Earth's landmass has split and come together several times. About 250 million years ago (MYA), our continents were part of a single landmass called *Pangaea*, with a single ocean known as *Panthalassa*. When *Pangaea* split up, the ocean was also split – but the different oceans are all connected and operate as one ocean. Changes in one will eventually affect all the others.

The Tower of London, England (UK), in winter

200 MYA

MOVEMENT OF THE EARTH'S CONTINENTS

135 MYA

EARTH TODAY

10 MYA

NORTH AMERICAN PLATE

A line of latitude

PACIFIC OCEAN

NORTH AMERICA

ATLANTIC OCEAN

THE EQUATOR

CARIBBEAN PLATE

PACIFIC PLATE

NAZCA PLATE

SOUTH AMERICA

The red lines indicate boundaries between tectonic plates.

SOUTH AMERICAN PLATE

SCOTIA PLATE

ANTARCTIC PLATE

GIANT JIGSAW

Imagine that the Earth's continents are all pieces in a giant jigsaw. If you could move them around, they would all fit together quite well. The bulge on the northwest side of Africa fits into the space between North America and South America. This is evidence that these continents were once joined together. The existence of identical fossils found on different continents also supports this theory.

The Earth's climate altered as the continents moved and as the oceans were formed. Scientists now fear that global warming may affect the oceans and currents, which would change weather patterns.

The Arabian Gulf (indicated on the map, above right) was formed only 3–4 million years ago. This is very recent on the geological time scale. Movements of the surrounding land caused a folding and sagging of the rocks. As a result, a shallow basin – the Gulf – was formed.

This photograph shows a shoal of chromis fish (Chromis species) above coral at the Great Barrier Reef, which extends along northeastern Australia.

CURRENT WEATHER

Ocean currents greatly influence climate and weather on land. London and Moscow should have similar climates because they are roughly the same distance away from the Equator – they have a similar "latitude" (see map). But London has much milder winters due to a current called the Gulf Stream, which carries warm water from the Caribbean to Britain. Moscow, far inland and away from the ocean, freezes up in winter with temperatures as low as -10°C (14°F).

Gorky Park in Moscow, Russia (Russian Federation), in winter

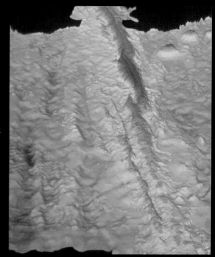

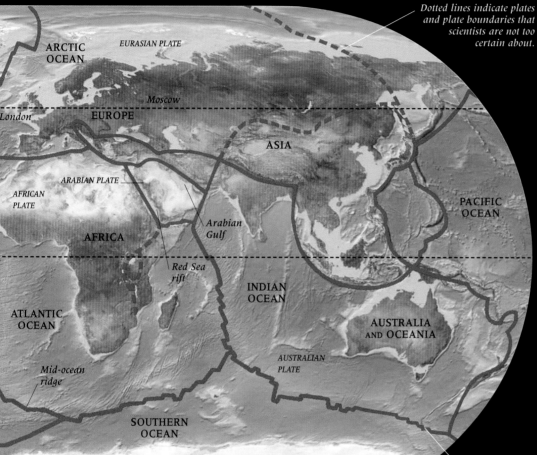

Dotted lines indicate plates and plate boundaries that scientists are not too certain about.

ARCTIC OCEAN · EURASIAN PLATE · Moscow · London · EUROPE · ASIA · ARABIAN PLATE · AFRICAN PLATE · Arabian Gulf · AFRICA · Red Sea rift · INDIAN OCEAN · PACIFIC OCEAN · ATLANTIC OCEAN · AUSTRALIA AND OCEANIA · AUSTRALIAN PLATE · Mid-ocean ridge · SOUTHERN OCEAN · ANTARCTICA

In a few more million years, a map of the world will look completely different from this one.

The tectonic plate boundaries follow lines of volcanic activity such as fault lines, oceanic trenches, and mid-ocean ridges.

GROWING OCEANS

This sonar image shows the East Pacific Rise, which is part of the mid-ocean ridge that runs down the Pacific Ocean. The ridge marks the line where two tectonic plates are pulling apart and where a new area of seabed is forming between them. This part of the Pacific is slowly getting wider as a result. Dark blue indicates the deepest depths while red shows up the shallowest areas.

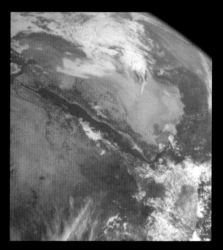

CONTINENTAL DRIFT

The Earth's continents are still moving and changing today – very, very slowly. This process is called continental drift. The Earth's strong outer "skin" – called the lithosphere – is cracked, like an eggshell, into about 12 large and small "tectonic plates". Volcanic forces deep within the Earth cause the plates to slide over the deeper, more liquid-like layers. In doing so, the plates carry the continents with them, like a giant game of "piggyback".

RED SEA RIFT

The Red Sea was formed about 50 million years ago, when Africa started to drift away from Arabia. This created a deep split, which eventually became the Red Sea. The Red Sea is still getting wider at a rate of about 2 cm (0.8 in) per year. In 150 million years' time it could even be as wide as the Atlantic Ocean.

THE BIG BLUE

THE OCEAN IS AN ENORMOUS, THREE-DIMENSIONAL living space. A lot of marine animals and plants live in or on the seabed, but many others spend their entire lives drifting or swimming near the surface and in mid-water. They have special adaptations to help them float effortlessly at their chosen depth. Most animals live within a particular depth range, but some change levels depending on whether it is day or night. In contrast, only a few specialized insects live a completely airborne life. For most of them, it takes up too much energy to stay permanently aloft in the thin air.

DIVISIONS OF THE MARINE ENVIRONMENT

Start of continental slope (200 m)

1. SEASHORE AND SUBLITTORAL ZONE:
0–200 M (0–650 FT)

2. CONTINENTAL SLOPE:
200–4,000 M (650–13,000 FT)

3. DEEPSEA: BED, VENTS, AND OCEAN TRENCHES

OPEN WATER ZONES

1. Sunlit or epipelagic zone, (including surface): 0–200 m (0–650 ft)

Marine life: plankton, jellyfish, flying fish, shoaling fish such as herring, fast predators such as tuna, swordfish and blue sharks, dolphins

2. Twilight or mesopelagic zone: 200–2,000 m (650–6,500 ft)

Marine life: animal plankton, small silvery fish with large eyes such as lantern fish, squid, prawns

3. Deepsea zones – bathypelagic zone and abyssopelagic zone (which includes deepsea trenches): 2,000–10,000 m (6,500–33,000 ft)

Marine life: small fish with large mouths and stomachs such as gulper eels, widemouths, anglerfish, rattail fish

THE MARINE ENVIRONMENT
Living in water is totally different from living on land. Water is much more dense than air and provides support. The blue whale is the largest animal that has ever lived on Earth. It can measure as much as 30 m (98 ft) in length. Nothing this size could ever survive on land – it would simply be too heavy to move. Sound travels much faster in water than in air, which aids communication between marine animals. Whales, for instance, can call to each other over huge distances.

COMMON STARFISH FEEDING ON MUSSELS

ECHINODERMS
Scientists believe that life on Earth began in the oceans and only later spread out onto the land. Most big groups (phyla) of animals found living in the sea also have representatives on land or in fresh water. Snails, for example, are found in the sea, on land, and in fresh water. However one large group, called the echinoderms (which means "spiny-skinned"), is only found in the oceans. Starfish, sea urchins, and sea cucumbers are all echinoderms.

SEA URCHIN

SEA CUCUMBER

SPERM WHALE (*PHYSETER MACROCEPHALUS*)

CRUSHING PRESSURE

Atmospheric pressure is commonly measured in units called atmospheres (atm). 1 atm is equal to about 1 kg of force per sq cm (15 lb per sq in). Going down into the depths of the oceans, water pressure increases by 1 atm for every 10 m (33 ft) of depth. Sperm whales can easily dive down to 1,000 m (3,300 ft), where the pressure – which is now 100 times greater than at the surface – crushes their chest and lungs. No human could survive this, but whales can. Whilst underwater they use oxygen already in their body tissues and re-inflate their lungs as they surface. Animals without any air spaces inside them, such as deepsea fish, are not affected by the increased pressure.

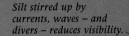

Silt stirred up by currents, waves – and divers – reduces visibility.

RED AND BLUE

Light is made up of the colours of the rainbow – red, orange, yellow, green, blue, indigo, and violet. In the ocean, red objects such as this lionfish appear a dull, bluish colour (top left) – as does a diver's blood! This is because the red part of light can only penetrate a short distance down into the ocean. Artificial flash light, from an underwater camera or torch, restores the true colour (bottom left).

FOGGY WATER

On a clear day, on land, it is possible to see mountains and hills many kilometres away. Even in the clearest tropical seas a diver can only see objects up to about 50 m (164 ft) away. On land, this would be considered a thick fog! Floating plankton and silt greatly reduce visibility in coastal waters.

OCEAN MOTION

WAVES ARE GENERATED BY wind blowing across the ocean surface. Strong, long-lasting winds blowing over great distances create the biggest waves. When a wave nears land its base catches on the seabed and slows, while the top part carries on, curls over, and crashes down as a breaker. Ocean currents, flowing like underwater winds, move water around the oceans in giant circles. Some currents are warm while others are cold, and this has a great influence on our weather.

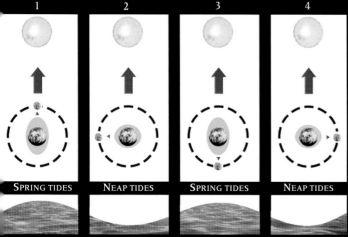

1	2	3	4
SPRING TIDES	NEAP TIDES	SPRING TIDES	NEAP TIDES

DIRECTED BY THE MOON

Tides are caused by the pull of gravity from the Sun and the Moon. The Moon is nearer to the Earth and so it exerts a stronger pull. The Moon moves around the Earth, and when the Sun, Moon, and Earth are in line (1 and 3) their gravities act together. This causes very high and low tides – the "spring" tides. When the Sun and Moon lie at right angles (2 and 4) the pull is weaker and there are smaller tides – the "neap" tides.

High tide in the Bay of Fundy   *Low tide in the Bay of Fundy*

HIGH AND DRY

Tides do not all behave the same around all the oceans' shores. In some places, such as the Mediterranean, the difference between the highest and the lowest water levels (the tidal range) is only about 1 m (3.3 ft) and the tide does not go out very far. In contrast, the tide in the Bay of Fundy, in Canada, falls by around 14 m (46 ft) and a huge expanse of seabed is revealed twice a day – leaving the boats there high and dry (above).

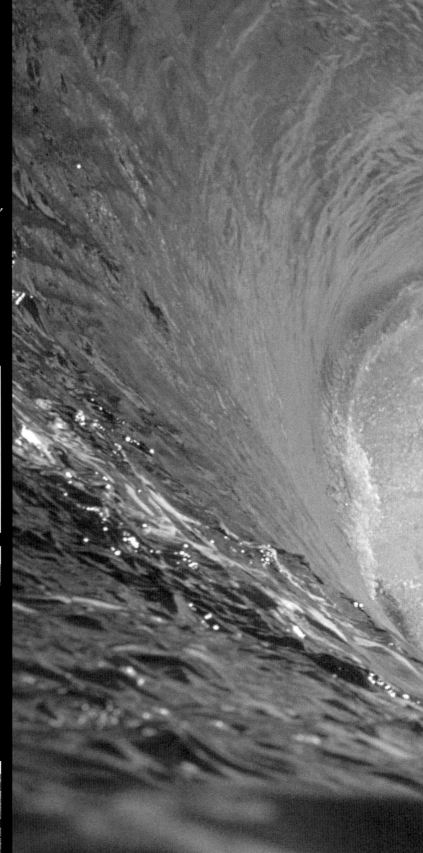

OCEAN SURFING
While most people fear the tremendous power of the huge breakers that roll onto the shores of Hawaii, surfers use this energy to experience the ride of a lifetime. With perfect timing and balance, a few expert surfers have skied down the smooth front of *Jaws*, the most dangerous and challenging wave system in the world – and lived to tell the tale. *Jaws* rears up to 18 m (60 ft) high along the edge of a hidden offshore reef near Maui, Hawaii. Most ocean waves are less than 3.7 m (12 ft) high.

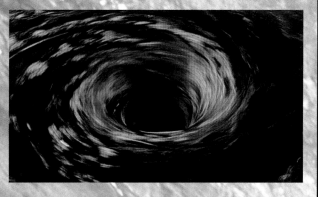

WHIRLPOOLS

Whirlpools such as this one (above) are created when strong tidal currents meet and clash. This usually happens where the water is channelled through narrow passages between islands and landmasses. Water roars so fast through the Saltstraumen Channel, off Norway's northwest coast, that the noise of the resulting whirlpools and eddies – where the water current reverses back on itself – can be heard several kilometres away.

Surfing waves this big is exhilarating but dangerous. The huge downward force and weight of the breaking wave can crush both people and boats.

CURRENT FOOD

Water currents can move up and down as well as sideways. Upwelling currents carry vital nutrients from the depths up to the surface. The nutrients provide food for tiny floating plants and animals (plankton), which multiply rapidly and are, in turn, eaten by small fish. Plankton in strong, upwelling currents off the coast of Peru feed gigantic shoals of silvery anchovies. Millions of these tiny fish are themselves caught by larger fish, birds, and fishermen. Nearly a quarter of all the fish caught worldwide are taken from here.

ROGUE WAVES

In the open sea, storm waves can stack together to form terrifying walls of water called rogue waves. Off Africa's southeast coast, rogue waves form where Southern Ocean storm waves meet the oncoming Agulhas Current. The waves slow and build to become steep and dangerous. Such waves have claimed many vessels.

WAVE ATTACK!

When wind-driven waves reach the shore, they have immense power. A wave 1 m (3 ft) high in shallow water can easily knock you off your feet. A series of pounding 10 m (33 ft) storm waves can cut back chalk cliffs by 1 m (3 ft) overnight. The sea is perpetually eroding and shaping exposed parts of the coast.

CREATING COASTS

AROUND THE WORLD'S COASTS an endless battle is fought where land meets sea. Every wave that crashes against the beach slowly wears it away. The damage is done by the sand, rocks, and debris that the waves fling against the shore. Soft sandstone and chalk cliffs are eroded quickly, while hard granite cliffs will hardly change over hundreds of years. On sheltered coasts, where waves are small, the sea may add land instead of taking it away. Currents and waves carry sediment in from deeper water and drop it in quiet, inshore areas. Sand and shingle bars, mud flats, and river deltas are built this way.

THE APOSTLES

Port Campbell National Park in the state of Victoria, Australia, is famous for its scenery. Twelve rocky stacks, known as the *Apostles*, stand like sentries guarding the rugged coastline. Each rock was once part of a headland that had been sculpted into an arch by the sea. Continual battering by waves broke each arch, leaving these dramatic rocks standing free.

This stack will eventually collapse into smaller pieces as its base is worn away by crashing waves. Meanwhile, new stacks are being created at other headlands.

UNDESIRABLE RESIDENCE

This house on the Norfolk coast in England was once a long way from the cliff edge. Waves have eroded the soft coastline, over many years, so that some ancient village sites are now several kilometres out to sea. Rock breakwaters have been built offshore at Sea Palling to help stop further erosion.

STEMMING THE TIDE

Building sea walls, such as this one in the USA, protects seaside towns from the full force of the pounding waves. But this can also cause erosion problems further down the coast if the wave patterns and water flow are altered.

ANIMAL EROSION

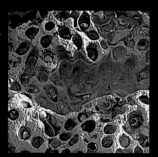

Cliffs and shores made of soft rock are eroded by shellfish such as piddocks. The animals drill into the rock when they are small and enlarge their holes as they grow.

The Fleet is a brackish (slightly salty) lagoon cut off by Chesil Beach. Its quiet, shallow waters hide some fascinating and rare marine creatures.

BUILDING STONES

Walking the length of Chesil Beach in Dorset, England, is extremely tiring! This bank of shingle was built entirely by the sea and stretches for 29 km (18 miles) between the Isle of Portland and the mainland. Strong waves move the pebbles along the coast and toss them up onto the shore.

CAVES AND GULLEYS

Coastlines that are exposed to the full force of ocean waves are often full of caves, carved out by the impact of the waves and the debris they carry. This spectacular blow hole in Hawaii was formed by waves pushing air and water into a small cave in a rock platform. The explosive force created inside the cave literally blew the roof off, creating an escape hole. With the exit hole clear, the air and water mixture can now be blown high into the air.

A diver shines his torch as he peers down into the blue water.

BLUE HOLES

Divers on the island of Gozo, Malta – in the Mediterranean – can walk into a beautiful pool in the shore, dive down into it, and swim out underwater through a huge archway. Over the centuries, this "blue hole" was carved out of fossilized rock by stormy seawaters. Some blue holes in the Bahamas open a long way inland.

SANDY SHORES

ASANDY BEACH IS A PERFECT PLACE to have a picnic, play games, and build sandcastles. This habitat is also a wonderful environment for wildlife. Compared to a rocky shore, the sand may appear lifeless. Seaweeds, limpets, and other fixed animals cannot attach themselves to the shifting surface. Instead, the animals live beneath the surface, protected from storms and safe from birds and other predators. The strand line left behind, as the tide goes out, provides clues as to what lives both here and further out to sea. Shells, egg cases, bones, seaweeds, fishing nets, and other rubbish are picked over by birds, crabs, and even foxes.

Common seals (Phoca vitulina) are also known as harbour seals.

NATURAL SWIMMERS

Common seal pups are often born on sand bars and sandy beaches that appear at low tide. They are able to swim within a few minutes of being born and so are not in danger of drowning when the tide comes in. The pups shed their first white coat before they are born, so they are not often hunted for their skins.

HUMAN TIDE

Sandy shores near towns and cities attract thousands of holidaymakers, especially in warmer climates. This crowded beach in Hawaii is typical. When large numbers of people trample over sand dunes, they can loosen or kill the vegetation that holds the dunes together. As a result, whole dunes may disappear when the wind blows.

HIDDEN VARIETY

Gazing along a sandy shore at low tide, it is hard to imagine that anything can live in such a bare desert. In fact, a surprising variety of worms, shells, crabs, starfish, and urchins lie safely hidden in the damp sand. When the tide returns, these animals emerge to feed.

The peacock worm (Sabella pavonina) extends a beautiful fan of tentacles from its muddy tube. At the slightest sign of danger, it instantly retreats back down its tube.

Ragworms are a favourite food of many wading birds – so, when the tide is out, they burrow into the sand to avoid being eaten. However, they themselves are also active hunters that search out their prey. Fishermen dig them out for bait – but, if handled carelessly, their powerful black jaws can give a painful nip.

SAND CREATURES

Sand is made of such small particles it is difficult to separate the individual grains. But, believe it or not, a whole community of animals – known as the meiofauna – lives in the water-filled spaces between the sand grains. The most common type are tiny worms such as the one shown here (*Derocheilocaris typica*, above) and minute, shrimp-like animals called copepods.

NATTERJACK TOAD

Although relatively common in western Europe, the natterjack toad (*Bufo calamita*) is rare in Britain, where it survives only in sand dunes and heaths. Here, it can burrow easily and lay its eggs in warm, freshwater pools at the back of the dunes.

Marram grass is holding these sand dunes together with its long roots and runners. Shifting sand stimulates it to grow upwards and send out side shoots.

Below is a sand mountain built by a male ghost crab (Ocypode quadrata) at the top of a beach in Oman. The crab lives in the burrow next door (bottom right). The tower (below left) is the marker for his territory.

SAND GHOSTS

Walk along a sandy, tropical shore as dusk falls and you will not be alone! Ghost crabs scurry in all directions, running swiftly on their long legs. They blend into the background so well that, if they stop, they seem to disappear. This is how they got their name. These crabs feed on debris brought in by each tide.

ROCKY SHORES

As THE TIDE GOES DOWN on a rocky shore, it uncovers a hidden seascape of rocks, cliffs, gulleys, and pools. Rocky shores in temperate (cool) regions, such as Great Britain and North America, are home to hundreds of different creatures. Masses of slippery brown seaweeds lie strewn in tangled heaps as the water drains away. Snails and crabs creep into damp crevices. Barnacles, mussels, and limpets stop feeding and tightly close up their shells to keep the life-giving seawater inside.

Green and brown seaweeds in an inter-tidal area along a temperate, rocky seashore on Bardsey Island, North Wales (UK). The brown seaweeds produce a slimy substance, called mucilage, which protects them from the wind and sunshine at low tide.

TIDAL TERRAIN
Exactly what sorts of plants and animals live on a rocky shore depends on where in the world the shore is. Seaweeds grow well on this shore on Bardsey Island, in North Wales (UK). In the picture, low spring tides have uncovered a part of the shore normally hidden from view, so that a kelp forest is revealed. A similar shore in the tropics would have very few plants. Exposed to the hot sunshine while the tide was out, such plants would soon die.

The sea scorpion (Myoxocephalus scorpius), below, can change its colour to suit the background.

SHORE TO BE A SAFE PLACE
Sheltered rocky shores are home to a wide variety of small fish, which hide amongst seaweeds and in pools. However, it is surprisingly difficult to spot them. As long as they do not move, they are safe from predators such as this sharp-eyed heron.

BLACK-
CROWNED
NIGHT HERON

With the tide in, this limpet (Patella species) can glide around, grazing on algae and leaving beautiful patterns of "teeth marks" on the rocks (above).

LITTLE SUCKERS

On rough, wave-exposed shores, seaweeds cannot grow well and so, instead, the rocks are covered with barnacles, limpets, and mussels. Limpets can cling on so tightly that it is almost impossible to dislodge them. Protected by their tough shells, periwinkles are rolled by the waves into crevices, while starfish grip on to rocks using thousands of tube feet, which act as suckers.

PERIWINKLES

ROCK POOLS

Rock pools are like miniature oases on the seashore, where delicate fish, anemones, and other soft animals can survive at low tide. However, living in a rock pool can be quite difficult. Small pools heat up and get very salty as the water evaporates on hot summer days. They also get diluted by rainwaters, which makes the water too fresh for many marine animals, and in winter small pools can freeze over. Pools high up on the shore pose the most difficult living conditions.

STARFISH IN ROCK POOL (USA)

These ochre sea stars (Pisaster ochraceus) are common in rock pools and on seashores in the USA. They vary in colour from orange to a greenish hue.

DUTIFUL DAD

The lumpsucker (*Cyclopterus lumpus*) visits northern European shores in late winter. The female lays her eggs, sticking them carefully onto a rock. But it is the male that stays behind to guard them. A strong sucker on his belly helps him to stay near the eggs when powerful waves come surging up the shore.

The pink and orange colours of the male lumpsucker are especially bright during the breeding season.

ON THE EDGE

WHEN THE TIDE GOES OUT along a mangrove-fringed shore, it reveals an almost alien landscape. Instead of a forest floor carpeted with leaves, humans and animals are faced by an almost impenetrable tangle of prop roots, which hang down, and aerial roots that grow up into the air instead of down into the soil! The prop roots support the trees while the aerial roots keep salt out and help the tree to breathe in salt water, which is normally fatal to land plants. Mangrove forests fringe muddy shores in tropical areas of the world.

MANGROVE SNAKE

These mud flats in Liverpool Bay, England (UK), provide wading birds with a feast of worms and shellfish.

BIRD LARDERS

Many northern European countries have coastlines with lots of river estuaries. Here, where fresh water meets salt water, great expanses of mud are deposited as the river drops its sediment load. At low tide, these mud flats provide feeding grounds for huge flocks of birds. British estuaries are important as they lie on the migration route for ducks, geese, and wading birds that fly south to spend the winter in the Mediterranean and Africa.

CRAB-EATING MACAQUE

HUNTING GROUND

Mangrove forests are a natural larder full of birds, insects, fish, crabs, and snails – an excellent hunting ground for those animals that can find a way in. Where mangroves merge into tropical rainforest, monkeys such as the crab-eating macaque are common. Fruit bats roost in the dense branches and estuarine crocodiles penetrate deep into the forest through twisting mangrove channels.

CARDINAL FISH

OYSTERS

PROP ROOTS

UNDERWATER NURSERY
The tangle of underwater roots and branches along the seaward edge of this mangrove forest, in the USA, provides a safe home for small fish. Many juvenile fish, including young sharks and barracuda, use the mangroves as a nursery area. Only when they are large enough to defend themselves will they venture out into the open ocean.

SEA LAVENDER

ESSEX SKIPPER BUTTERFLY

SEA DEFENCES
In cool areas such as northern Europe there are no mangroves. Instead, sheltered, muddy shores are often bordered by salt marshes. Salt-tolerant plants such as sea lavender grow over the marshes, which are rich in wildlife. Salt marshes and mangroves both form vital sea defences, helping to stop erosion and flooding. They can adjust to rising sea levels by growing further inland.

RIVER DELTAS
This aerial view of the River Volga delta shows how land is formed where a mighty river meets the sea. The river carries mud particles that settle on the seabed and build up into banks. As these become higher, plants colonize the mud and stabilize it, forming a delta crossed by many river channels. Human settlements on dry deltas are at serious risk from flooding.

TREE FISH
Finding a fish on land is surprising enough but finding one in a tree is truly extraordinary! Mudskippers climb up mangrove tree branches as the tide comes in, to avoid predatory fish. They use their strong front fins like arms and cling on with a sucker situated on their belly.

Whilst out of water, mudskippers keep their gills full of a frothy mixture of air and water so that they can still breathe. At low tide, they drop off the trees to feed on creatures in the mud flats.

115

CORAL REEFS

THE GREAT BARRIER REEF IS ONE OF the longest reefs in the world. It extends for more than 2,000 km (1,240 miles) along the northeast coast of Australia. It seems incredible that this huge structure – visible from space – was built by tiny coral animals (polyps) less than 1 cm (0.4 in) high. Thousands of these polyps live, joined together, inside every coral.

CORAL ATOLL FORMATION

Coral atolls start life as fringing reefs growing around volcanic islands far out in the ocean.

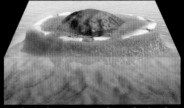

Geological processes and weathering have caused the volcano to sink and disappear, leaving a ring of coral behind it.

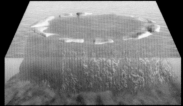

Sand and rubble build islands on top of the coral. Larger islands are colonized by plants and animals.

CORAL REEF FORMATIONS

Coral reefs can only grow in shallow waters, where there is a hard seabed to which they can attach themselves. This is why most reefs grow along the edges of continents (barrier reefs) or around islands (fringing reefs). This fringing reef (below) is typical of those surrounding islands throughout Micronesia, in the Pacific Ocean.

NATURAL PREDATORS

The prickly crown-of-thorns starfish eats living coral. Whole reefs can be killed when large numbers invade an area. Sitting on top of the coral, the starfish extends its stomach out through its mouth and digests the soft coral polyps.

Lophelia pertusa

Brightly coloured soft corals and sponges grow amongst the white Lophelia coral.

COLD WATER CORALS

Deep down in the cold, dark waters off Norway and western Scotland there are also coral reefs! These reefs consist of only one type of hard coral – *Lophelia*. This coral grows slowly as it does not contain *zooxanthellae* (tiny plants), which provide extra food for growth.

BOMBS AWAY

In Malaysia, Indonesia, and the Philippines, irresponsible fishermen toss home-made bombs onto reefs to stun and kill fish. Unfortunately, the bomb blast also smashes up the coral, which may take many years to re-grow. Sometimes the fishermen themselves are injured. With the reef gone, fishing will be poor for other fishermen.

CORAL LANDSCAPES

This photograph shows the beautiful coral landscape that surrounds Komodo Island in Indonesia. The corals grow well in the clear, sunlit waters of this region. Although they are animals, coral polyps need light to build their massive skeletons. This is because the polyps carry single-celled algae called *zooxanthellae* inside their bodies. These minute plants use the energy in sunlight to make their own food and pass some of it on to the coral polyps.

REEF LIFE

A VISIT TO A CORAL REEF is an amazing experience for divers to enjoy. A healthy reef simply bursts with life and colour in just the same way as a tropical rainforest does on land. Even a small reef in the Indian Ocean may have many hundreds of different sorts of corals, fish, crabs, starfish, sea urchins, and other animals. Millions of people in coastal communities worldwide rely on coral reefs to provide fish, medicines, and many other materials. But reefs are important to all of us. Corals use up carbon dioxide to make their skeletons and so help to prevent global warming.

These whitetip reef sharks are hunting surgeonfish in coral around Cocos Island, Costa Rica.

PURPLE TUBE SPONGE

A beautiful purple tube sponge from the Caribbean. Sponges come in a wide variety of shapes and colours and are common on most coral reefs.

EMPEROR ANGELFISH

RED SEA REEFS

The coral reef scene shown in the main photograph (above) is typical of the Red Sea. The corals come in many different shapes and sizes and jostle with one another for space. Each coral colony has grown up from a single small larva that drifted in and settled on the reef. Clouds of small, pink anthias fish are "picking" plankton from the water, while emperor angelfish search for sponges to eat.

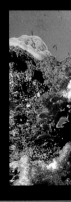

SHARK PATROL

This photograph, from Cocos Island in the Pacific Ocean, shows a pack of whitetip reef sharks (*Trianodon obesus*) hunting at night. During the day, the sharks rest peacefully in sandy coral caves and gullies – but as darkness falls they burst into frenetic activity, sniffing out coral fish hidden deep in the reef.

Tubastrea *coral with polyps retracted*

Tubastrea *coral with polyps extended*

FISHING AT NIGHT

Divers visiting a coral reef at night are often amazed at how colourful the corals appear in their torch beams. This is because it is at night that the coral polyps extend their bright tentacles to feed. During these hours of darkness tiny plankton animals, on which the corals feed, swim up onto the reef from deeper water.

BLACKTIP
REEF SHARK

The blacktip reef shark (Carcharhinus melanopterus) *hunts over shallow reefs for fish, squid, and octopuses, sometimes within an arm's length of the shore.*

CORAL RELATIVES

Colourful soft corals, such as these *Dendronepthya* species from Fiji, are close relatives of reef-forming corals. As their name suggests, they do not have a hard skeleton and collapse into a soggy heap when out of water. Unlike true corals, they do not need sunlight and can live on the deeper, darker parts of the reef.

TUBE WORMS

TUBE
WORM

Coral polyps are not the only animals to make reefs. The beautiful red worm (*Serpula vermicularis*) shown on the left lives in European coastal waters. In some sheltered Scottish sea lochs, these worms grow so well that they form mini-reefs with their hard, chalky tubes.

FORESTS AND MEADOWS

WITHIN EASY REACH of the teeming bustle of many European and American cities, there are immense, tranquil forests. These forests lie not on land but under the sea and are formed by giant seaweeds known as kelp. Giant Californian kelp can reach nearly 60 m (197 ft) long. These huge plants provide a habitat for a wide variety of fish, which in turn are hunted by seals, sea lions, and dolphins. Kelp forests grow only in cool, sunlit waters and are not found in the tropics. European kelps shed their tops each year just as trees lose their leaves.

Harbour seals (right) rest and play in the kelp forest, safe from the predatory sharks that patrol the open waters further out to sea.

SEA MEADOWS

Cows grazing peacefully in a grassy meadow are a common sight on land – but, surprisingly, you might come across a similar scene underwater! Sea grasses, which look quite like ordinary grass, grow on shallow, sandy seabeds – often covering large areas next to mangroves and coral reefs. In northern Australia and Southeast Asia, sea grass meadows are the favourite haunts of sea cows. European sea grass beds are extensively grazed by brent geese.

SAFE HAVEN

Baby lemon sharks are born live but their mother does not look after them. In the open ocean they would be very vulnerable to predators, so the sharks give birth to them in safe areas such as sea grass beds in shallow lagoons.

A dugong or sea cow (Dugong dugon), left, munching happily on an undersea lawn of sea grass.

SEAHORSES

Sunlight filters through the dense canopy of a giant kelp (Macrocystis) forest off the coast of California, USA. Air bladders (small capsules of gas along the kelp) help to keep the plants upright in the water.

A close search through clumps of sea grass may reveal some of the many small creatures that live there. Seahorses thrive on tiny shrimps that dart through the grass beds.

SEA OTTERS

Californian giant kelp forests are home to the delightful sea otter. These charming creatures are vital predators of kelp pests. Diving down to the seabed, this otter (below) has collected a sea urchin, cracked it open with a rock, and is now busy munching into its tasty insides. Without the otters, sea urchins can overgraze and destroy large areas of kelp forest.

Giant kelp can grow up to 0.6 m (2 ft) in length every day. This growth rate is almost as quick as giant bamboo, the fastest-growing plant on land.

GIANT
KELP

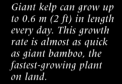

HUMAN
BEING

PLANT-LIKE ANIMALS

Anemones, sponges, and sea squirts are all examples of marine animals that look and behave rather like plants. Instead of searching for their food, they can stay fixed in one spot because water currents carry tiny, floating planktonic creatures into their reach. The understorey in a kelp forest has many such animals.

Soft corals such as these European dead man's fingers grow as fixed colonies. Hundreds of individual feeding heads, called polyps (left), catch passing plankton.

Colourful anemones often form part of the undergrowth in kelp forests. Their stinging tentacles can capture small fish and shrimps.

ANIMAL HOMES

Kelp plants provide a home for many small animals that live and feed on them. Hundreds of different species have been counted living on a single plant! In the photograph (above) a group of beautiful blue-rayed limpets are chewing holes in a kelp stem, which may eventually snap.

SUNLIT WATERS

THE SUNLIT SURFACE WATERS of the oceans teem with life. Huge numbers of microscopically small plants and animals, the plankton, drift in the water currents. Almost all life in the oceans ultimately depends on this floating food source. Shoals of silvery fish feed on the plankton, closely followed by hungry sharks, sailfish, and other predators. Larger jellyfish and other floating animals are blown along the surface by ocean winds.

DIVING BIRDS

Guillemots spend much of their life out at sea, feeding, resting, and sleeping on the ocean surface. They only come ashore to breed – in noisy colonies on steep cliffs. The birds fish for sprats, sand eels, and herring by dipping under the surface and then swimming underwater by flapping their wings. They can easily swim to a depth of 20 m (66 ft), and

TOOTHLESS WONDER

The whale shark is the largest fish in the sea and can grow to at least 14 m (46 ft) long – the size of a bus! If it had teeth, like other sharks, it could eat a person in one bite. Luckily, its huge mouth is simply used to take in gallons of seawater containing the tiny shrimps, and other plankton,

SARGASSUM
FROGFISH IN
SARGASSUM
WEED

FLOATING FORESTS

The surface of the
Sargasso Sea, near
Bermuda, is still and
warm for most of the
year. These conditions
have allowed a strange,
floating forest to develop
– a vast, tangled raft of
seaweed held up by gas-
filled bladders. Sea snails,
urchins, and limpets
graze on the seaweed,
while sea snakes hunt
for fish and shrimps.

*A shoal of jackfish
(Caranx sexfasciatus),
otherwise known as
big-eye trevally*

SAFETY SHOALS

Fish living in sunlit surface waters protect themselves
from predatory fish and seabirds by forming large
shoals. When attacked, all the fish in the shoal move
together and confuse the predator. Their darker backs
and silvery bellies help to camouflage them from
both above and below.

OCEAN WANDERERS

Leatherback turtles are
true ocean wanderers.
Satellite tags fitted to
these gentle giants have
shown that they travel
thousands of miles in
search of food. They
can grow to nearly 2 m
(6.5 ft) long and weigh
up to 650 kg (1,430 lb),
all on a diet consisting

*The violet sea snail builds itself a
floating "raft" by entangling air*

DRIFTING FREE

While most sea snails
live on the seabed,
the violet sea snail
(*Janthina janthina*)
is completely at home
drifting at the ocean
surface. It feeds on
other ocean drifters
such as the blue jelly
Porpita and the by-the-
wind-sailor *Velella*.

Submarine Landscapes

THE OCEAN DEPTHS REMAIN MYSTERIOUS, even today. Sunlight penetrates to no more than a few hundred metres. Further down is an alien world of abyssal plains, mountains, and trenches inhabited by creatures rarely seen by humans. Until the 20th century, the only way to map the sea floor was by plumbing its depths with a weight and line. The invention of sonar – using sound waves to "see" – has revolutionized our knowledge of the sea floor. Scientists now know that the oceans hide many more volcanoes than are found on continents, and that the largest mountain ranges on Earth are found in the inky depths of the sea, not on land. However, the crushing pressure of deep water makes these places very difficult to visit.

LAUNCHING GLORIA
This torpedo-shaped sonar device, called GLORIA, is being launched from a research vessel. Towed behind the ship, it bounces sound waves off the sea floor. The returning signals are analysed to build up a 3-D map. This helps scientists to identify hazards on the sea bed, determine routes for laying cables, and locate areas for exploring minerals and oil.

MOUNTAINS AND TRENCHES
This map shows some of the rugged landscape of the sea floor. Long ridge systems of steep mountains meander through the world's oceans. Some rise to more than 2 km (1.2 miles) above the sea floor. Elsewhere, ocean basins plunge into deep-sea trenches that are nearly 11,000 m (36,000 ft) below the surface – the deepest places on Earth.

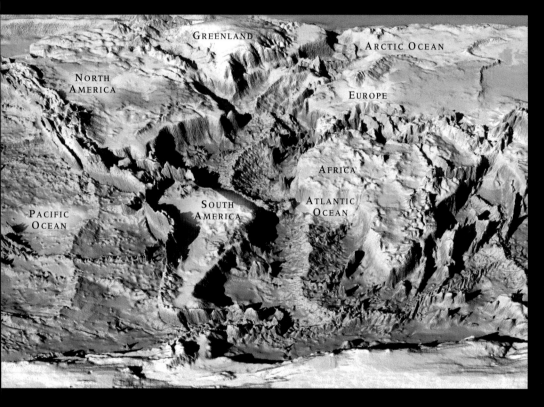

GREENLAND
ARCTIC OCEAN
NORTH AMERICA
EUROPE
AFRICA
SOUTH AMERICA
ATLANTIC OCEAN
PACIFIC OCEAN

OCEAN FLOOR
Ocean basins are places where dense crust has settled down to form depressions filled with seawater. The ocean floor is the bottom of the basin. A continental slope marks the edge of the ocean basin and is the true geological boundary between continent and ocean. Giant cracks in the continental slope, or submarine canyons, deposit fans of sediment onto the basin. Underwater avalanches, called turbidity currents, occasionally rush down the canyon with such speed and power that they snap underwater telephone cables.

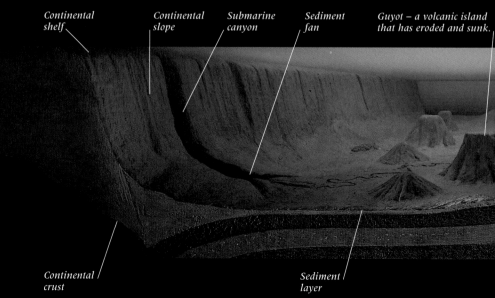

Continental shelf

Continental slope

Submarine canyon

Sediment fan

Guyot – a volcanic island that has eroded and sunk.

Continental crust

Sediment layer

BLACK SMOKERS

On the deep sea floor, close to spreading ocean ridges, strange structures belch out clouds of volcanically heated water filled with minerals. They are hydrothermal vents, or "black smokers" (*left*). The sulphur-rich water coming from the smokers can be as hot as 400°C (752°F), but does not boil due to the immense pressure of the water. A mound of mineral deposits builds up around the vents.

RADIOLARIAN

Giant deepsea clams and squat lobsters live around vents at a depth of 2,600 m (8,500 ft) off Mazailán, Mexico.

UNDERWATER OASES

The discovery of hydrothermal vents in the 1970s amazed marine scientists. Bacteria thrive on the minerals and provide food for the many strange animals that live around the vents. Other vent animals prey on each other. Thus, the whole community survives without getting any energy from plants and sunlight.

DIATOMS

Abyssal plain – the flat expanse of ocean floor.

Spreading ridge, where two tectonic plates are moving apart.

Ocean trench plunging to great depths.

Magma rising from the mantle.

Oceanic crust

Solid upper mantle

OOZE

These distorted discs are the silica skeletons of diatoms – single-celled algae that float in surface waters. Diatoms photosynthesize (trap light to make food), just as plants do on land. The spiny ball is a radiolarian – a single-celled animal that feeds on diatoms. When diatoms and radiolarians die, they sink to the sea bed to form a carpet of ooze that can be 500 m (1,640 ft) thick in places. The tiny organisms living in ooze feed a variety of bizarre creatures that have adapted to life in the darkness of the deep ocean.

125

MIDWATER MYSTERIES

IMAGINE FLOATING WEIGHTLESS IN DARK, COLD WATER with nothing to tell you which way is up or down. Many animals spend their entire lives swimming or drifting in mid-water, where there is very little or no light. So how do the animals find food or a mate? Some fish and crustaceans have enormous eyes to use what little light there is. Others have tiny eyes but an excellent sense of smell and antennae sensitive to vibrations.

BIOLUMINESCENCE

Bioluminescence is a beautiful, bluish light produced by living animals and plants. In the deep mid-waters, many fish, squid, jellies, and crustaceans light up with this eerie glow, which they use to navigate, hunt, signal, frighten, and even to camouflage themselves. The light is created when a chemical called luciferin is mixed with oxygen.

The anglerfish uses this glowing lure, like a fishing rod, to entice prey. It appears ferocious but, like most deepsea fish, it is only centimetres long.

FLASHLIGHT FISH

This fish keeps bioluminescent bacteria in special sacs under each eye. The bacteria glow constantly, but the fish can blink the lights on and off using a flap of skin.

INKY LIGHT

Many different species of squid live in the midwater darkness and are eaten by predatory fish – if the fish can catch them. Most are only centimetres long, but they shimmer and glow with hundreds of tiny, bioluminescent lights. Some can even squirt out a luminous, inky "smokescreen".

This small squid, called Histioteuthis, waits quietly for passing prey to bump into its tentacles.

CREEPY HITCH-HIKER

There are no solid surfaces to cling on to and make a home of in mid-water. The *Phronima* – a small, shrimp-like animal – steals itself a floating home. Gripping on to a floating sea squirt (salp) or jelly, this ingenious creature eats the insides of its prey and then uses the transparent skin as a shelter for itself and its young.

WHY RED?

This red shrimp (*Pasiphaea* species) lives in deep, dark waters lit only by bioluminescent glows. Red light does not penetrate this deep, and so red things appear black. In mid-water, therefore, the shrimp is almost invisible. However, a small, black fish called *Malosteus* captures and eats these shrimps by locating them with a beam of *red* bioluminescence.

Slipping in and out of its floating "barrel", the Phronima can search for food in safety.

DEEP PLAINS

ONLY 150 YEARS AGO, biologists still believed that no marine creatures could possibly survive below a depth of 1,000 m (3,300 ft) because of the huge pressures and icy cold. The deepsea vehicles *Trieste* and *Kaiko* have since visited the very deepest part of the ocean and seen animals there. Much of the deep ocean floor consists of immense plains of soft mud, peppered with holes and mounds made by buried worms and other small animals. There are far fewer large predatory animals, such as starfish, because food is very scarce.

ELBOWS ON THE TABLE

Tripodfish "perch" just above the mud surface by propping themselves up on the tips of their long tail and front fins. Sensitive antennae help them to detect and pounce on passing small fish and shrimps.

TRIPODFISH

UNDERWATER VACUUM CLEANERS

Believe it or not, this strange-looking creature – a sea cucumber – is a close relative of the familiar starfish. Sea cucumbers are common on the muddy, deepsea floor all over the world. They get by very well here because they "hoover" the surface, sucking in a mixture of mud and edible snacks. Undigested mud passes through their gut and is left in neat little piles, called faecal casts.

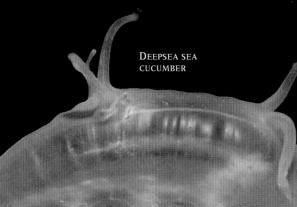

DEEPSEA SEA CUCUMBER

The sea pens shown in this picture are examples of a deepsea variety known as the "droopy" sea pen.

BLUNTNOSE SIX-GILL SHARK
(*HEXANCHUS GRISEUS*)

HIGH TEA

On the great African plains there are plenty of antelope for swift land predators, such as cheetahs, to hunt and kill. In contrast, there are very few large hunters down on the deepsea plains. Chasing prey uses up a lot of energy and food is scarce. The bluntnose six-gill shark (above) scavenges for left-overs in the depths, during the day, but hunts its live prey at night near the surface, where more food is available.

DEEPSEA BONANZA

One of the reasons there is not much food available on deep plains is that most of it gets eaten by midwater animals on the way down. But on rare occasions something really large, such as a dead whale, may reach the deepsea floor. Scavenging rattail fish, hagfish, and deepsea sharks – the "vultures" of the ocean depths – smell the carrion and move in for a feast.

Rattail fish get their name from their long, thin tails. They feed on anything they can catch – whether it is alive or dead.

DEEPLY DELICATE

Delicate deepsea animals such as this pom-pom anemone (*Liponema brevicornis*) are known mainly from photographs taken from submersibles. Collecting specimens using clumsy submersible arms is very difficult. In addition, many specimens disintegrate on the way to the surface because of the changing temperature and pressure.

POM-POM ANEMONE

POISED PENS

Sea cucumbers and crabs crawl and plough their way through the muddy floor of the ocean's abyssal plains in search of things to eat. Meanwhile, plant-like animals, such as the floppy sea pens in this photograph, filter the water currents to catch drifting food. These sea pens have long, flexible stalks to keep them well above the soft mud that might otherwise clog up their mouths and tentacles.

ISLAND REFUGE

IN THE VAST EXPANSES OF the open ocean, islands are like desert oases where life can settle and grow. When an island is first formed, it may be colonized by floating plants and seeds, flying insects and birds, and by marine larvae brought to shore by the ocean currents. Fewer creatures will reach isolated islands that are situated far away from reefs, land, or other islands.

A model of the now extinct dodo (Raphus cucullatus)

Cactus ground finch on Plaza Island, Galápagos

OLD SPECIES, NEW SPECIES

There were no predators on the island of Mauritius before people arrived. The flightless dodo was totally unafraid and was soon hunted to extinction. When the remote Galápagos Islands were formed, flocks of finches were blown there by storms. These birds evolved to suit the particular conditions on each island. Each island now has its own specific species.

Komodo dragons grow to between 2 m and 3 m (6.5 ft and 9.75 ft) in length.

LIZARD AT LARGE

Small islands can be home to some very large animals. On a few small islands in Indonesia you can meet the world's heaviest lizard, the Komodo dragon (*Varanus komodoensis*). These ferocious predators can weigh more than 70 kg (155 lb) and can run fast enough to kill deer and wild pigs for food. However, their usual tactic is to ambush prey.

These tank-like tracks were made by a female turtle as she dragged herself up the beach.

TURTLE HOMES

This green turtle (below) is digging her nest on a sandy beach in the Philippines. Remote islands provide safe nesting sites with fewer predators to eat the eggs and young. Unfortunately, many nesting beaches have now become tourist resorts. Turtles will travel thousands of kilometres to reach their traditional nesting sites – often the very same island on which they were born.

EGGS

BIRD CITIES

Many seabirds breed in noisy,
densely crowded colonies. In spring,
thousands of gannets gather to breed
on isolated, rocky islands around
Scotland. The colony on Saint
Kilda has over 50,000 breeding
pairs. They create a spectacular
air show while wheeling and
plunge-diving to catch
sprats and herring to
feed to their young.

COCONUT THIEF

The Seychelles are
home to one of
the strangest of all
crabs – the coconut
or robber crab
(*Birgus latro*). This
giant, at 20 cm
(8 in) long,
has claws
strong enough
to pinch off your
finger. It uses these
claws to climb
trees and cut
open young
coconuts.

FROZEN SEAS

THE SOUTHERN OCEAN surrounding Antarctica is surprisingly rich in animal life. In winter, pack ice covers more than half the ocean and air temperatures drop to between -20°C (-4°F) and -30°C (-22°F). But in summer, when the ice retreats, huge numbers of birds, seals, whales, fish, and squid hunt for food in the icy waters. Animals such as sponges, anemones, crabs, and starfish thrive on the seabed, even in winter. Under the cover of ice there are no howling gales, and the water temperature remains between 0°C (32°F) and -2°C (28°F).

Antarctic pack ice helps to keep the Earth cool by reflecting the Sun's rays back into space.

A giant Antarctic spider out on a hunt

GIANT SPIDERS

Animals living on the Antarctic seabed grow very slowly in the icy-cold water. However, most species live for a long time and grow much bigger than their relatives in warmer waters. The giant Antarctic sea spider in the picture (above) is around the same size as a person's hand. Sea spiders in British waters, for example, only grow to about 1 cm (0.4 in) long.

Icefish have thin, pale blood with no red blood cells, so that the blood can circulate easily in the cold conditions.

ANTIFREEZE

In winter, the water temperature around Antarctica often falls below the freezing point of normal fish blood. Icefish survive these conditions because their blood contains glycoprotein. This substance freezes at a lower temperature than water, so the fishes' blood does not freeze, even if trapped in ice. The antifreeze used in car radiators works in the same way.

Adelie penguins spend the winter on the Antarctic pack ice. This one is hesitating before taking a dive into the water, aware that a leopard seal might be lying in wait for it.

THE EMPERORS

Emperor penguins are bigger than any other seabird. They live in huge colonies on the pack ice that surrounds Antarctica. Their large size helps them to survive the hurricane-force winds and temperatures that can drop to as low as -30ºC (-22ºF) in winter. They can dive down to depths of 200 m (650 ft) or more, and stay down for about 20 minutes while they hunt for fish.

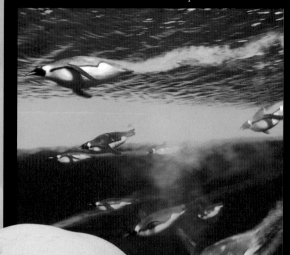

ICY TOMB

The underside of the winter pack ice is riddled with small channels filled with microscopic plants called algae. These give the ice an eerie green colour. In spring, when the ice melts, the algae are released and quickly multiply. The algae are eaten by tiny shrimps called krill, which also breed rapidly. This wealth of food is the reason why so many birds, seals, whales, and fish can live in these icy waters.

Starfish gather below seal breathing holes to feed on the seals' faeces (deposits of solid waste).

SEALED IN

The leopard seal is a ferocious predator. It is fast and agile underwater and can even out-manoeuvre a penguin. The seal uses up a lot of energy while chasing its prey, but uses an extra-thick layer of fat, called blubber, to store up energy and keep warm. Young leopard seals mostly eat krill – a tiny shrimp that is also the main food source of the great blue whale.

Although only about 5 cm (2 in) long, krill (Euphausia superba) occur in swarms that may be thousands of metres across, and which could contain several million tonnes of these tiny shrimps.

KRILL

An Antarctic sea urchin (Sterechinus neumayeri) grazing on the seabed

MARINE MIGRATIONS

In 1969–70, SIDNEY GENDERS ROWED 6,114 km (3,800 miles) across the Atlantic Ocean in 74 days. Ten years later, Sir Ranulph Fiennes trecked 2,170 km (1,348 miles) to the South Pole (1979–82). These are epic voyages, and yet much longer journeys are made by many ocean animals every year. Some, like the salmon, can navigate so accurately that they can return from rich feeding grounds in Greenland to the very same river in Europe where they were born. There, they recognize the smell of their home waters. Birds, fish, and whales may all be able to sense the Earth's magnetic field and use it to guide their way. Birds can also navigate using the Sun and stars. By travelling so far, these animals can feed in one area but breed in a much safer spot.

Grey whales were once hunted almost to extinction. Today, their numbers have recovered and boatloads of tourists travel to watch them instead.

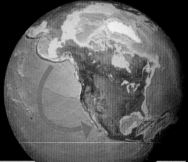

THE WHALE ROAD
Every year, grey whales travel from their rich (but icy-cold) feeding grounds off Alaska to the safe, warm coastal lagoons of Baja California, Mexico. Here, they give birth to their calves after an incredible 9,650-km (6,000-mile) journey. The calves are sometimes attacked by killer whales on their way back north.

INCREDIBLE JOURNEY

European eels swim right across the Atlantic Ocean to the Sargasso Sea, near Bermuda, to lay their eggs. Exhausted, they all die. The eggs hatch into tiny, leaf-shaped *leptocephalus* larvae. These drift back to Europe, pushed along by the ocean currents.

The Arctic tern always migrates over the ocean so that it can feed on small fish during its long journeys.

MAGNETIC NOSE

Blue sharks travel in a loop around the North Atlantic. They go clockwise with the ocean currents to Europe, Africa, then back across to the Caribbean. They may find their way using an in-built "compass" that detects changes in the Earth's magnetic field.

TURTLE TRIPS

Marine turtles roam the oceans, but when it is time to lay eggs many return to the beach where they hatched. Atlantic ridley turtles all return to a few remote beaches in the Gulf of Mexico – once in their thousands, but now only a few are left.

This European eel (Anguilla anguilla) will spend up to 20 years in fresh (not salty) water before setting out on its long ocean journey to breed.

ARCTIC TO ANTARCTIC

Arctic terns travel up to 35,000 km (21,750 miles) a year. They nest in summer near to the Arctic Circle. Then, as winter approaches, they fly south to Africa, Australia, and the Antarctic where it will be summer.

The blue shark (Prionace glauca) was once very common, but is now endangered due to overfishing.

These Atlantic ridley turtles (Lepidochelys kempii) are coming ashore to lay eggs on a Costa Rican beach.

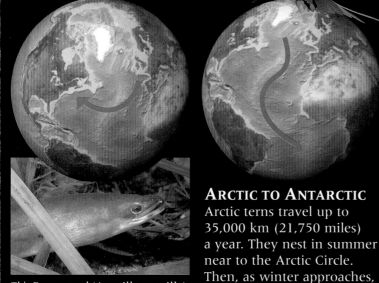

LOBSTER LINE

Tropical spiny lobsters (*Panulirus argus*) spend most of their time hiding in rocky crevices with only their long antennae sticking out. So divers are often very surprised to see long lines of them marching purposefully across the seabed. Each year, the lobsters walk to special areas, close inshore, where they lay their eggs. Afterwards, they walk back again.

PERFECT BALANCE

LIFE ON EARTH AND IN OUR OCEANS depends on plants. Without them, animals would not exist. Powered by sunlight, plants make their own food by changing water and carbon dioxide gas into sugar and starch – a process known as photosynthesis. Animals eat plants, but they also breathe out carbon dioxide and produce manure that provides nutrients for the plants. In the ocean there is only enough light for seaweeds and sea grasses to grow in shallow water around the ocean edges. The rest of the ocean's plant life consists of billions and billions of tonnes of phytoplankton – the microscopically small plants that float in the sunlit waters near to the surface.

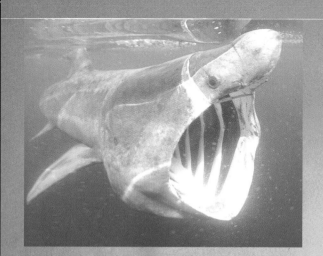

NO CHAIN
The basking shark (*Cetorhinus maximus*) is found in cool seas. It can grow to up to 10 m (33 ft) long, which makes it the second-largest fish in the ocean. (The whale shark is the biggest.) In spite of its great size, this fish feeds entirely on plankton. Most other sharks are predators at the top of the food chain. Using its huge, gaping mouth the basking shark can filter many gallons of seawater every hour.

Sharks are top predators. Large hunting species, such as great white sharks, can eat dolphins and seals as well as fish. Bottlenose dolphins eat large numbers of fish that live near the seabed, including cod.

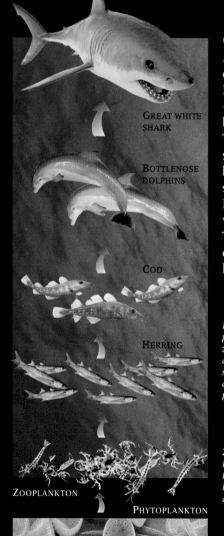

GREAT WHITE SHARK

BOTTLENOSE DOLPHINS

COD

HERRING

ZOOPLANKTON

PHYTOPLANKTON

OCEAN FOOD CHAINS
Most large animals cannot eat plant plankton directly. Instead, the plant plankton (phytoplankton) is "grazed" by tiny animals (zooplankton). These in turn are eaten by small fish, which are eaten by bigger fish, and so on. This system is called a food chain. However, most animals eat a variety of different creatures. They are, therefore, part of a more complex system, known as a food "web".

Herring and sprat are "plankton pickers" that eat the larger zooplankton animals. Herring and sprat are eaten by larger fish such as cod. Cod also eat many other marine creatures and are part of an extensive food web.

Zooplankton consists of animals like copepods, which spend all their life in the plankton, plus the larvae (young) of bottom-dwelling animals such as crabs.

A scanning electron microscope photograph (left) of diatoms, one of the most common types of plant plankton.

BALANCED
Giant tube worms (*Riftia pachyptila*), as tall as a person, live around deepsea volcanic vents. They have no mouth or gut and so cannot feed. Instead, the worms absorb chemicals from the hot vent water. Bacteria that live inside the worms' bodies use the chemicals to make food for themselves, and also for the worms – a perfectly balanced system.

The worms' bright red gills stick out from their hard, white tubes.

KING RAY

Tropical manta rays (*Manta birostris*) used to have a fearsome reputation – the result of their huge size, strange-looking "horns", and their unnerving habit of jumping up out of the water. They were given the name "devilfish" and were believed to be as dangerous as sharks. When scuba diving began, divers soon found that these graceful animals were so docile they could be stroked. Like basking sharks and whale sharks, these giants only eat plankton and use their "horns" to funnel plankton-rich water into their mouths.

UNBALANCED

California is famous for its beautiful underwater forests of giant kelp seaweeds. Unfortunately, armies of sea urchins are damaging some forests, eating every plant in their path. Humans have broken the delicate food chain by overfishing sheephead fish and, in the past, by hunting sea otters. Sheephead fish and sea otters both eat sea urchins. Without them, the urchins are taking over!

137

PARTNERS AND PARASITES

FINDING A SAFE HOME IN THE SEA is a problem faced by many defenceless, bite-sized animals such as juvenile fish, shrimps, and small crabs. One ingenious solution involves living with a partner, who acts as a bodyguard. A favourite choice on coral reefs is the giant sea anemone, because it has powerful stinging tentacles. Anemonefish live with these anemones and wear a special coat of slimy mucus that prevents them from being stung. In return for this service, these small fish serve as housekeepers, removing debris in and around the anemone.

Here, a large grouper is having bits of food and debris removed from between its teeth by a hard-working cleaner wrasse.

CLEANER AT WORK
Just as animals such as rabbits and hedgehogs harbour fleas, many coral reef fish suffer from tiny, shrimp-like skin parasites. When these become too troublesome, the fish go for a wash and brush-up. Certain small fish and shrimps get their food by eating these parasites along with dead skin and scales.

The clownfish (Amphiprion cellaris), a type of anemonefish, always remains close to its chosen anemone and sleeps deep within the tentacles at night.

CURTAIN OF DEATH

Jellyfish have some of the most powerful stings of all animals, and large ones can kill and eat fish. Most predators therefore steer well clear of them. Some baby fish have learnt to take advantage of this by hiding amongst the trailing net of a jellyfish's tentacles. Out in the open ocean, where the jellies drift, there is little other cover. Slipping easily between the tentacles, these juvenile fish come to no harm.

LION'S MANE JELLYFISH

Tiny juvenile jackfish hide amongst the deadly tentacles of a giant pelagic jellyfish (Chrysaora achlyos).

CLOWNFISH WITH LARGE SEA ANEMONES

HITCHING A RIDE

Some animal partnerships involve getting a free ride and perhaps sharing the host's meals. This rather one-sided relationship suits the remora, a small fish that clings on to sharks, turtles, and whales. The remora can swim by itself and often changes partners. Anemones remain with their hermit crab hosts until the crab "moves house" and finds a bigger shell.

This closed-up sea anemone (Calliactis parasitica) *is perched on a hermit crab shell.*

Close-up of barnacles and lice attached to a grey whale. Barnacles often settle on the thick skin of whales.

Two remoras, also known as "shark suckers" (Echeneis naucrates), *are hitching a free ride on a loggerhead turtle* (Caretta caretta).

DEADLY FOOD

Some sea slugs – colourful relatives of garden slugs – are able to eat the stinging tentacles of anemones and sea firs. Instead of digesting the stinging cells, they store them in special feathery extensions on their backs. They use the stolen stings to ward off attacks by fish. This rainbow sea slug *Dendronotus iris* (below) has eaten all the tentacles off a large tube anemone.

SURVIVAL

THERE ARE NEARLY AS MANY DIFFERENT sorts of fish in the ocean as there are land mammals and birds put together – around 14,000 species. Each species is faced with the problem of finding food whilst, at the same time, trying not to become a meal for something bigger than itself. Many are expertly camouflaged, while others are armed with a supply of weapons that are used either for defence or attack – and sometimes for both. As a result, there are some weird-looking shapes and extraordinary lifestyles in the world of fish.

SLEEPING PARROT
Like their bird namesakes, parrotfish are brightly coloured and have their teeth joined together into a tough, parrot-like beak. They spend their days busily scraping and biting into the corals (their food). At night, exhausted by all this activity, they go to sleep while wedged into a rock crevice. Many cover themselves in a cocoon of slimy mucus, which prevents predators from sniffing them out.

STAYING PUT
Garden eels survive by retreating deep into their burrows when danger threatens. Large colonies of these strange fish live in sandy areas near to coral reefs. Swaying gracefully from side to side, the eels rise up out of their burrows to feed on passing plankton. They are very sensitive to vibrations and to the noise made by scuba divers' air bubbles. As a result, they are very difficult to photograph underwater.

The spotted garden eel (Heteroconger hassi) lives in the warm waters of the Red Sea and the Indian Ocean.

SELF DEFENCE

When a porcupinefish is out hunting for crabs and snails, it keeps its spines folded back along its body and looks quite harmless – just like an actual porcupine does. If it is attacked, it immediately swallows huge mouthfuls of water and inflates itself into a ball-shape. Surgeonfish defend themselves by extending sharp spines at either side of their tails.

PUFFERFISH

Few predators would dare attack a fully inflated porcupinefish or pufferfish, like this one (above).

LEAFY SEA DRAGON

Long skin tassles help to camouflage this weird relative of the seahorse, which lives amongst seaweeds.

HAMMER-VISION

HAMMERHEAD SHARK

As well as an excellent sense of smell, sharks have extremely good eyesight. A hammerhead's eyes are at each end of a flattened, hammer-shaped head. The head is kept moving at all times – so that the shark can see in every direction – and is also used as a rudder.

This blenny pretends to be a cleaner fish, ready to remove irritating parasites from larger fish – but instead it darts in and takes a bite out of its surprised target.

FALSE CLEANER BLENNY

SHOCKING TACTICS

The electric ray has a very unusual ability – it can give a diver, fisherman, or predator who touches it a nasty shock! The electric shock is produced in special organs on the ray's "wings". The ray also uses this ability to stun or kill fish to eat. It lies quietly in wait on the seabed until a fish swims within reach.

MARBLED ELECTRIC RAY

THE KILLERS

WHEN WE THINK OF really dangerous marine creatures, most people would name sharks as the villains. However, whilst all sharks should be treated with respect, they rarely attack humans. Most other sea creatures that can hurt – or even kill – humans are small and do not look dangerous at all. Jellyfish, sea snakes, and some fish, seashells, and octopuses are armed with a venomous bite or sting. Some use their venom to help capture and subdue their prey, but when they sting or bite us it is because we have accidentally trodden on them or picked them up. They are simply trying to defend themselves.

SEA SNAKES

Sea snakes are found mostly in the warm, tropical waters of the Indian and Pacific oceans. The banded sea krait, *Laticauda colubrina* (right), is often seen on coral reefs by divers and snorkellers. Using its specially flattened tail to swim efficiently from place to place, it hunts for small fish hiding in coral crevices or sandy burrows. A bite from a sea snake can be as deadly as that of a cobra, but most are shy and docile and will not attack humans unless provoked. Most sea snake-related deaths are of fishermen who are bitten by snakes that get tangled up in their nets.

DEADLY BOX

At certain times of the year, many beaches along the northern coast of Australia are closed to swimmers. This region is the haunt of the box jellyfish (*Chironex fleckeri*), one of the most venomous animals in the world. The intensely painful sting of this beautiful creature can kill in just a few minutes. The deadly tentacles hang down in bunches from each corner of the box-shaped top, and survivors often have dramatic scars to remind them of their brush with death.

Most victims of the blue-ringed octopus are Australian holidaymakers who find the little octopus in sea shells or under rocks on the seashore.

BLUE-RINGED
OCTOPUS

COLLECTING SHELLS

The beauty of cone shells belies their deadly nature. These tropical shells crawl over coral reefs and shores searching for fish and other prey. They attack by thrusting out a minute "harpoon" on the end of a long proboscis. One stab of venom and it is all over. Not all species are poisonous, but some can kill a person – so these shells should never be handled.

CONE
SHELLS

The tiny, poisonous "harpoon" of a striated cone (Conus striatus)

BLUE-RINGED BITER

Compared with the giant octopus, whose stretched-out arms could envelop a bus, the tiny blue-ringed octopus – often smaller than a human hand – seems quite harmless. Nothing could be further from the truth. Although its bite is painless, it can kill a man in only a few minutes. The victim becomes paralyzed and stops breathing.

RED TIDES

Not oil or pollution, but billions of tiny, single-celled creatures called *dinoflagellates* have caused this red slick on the sea (below). The presence of sewage in the water has caused a population explosion. *Dinoflagellates* are a type of floating plant plankton that multiply very quickly. Some species are poisonous and humans can become seriously ill after eating shellfish that have been feeding in the area.

LIONFISH

The lionfish or turkeyfish (Pterois volitans) has an extremely painful sting, but it is unlikely to kill a person.

STONEFISH

Stonefish (Synanceia species) live in shallow tropical seas and are the world's most venomous fish.

SWORD IN THE STONE

Stonefish and lionfish are safe from attack by predators because they have an armoury of sharp, poisonous spines in their fins. The flamboyant red and white lionfish is easy to spot; its colours warn us to stay away. In contrast, the stonefish is a master of disguise. Treading on a stonefish may be the last thing you do, since a sting from its sword-like spines can be fatal.

Dinoflagellates come in many intricate shapes and not all of them produce poisons.

GOING DOWN

TODAY'S SCUBA-DIVING EQUIPMENT IS LIGHT and easy to use – and also colourful! With the correct training, children as young as 12 years old can now learn to dive safely, carrying their air supply in a cylinder mounted on their backs. The normal depth limit for a scuba diver (breathing air) is around 50 m (164 ft). By using special vehicles and equipment, scientists, explorers – and even film crews – can now go beyond this limit and visit all except the very deepest parts of the oceans.

UNDERWATER PHOTOGRAPHY

The equipment needed to make professional underwater films is still quite large and expensive. However, there is now a huge range of relatively inexpensive underwater cameras available for ordinary divers to use. Tourists can even buy disposable underwater cameras. Louis Boutan, who took the very first underwater photographs in 1893, would have been amazed by these new gadgets.

This diver is doing some underwater filming using a Betacam SP video camera.

A demand valve, or "regulator", controls the flow of air from the cyclinder to the diver, providing air whenever the diver sucks on the mouth piece.

HS1200
PRESSURE
SUIT

HS2000
PRESSURE
SUIT

The hydraulic pincers on these pressure suits act as hands.

PRESSURE SUITS

Imagine walking around on the seabed in your own personal made-to-measure submarine! That is what it is like to wear a pressure suit. The pressure inside the tough, hard suit is kept the same as it is at the surface of the ocean. This means that the diver is not crushed by the much higher pressure at greater depths.

The diver in this HS2000 suit can work as deep as 500 m (1,640 ft) for approximately six to eight hours.

SUBMERSIBLES

Submersibles are like miniature submarines. They are mainly used to take research scientists into the deep sea, but some now carry tourists. The people on board a submersible are protected inside a strong, pressure-resistant capsule. The hull is filled with a lightweight material called syntactic foam, which helps it to float.

The RSL submersible has a transparent viewing sphere made of thick acrylic plastic. This gives its passengers an excellent view. However, it can only go down to around 244 m (800 ft).

REMOTELY OPERATED VEHICLES (ROVs)

ROVs are unmanned craft used to explore, film, measure, and collect samples underwater. They are connected to a mother ship by long cables. Cameras transmit images to operators on the ship, who can steer the vehicle as though they were in it. Satellite links allow scientists to follow the action as it happens, via the Internet.

Solo (above) is an ROV used for pipeline surveys and other underwater work in the North Sea oil fields.

UNDERWATER HOTELS

As with space tourism, underwater holidays are now a possibility. Tourist submarines operate in the Caribbean, and in Florida, USA, guests can stay in a hotel called *Jules' Undersea Lodge*. The record for living continuously underwater is 69 days and 19 minutes.

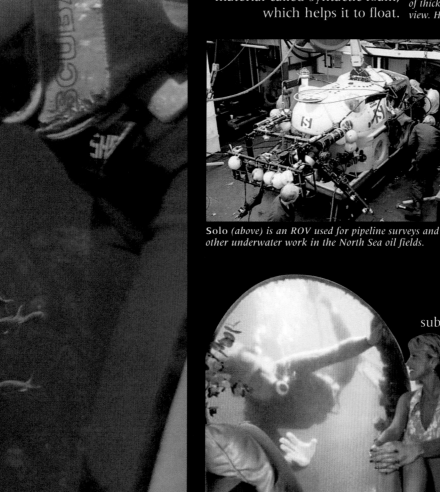

MARINE ARCHAEOLOGY

THE SEA RUSTS METAL, ROTS WOOD, and breaks up glass, but it can also preserve shipwrecks and artefacts for many centuries by burying them under shifting sand and mud. Such "time capsules" are a treasure trove of information for historians and archaeologists. Others hunt for wrecks in the hope of finding precious treasure – coins, gold, valuable china, and even wine! Few succeed, but in 1985 an American called Mel Fisher found a Spanish wreck off the coast of Florida (USA) that sank in 1622, carrying 40.6 tonnes (40 tons) of gold, silver, and emeralds.

The Sankisan Maru *under attack in Pearl Harbour, 1944*

THE *MARY ROSE*

On 11 October 1982, King Henry VIII's flagship, the *Mary Rose*, saw the light of day for the first time in 437 years. Her hull was raised to the surface and is now in a museum at the Royal Naval base in Portsmouth, England (UK). Divers and archaeologists spent ten years carefully measuring, recording, and excavating the ship before she was raised. They recovered thousands of objects, from shoes and hair combs to bows and arrows.

Wreck of the Kasi Maru, *New Georgia, Solomon Islands*

The picture to the right shows the Mary Rose *being sprayed with preserving chemicals in the museum.*

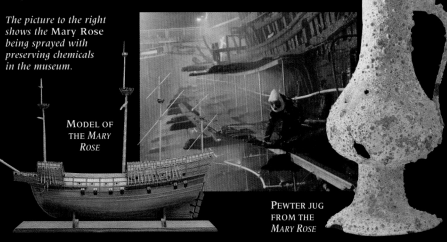

MODEL OF THE *MARY ROSE*

PEWTER JUG FROM THE *MARY ROSE*

NEW FROM OLD

During World War II, many ships and aeroplanes were sunk. Whilst this was a tragic end for many brave servicemen, it was the start of a new life for the wrecks. Soon after they sank, plants and animals quickly began to settle on the Japanese freighters shown above. In the tropics, a rusting hulk can transform into a living, artificial reef in a matter of months.

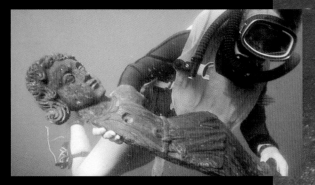

BURIED AT SEA

Walk along the shore at Lyme Regis in Dorset, England, and you will be walking over millions of years of history. The cliffs and shores there are full of the fossilized remains of ancient animals, such as the ammonite shown in the picture below. When it died, the ammonite was first buried in silt at the bottom of the ocean and later turned to stone through a complex chemical process.

TREASURE HUNTERS

Every shipwreck is owned by somebody. Ancient wrecks are usually the property of the government of a country. Most countries have rules about how much "treasure" can be kept by the finder. Salvage companies usually make a deal with the wreck owner or with the government.

This ammonite fossil is about 200 million years old.

ROMAN JAR COVERED IN SEA CREATURES

18TH CENTURY GOLD DOUBLOONS (SPANISH COINS)

The remains of this US fighter plane, a Grumman F6F-3 "Hellcat", has attracted a variety of reef fish and is of great interest to divers and marine historians.

TSUNAMI

TSUNAMIS ARE GIANT WAVES TRIGGERED BY volcanic eruptions and underwater earthquakes. They begin as broad, low ripples in the open sea, often passing unnoticed beneath ships. Although tsunamis start small, they are incredibly fast, travelling across deep water at more than 700 kph (435 mph), the speed of a jet aircraft. When they reach shallow water, they slow down and begin rising to a terrifying size – sometimes up to 60 m (200 ft) high. Water is usually drawn away from the shore before a tsunami arrives, leaving fish stranded and wrecks exposed. People who come to look at these strange sights are often swept away when the wave suddenly rears up out of the sea.

NO ORDINARY WAVE

Tsunamis are not related to ordinary waves blown up by the wind. Wind waves are steep, narrow, and slow-moving. They are clearly visible as they cross the water. Tsunamis remain hidden until the last minute. They move by stealth, and are very hard to detect as they race over thousands of kilometres of sea. When they reach the shore, they are sometimes mistaken for tidal waves (caused by a tidal surge), although they have nothing to do with tides.

BIRTH OF A TSUNAMI

When seismic activity causes the seabed to rise or fall abruptly, the surrounding sea bulges and spreads out in a sequence of ripple-like waves. This can produce a series of tsunamis, one after the other. The ripples are usually very broad, and can reach more than 200 km (124 miles) in length, even though they may be less than 0.5 m (20 in) high in the open ocean.

When a section of seabed subsides, it creates a trough of one or more giant waves.

In deep water, tsunamis travel in a series of very long, low ripples.

As they reach land, tsunamis rear up, sucking water away from the shore.

THE GOOD FRIDAY TSUNAMI

On Good Friday, 27 March 1964, a massive earthquake under the sea near Alaska, USA, sent a tsunami down the northwest Pacific coast. Alaskans were familiar with tsunamis, but the residents of Oregon and California were not. When the civil defence chief of Crescent City, California, received a tsunami warning, he had to seek advice to find out what a tsunami was! Later that day, Crescent City was struck by the wave, and 16 people died. Crescent City got off lightly. In 1883, a tsunami caused by the eruption of Karakatoa, Indonesia, killed 36,000 people.

HILO, HAWAII

This picture shows some of the devastation caused by a tsunami that struck Hilo, Hawaii, in 1946. The wave travelled 3,000 km (1,865 miles) from the coast of Alaska, taking five hours to reach Hilo Bay. The horseshoe shape of the bay funnelled the tsunami's force onto the town, killing 159 people. Today, the Pacific Tsunami Warning Centre, based on Hawaii, alerts coastal towns to unusually large sea waves.

DEVASTATION

The tsunami of December 2004 began with a massive earthquake off the coast of Indonesia, and the resulting waves spread from there. The earthquake was the second largest ever recorded, as well as lasting the longest time – at up to 10 minutes.

Before Banda Aceh in Indonesia was close to the epicentre of the 2004 earthquake and was the first place the tsunami struck.

It took time for the 2004 tsunami to reach the surrounding countries, as shown on this map, and the effects were devasting. The wave was eventually felt as far away as Iceland and Chile.

AFTER Most of the northern shore was submerged by the tsunami. An estimated 230,000 people in eleven countries died when the waves hit land.

HARVEST FROM THE SEA

PEOPLE THE WORLD OVER HAVE ALWAYS harvested what they need from the sea, and many people in poor, coastal regions depend entirely on fishing for their food and livelihood. In Southeast Asia, many such coastal communities rely on aquaculture – the "farming" of the sea. Seaweed, giant clams, oysters, tiger prawns, and milkfish are just some of the famers' "crops". The Bajau Laut, or sea gypsies, in Malaysia spend their entire lives out at sea on their boats. Usually, they only come ashore to bury their dead.

A WAY OF LIFE

Fishing is also a way of life for thousands of people in developed regions such as Europe and the USA. The photograph (above) shows a European double-beamed shrimp trawler collecting its catch. Many families have been fishing for generations, but overfishing has drastically reduced fish stocks throughout the oceans. In some places, whole communities have stopped fishing. In the future, fish farms and indoor hatcheries on land may become the main source for popular fish such as cod.

MUSSELS   WINKLES   COCKLES

As long as they are adequately washed, hand-collected shellfish can provide an excellent free meal.

"ALIVE, ALIVE-OH!"
Cockles, mussels, and periwinkles can easily be collected on shores around Europe. Hand-collecting causes few problems for worldwide stocks, but in areas where commercial machines – such as cockle dredgers – are used, these shellfish soon become scarce.

MARINE MEDICINES
Many colourful sponges grow on coral reefs around the world. Some produce powerful chemicals that prevent other creatures from growing over them. Scientists have found that some of these chemicals can be used to combat illnesses such as malaria and cancer. Whenever a useful sponge chemical is discovered, scientists try to reproduce it in the laboratory to save collecting up too many wild sponges.

An azure vase sponge (right) from the Caribbean. New sponge species are discovered on coral reefs every year.

SEAWEED STRINGS
Seaweed is farmed in many developing countries in tropical parts of the world, and provides an income for local families. It can be sold as food, fertilizer, and as an ingredient for other products. Small pieces of seaweed are tied on to ropes and staked out in the sea (right), often with plastic bottles attached to the ropes as floats. When it has grown big enough, the seaweed is collected and dried out on land.

A STRING OF PEARLS

Pearls are one of the most valuable natural products found in the sea. When an oyster gets a bit of irritating material inside its shell, it covers it with shiny, smooth layers of a precious material called mother-of-pearl. Pearl farmers in the South Pacific hang oysters on ropes and slip small pieces of broken shell into them so that they make pearls.

A diver is inspecting his pearl oysters to check that they are healthy, and that the ropes are not frayed or damaged.

A FARMED SALMON

Many different species of oysters and mussels can produce pearls, but they are not always as perfectly formed as these ones (above right).

SALMON FARMING

In northern Europe, salmon can be bought in most supermarkets. Most of it now comes not from wild-caught stocks, but from Scottish and Norwegian fish farms. The fish are grown in suspended pens and, as in the photograph (left), are fed pellets made from fish-meal.

IMPACT ON THE OCEANS

PEOPLE ONCE THOUGHT THAT THE OCEANS were so huge that nothing we did could ever affect them. Unfortunately, this is no longer true. Modern technology, huge increases in the world's population, and a lack of management have resulted in some serious problems. Today, overfishing is one of the most serious. Catching large numbers of a few species upsets the delicate balance of nature. Other serious problems include pollution from poorly treated sewage, effluents from oil spills, litter, and the destruction of coral reefs. These problems can be solved – but only if nations and governments work together.

A humpback whale lifts its huge tail fluke before diving into

Spermaceti oil from sperm whales was used as a lubricant and for making candles.

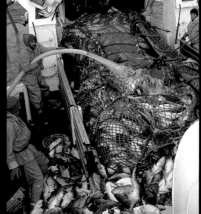

IN FOR THE KRILL

Most countries have banned commercial whaling and a large part of the Southern Ocean around Antarctica is now a whale sactuary. But Japan and Norway still catch whales legally. Krill, the tiny shrimps on which many whales feed, is now harvested from the Southern Ocean –

OVERFISHING

Cod was once the most plentiful fish in the North Atlantic. It was so common that whole communities depended on it for a living. Today there are far fewer, due to modern fishing methods that track where the fish are and trawl them up in huge quantities. Fishing for cod has now been stopped or restricted in some areas, which should allow their numbers to increase.

Although cod can live for at least 20 (and possibly 30) years, there are now virtually no cod in the

This small wooden house by the sea, in Indonesia, is protected by a wall built from coral blocks.

ARCTIC IMPROVEMENTS

The inhospitable Arctic Ocean is perhaps the least exploited ocean region, mainly because it is so difficult to work there. In the 1970s and 1980s, thousands of baby harp seals were killed each year for their white fur – but no longer. Inuit people hunt walruses and seals, but they only take what they need for food and clothing.

CORAL MINING

Throughout the Indian Ocean there are many small island nations such as the Maldives. Island resorts are becoming popular with tourists who want to visit the coral reefs and beautiful beaches. Many hotels and jetties used by these tourists are built using coral rock mined from the reefs, which are damaged as a result.

the depths. Individual whales can be recognized from markings on their tails.

OIL SPILLS

Oil spills occur in oceans and seas throughout the world. They are mainly caused by oil tankers that run aground. Considerable damage can occur when the oil goes ashore, especially if there are major seabird or seal colonies nearby. Smaller – and more frequent – spills from ships illegally washing out their tanks can be just as damaging to marine life. Out at sea, spills can be treated with detergents – but many

This auk is covered in oil from the 1996 Sea Empress disaster in Wales, UK. Most oiled birds die even if they

REMOTE SENSING

U NDERSTANDING HOW THE OCEANS work is the job of oceanographers. These scientists used to spend many weeks at sea measuring water temperature, currents, waves, and water clarity. Nowadays, satellites can obtain information about the sea by measuring electromagnetic radiation. The data is sent to powerful computers that convert the readings into temperature, colour, wave height, and current speed information.

EUROPEAN
REMOTE-SENSING
SATELLITE *ERS-1*

ERS-1 *was launched into orbit by the* Ariane 4 *rocket on 17 July, 1991.*

OCEANOGRAPHIC SURVEYS

The *ERS-1* satellite orbits Earth and is used to collect data on coastlines, oceans, and polar ice. Scientists around the world are using it to study climate change. Sensors on the satellite detect microwaves, which can pass through clouds, unlike the visible light needed to take photographs.

CURRENTLY WARM

Sea surface temperatures are measured by satellite sensors that detect infra-red radiation. This image, from the *NOAA 11* satellite, shows the origin of the Gulf Stream – a current that carries warm water from around Florida, USA, to the shores of Britain. Without it, Britain would have a climate as cold as Greenland. Red and yellow indicate warm water. Blue and grey show cool water.

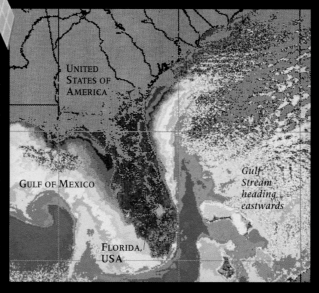

UNITED
STATES OF
AMERICA

GULF OF MEXICO

Gulf Stream heading eastwards

FLORIDA,
USA

JAPANESE
TUNA

TUNA TROUBLE

Modern fishing boats make full use of satellite technology, computers, and sonar to help them locate and catch fish shoals. With sonar, pulses of sound are sent down into the water and "bounce" back if they hit shoals of fish. The time taken for echoes to return is measured and these readings help to pin-point large shoals of fish, worthy of pursuit. Valuable tuna shoals are also "spotted" by light aircraft. Sadly, these methods are so efficient that some species, such as bluefin tuna, are becoming very scarce.

A shark is caught using a baited line and brought safely aboard the ship in a netted "hammock".

BIRD'S EYE VIEWS

Aerial photographs can be used to survey coastlines and coral reefs, and to monitor the effects of oil spills. Photographs taken from aeroplanes give a closer view, while satellites can cover very large areas. This photograph shows Kayangel Atoll, a ring of coral reefs (an atoll) in the Pacific Ocean. By repeating the survey at a later date, changes in the shifting sand banks – and the vegetation trying to grow on them – can be documented.

Shallow sand banks show up as pale blue areas, while deep water channels or lagoons are dark blue.

The build-up of sand, and other sediments, drifting across the reef eventually causes sandy islands to form. Wind-borne plant seeds bring new vegetation to these young islands.

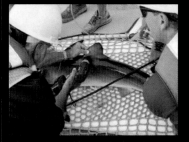

The tag is quickly attached to the shark's dorsal fin using a special tool.

This is an example of the sort of tag used to track sharks and other large marine animals.

Once the satellite tag has been attached, the tag's number is recorded and the shark is carefully returned to the sea.

SATELLITE TRACKING

Satellite tags are used to track the movements of large animals such as sharks, whales, and turtles. The tags record where the animal is and transmit the data to a satellite when the animal is on the surface. By following the movements of endangered species, such as blue whales and bluefin tuna, scientists will be able to make plans to protect these animals.

FLUID WORLD

WHEN THE ENGINEER NIKOLAUS OTTO DEVISED the first four-stroke internal combustion engine, in 1876, he could never have dreamed that one day his invention would affect our climate and our oceans. Cars use engines based on his design and each day, tens of millions of them belch out carbon dioxide gas in their exhaust fumes. This gas traps the Sun's heat and is one of the causes of "global warming". Some scientists predict that global warming will cause sea levels to rise – firstly because the polar ice will melt, and secondly because warm water takes up more space than cold water does.

MELTING ICE

Nobody can yet say for sure whether global warming is affecting the ice caps in the Arctic and Antarctic. However, there are some worrying signs. Glaciers such as the Hubbard Glacier in Alaska (left) are retreating and growing smaller, iceberg numbers have increased, and temperatures in the Antarctic are rising.

EL NIÑO

Every few years, changes in wind patterns and water currents in the Pacific Ocean cause an event called *El Niño*. Unusually warm water moves eastwards towards South America. This causes heavy rain, violent storms, and cuts off the food supply for fish such as anchovies.

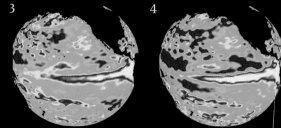

This computer-enhanced satellite image, taken on 25 April 1997, shows an area of unusually warm water – the start of an El Niño event. Global warming could be making El Niño *events worse.*

By 5 September 1997, the warm water has reached the coast of Peru, where the anchovy population is affected. Without the anchovies, many birds die and fishermen face great hardship.

NOT SO SILENT WORLD

The famous diver Jacques Cousteau gave the title *Silent World* to his book about the oceans. Sadly, our seas are no longer silent places. Loud noises from oil exploration, commercial shipping, scientific experiments, and naval exercises may be confusing whales and dolphins. This could be one reason why these animals sometimes get stranded on the shore.

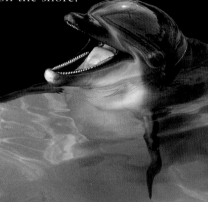

Bottlenose dolphin (Tursiops truncatus)

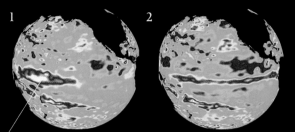

"Alternative", or "renewable", energy sources – such as wind power – do not produce carbon dioxide or other wastes. However, they are not yet efficient or cheap enough to completely replace fossil fuels.

CLEAN ENERGY

Burning oil, coal, and other "fossil fuels" in power stations releases carbon dioxide into the atmosphere, which adds to global warming. This is why "clean" ways of making electricity are being developed, using the power of the wind, Sun, and tides. This picture shows the Livermore Wind Farm in California, USA.

TIDAL POWER

This tidal barrage, built across the French River Rance, generates power from every tide. The tide is allowed to swirl in through the sluice gates to fill the river estuary. The gates are then closed, as the tide starts to fall, and the water is released through 24 turbines, which generate approximately 240 million watts of electricity.

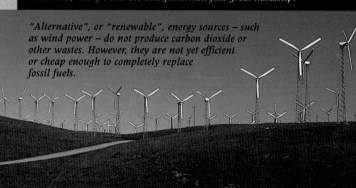

Tidal barrages only work where there are big tides. The tidal range at this dam reaches 13.5 m (44 ft). The barrage is 750 m (2,500 ft) long and creates an artificial lake 22 sq km (8.5 sq miles) in area.

Huge chunks of ice are falling from the front edge of the glacier, where it reaches the sea.

TIDES OF CHANGE

THERE IS NO DOUBT THAT OUR WORLD and its oceans face many problems. We hear on the news of global warming, overfishing, and massive oil spills. Government action is needed to tackle these issues, but individuals can take action, too. For example, if tourists refuse to buy souvenirs such as shark jaws and turtle shells, fishermen will stop catching the animals. Sharks in popular diving spots are now worth much more alive than dead because diving tourists will pay to see them.

MARINE ALIENS

When ships sail around the world's oceans they sometimes carry "stowaway" plants and animals on their hulls or amongst their cargo. Japweed (*Sargassum muticum*) came to the UK from Japan. It now grows all along the south coast of England and getting rid of the stuff has proved impossible.

Once plentiful, Kemp's ridley sea turtles are now the most endangered of all turtle species. Sometimes, ocean currents carry young ones over to Europe from America.

FISHING FOR PUFFINS

ATLANTIC PUFFIN
(*FRATERCULA ARCTICA*)

The Shetland Islands, off northern Scotland, are home to many thousands of puffins that nest in cliff-top burrows. In the 1980s, the numbers of puffins fell dramatically. Fishing boats had caught so many sand eels that few were left for the puffins to feed their chicks.

Puffins rely on a good supply of sand eels to feed to their chicks. Recent fishing restrictions have made the eels more plentiful.

BRENT SPAR

The *Brent Spar* was a massive, 4,000-tonne (3,900-ton) North Sea oil platform. When it was no longer needed, the owners planned to sink it into the ocean depths. There followed a public outcry over the contamination this would cause, and it was eventually dismantled onshore in spite of the cost. Ordinary people had won the day.

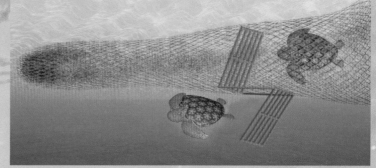

TURTLE EXCLUSION DEVICE (TED)

SHRIMPS IN, TURTLES OUT

Kemp's ridley turtles are the rarest of the six species of turtle found in our oceans. In the Gulf of Mexico, many turtles get caught in nets towed by fishing boats that are trawling for shrimps. The turtles usually drown because they cannot get to the surface to breathe. Luckily, scientists have developed nets with special "escape hatches" (above) that allow the turtles to get out without losing the shrimp catch.

KEMP'S RIDLEY SEA TURTLE
(*LEPIDOCHELYS KEMPII*)

This snorkeller is swimming with fish in a marine reserve area in Belize, Central America.

THE PLASTIC PERIL

Litter on beaches is a big problem. It comes from ships, fishing boats, tourists, and sewers. Plastic is especially dangerous as it lasts a long time and can injure or kill wildlife. Dumping plastic waste from ships is banned in many sea areas but the problem remains. Volunteers sometimes help out in organized beach "clean-ups".

MARINE RESERVES

There are many marine parks and reserves around the world where fishing and collecting are banned or restricted. Marine reserves provide a safe haven for fish and other ocean creatures. As in the picture (above), such fish can become very tame. However, the amount of ocean that can be protected in this way is tiny.

OCEAN DATA

OCEAN RECORDS

Highest storm wave In 1933, an American ship, the *USS Ramapo*, encountered a terrible storm on its way from Manila, Philippines, to San Diego. One of the crew measured a wave 34 m (112 ft) high.

Highest recorded wave The greatest wave ever recorded was created by a massive landslide in an inlet in Alaska, USA (9 July, 1958). The falling rock caused a wave to surge up the opposite side of the bay, which reached a height of 530 m (1,740 ft).

Deepest part of the ocean The Challenger Deep in the Mariana Trench, between Japan and Papua New Guinea, has a maximum recorded depth of 11,033 m (36,198 ft).

Deepest manned craft On 23 January 1960, the bathyscape *Trieste* descended to a depth of 10,918 m (35,820 ft) in the Challenger Deep with two people on board. The record still stands.

Worst whirlpools The Malstrøm is a famous whirlpool that forms when strong tides run through narrow passages between the Lofotodden Islands off Norway's rugged west coast.

Biggest tides (and tidal range) The difference in height between high and low water in the Bay of Fundy, in Canada, is 16 m (53.5 ft).

Most dramatic tidal bore In the Qiantang River estuary, in China, the incoming tide funnels seawater up the river as a fast wave called the *Black Dragon*, which reaches heights of up to 9 m (30 ft).

Highest submarine mountain The top of Mount Kea in the Pacific Ocean is 10,203 m (33,476 ft) above the sea floor. It is significantly higher than Mount Everest, the tallest mountain on land, which is 8,850 m (29,037 ft) tall.

MARINE WILDLIFE RECORDS

Biggest marine animal Blue whale. Largest recorded length: 31 m (102 ft). Largest recorded weight: 196 tonnes (212 tons). Bigger examples may exist.

Biggest invertebrate Giant squid. Largest known specimen: 16.8 m (55 ft) long. Much larger examples may exist.

Biggest jellyfish Lion's mane jellyfish (*Cyanea capillata*). Bell diameter: 2.3 m (7.5 ft). Tentacle length: 36.5 m (120 ft).

Smallest vertebrate Dwarf goby fish. Adults average 8.8 mm (0.35 in) long.

Tallest seaweed Giant kelp (*Macrocystis*) can reach nearly 60 m (197 ft) tall – see pages 120-121.

Longest migration (swimming) Grey whale. A round trip of 20,000 km (12,400 miles) – see page 134-135.

Most dangerous vertebrate Great white shark. Grows to at least 6.5 m (21 ft) long. Mainly eats seals, sea lions, dolphins, and large fish – see page 136.

Smallest shark Spined pygmy shark. Adult males are only 15 cm (6 in) long; females are 17–20 cm (7–8 in) long.

Most common shark Spiny dogfish. Common worldwide and sometimes caught by the million by fishermen.

Most dangerous invertebrate Box jellyfish (*Chironex fleckeri*). Its sting can kill – see page 142.

Most venomous fish Stonefish (family Synanceiidae). These well-camouflaged fish are easily touched by accident and possess sharp spines containing a lethal nerve poison.

Slowest fish Sea horses. They are weak swimmers because their only source of propulsion is a small fin that flickers to drive them forwards in an upright posture. Sea horses cannot swim against the current and must cling to seaweeds with their curled tails to avoid being swept away.

Deepest diver Sperm whale. Can probably reach depths of at least 3,000 m (9,800 ft) – see page 105.

Living fossil Coelacanth. This fish belongs to a group that was thought to have been extinct since the Cretaceous Period (135–70 MYA). However, a specimen was caught in 1938.

Loudest sound produced Some baleen whales produce sounds that can travel all the way across entire oceans.

OCEAN HISTORY

OCEAN TIMELINE:

• **4.6 billion years ago** Earth forms
• **3.8 billion years ago** The condensation of atmospheric water causes the true oceans to form
• **500 million years ago** Life exists only in the oceans
• **300 million years ago** The age of fish
• **200–180 million years ago** The supercontinent *Pangaea* begins to break up
• **100 million years ago** The age of reptiles, dinosaurs (on land), and ichthyosaurs and plesiosaurs in the ocean
• **65 million years ago** Primitive whales swim in the oceans
• **c. 2.5 million years ago** Primitive human beings appear

HISTORY OF EXPLORATION:

• **1831–36** Charles Darwin travels on his famous voyage on board the *Beagle*, making observations (regarding wildlife) that lead to his revolutionary theory of natural selection
• **1872–76** The voyage of the *HMS Challenger* – the first comprehensive oceanographic research expedition
• **1912** The *RMS Titanic* sinks
• **1920** Echo sounding equipment first used
• **1940s** Aqualung (scuba) equipment is invented
• **1960** The bathyscape *Trieste* reaches the deepest part of the ocean
• **1977** Extraordinary animals are found around deepsea volcanic vents
• **1985–87** The wreck of the *Titanic* is found and filmed by a submersible

DID YOU KNOW...

The amount of water contained by the oceans is around 1.4 billion cubic km (326 million cubic miles).

The five oceans (biggest to smallest) are the Pacific, Atlantic, Indian, Southern (Antarctic), and the Arctic.

The Pacific Ocean is the biggest of the five oceans. It covers an area of more than 163 million square km (63 million square miles).

Seas of the world Seas are smaller than oceans. Oceanographers recognize about 54 official seas.

Inland seas Some seas (e.g. Dead Sea, Caspian Sea) are land-locked and have no connection to the ocean.

Salinity The saltiness (salinity) of the ocean is measured in parts per thousand (ppt). The average salinity is 35 ppt, which means 35 units of salt in every 1,000 units of water.

Elements The ocean contains all the known elements, although some are only present in tiny amounts.

Temperature varies widely in the ocean. It ranges from -2°C (28°F) in the Arctic and Southern oceans to 36°C (97°F), during the summer, in the Arabian Gulf.

Sound travels 4.5 times faster through seawater than it does through air.

SEA STATE: THE BEAUFORT SCALE (simplified)

Force	Wind speed (knots)	Descriptive term	Sea state	Probable wave height (metres)
0	< 1	Calm	Sea like a mirror	0.0 m (0.0 ft)
1	1–3	Light air	Ripples with the appearance of scales	0.1 m (0.3 ft)
2	4–6	Light breeze	Small wavelets	0.2 m (0.7 ft)
3	7–10	Gentle breeze	Large wavelets; crests begin to break	0.6 m (2.0 ft)
4	11–16	Moderate breeze	Small waves becoming longer; fairly frequent "white horses" (white-topped waves)	1.0 m (3.3 ft)
5	17–21	Fresh breeze	Moderate waves; many white horses	2.0 m (6.6 ft)
6	22–27	Strong breeze	Large waves; white horses everywhere; probably some spray	3.0 m (9.8 ft)
7	28–33	Near gale	Sea heaps up; white foam from breaking waves begins to be blown in streaks along the direction of the wind	4.0 m (13.0 ft)
8	34–40	Gale	Moderately high, long waves; foam from crests is blown in well-marked streaks along direction of wind	5.5 m (18.0 ft)
9	41–47	Strong gale	High waves; dense streaks of foam along direction of wind; crests of waves begin to topple, tumble, and roll over	7.0 m (23.0 ft)
10	48–55	Storm	Very high waves with long, overhanging crests; the resulting foam is blown in dense, white streaks along direction of wind; surface takes on a white appearance; tumbling of the sea becomes very heavy and shock-like	9.0 m (29.5 ft)
11	56–63	Violent storm	Exceptionally high waves; sea completely covered with long, white patches of foam lying along direction of wind; everywhere the edges of the wave crests are blown into froth; visibility affected	11.5 m (37.7 ft)
12	64 +	Hurricane	Air filled with foam and spray; sea completely white with driving spray; visibility very seriously affected	14.0 m (46.0 ft)

MYTHS AND MONSTERS

The Kraken
Stories about the legendary Kraken came out of Norway in the 12th century. They told of a giant, octopus-like creature that was believed to sink ships. This mythical beast is probably based on the giant squid (see "Marine wildlife records", left).

Sea monsters
Sailors used to believe that the sea was filled with deadly sea monsters. Sightings of huge whales probably gave rise to some of these stories.

Mermaids
Mermaid legends, from as early as the 8th century BC, refer to creatures with a human, female top half and a scaly, fish tail as a bottom half. Sea cows (dugongs) may be the basis of this myth, although their whiskery faces are not particularly beautiful!

Sea serpents
Oarfish have an eel-like body, of up to 7 m (23 ft) long, and a bright red crest along their back. They probably inspired many stories about sea serpents.

Devilfish
The huge but harmless manta ray (see page 137) was once thought to be able to drag ships out to sea by their anchor chains.

WEBSITES

www.noaa.gov
The US Government's official National Oceanic and Atmospheric Administration (NOAA) website. Offers news and educational information.

www.bbc.co.uk/nature/blueplanet
The BBC's online guide to the natural history of the oceans.

http://earth.google.com/ocean/
Google Earth's ocean section allows you to dive below the waves and explore the sea floor. You will need to download the latest version of Google Earth to use its new ocean feature.

www.montereybayaquarium.org/
Watch sea otters, turtles, a kelp forest, and many other marine wonders on the live webcams at Monterey Bay Aquarium in California, USA.

www.fishbase.org/search.cfm
Information on almost all species of fish. Photographs help to identify each species.

www.ocean.udel.edu/deepsea
Voyage to the Deep. Plunge into the ocean depths with deep submersible craft *Alvin*.

www.mcsuk.org
Information on how you can help conserve the oceans. Includes details of beach clean-ups and projects such as "Adopt a Turtle".

www.sharktrust.org
Fascinating facts about sharks and the problems they face due to overfishing.

http://dsc.discovery.com/ convergence/sharkweek/ ultimate-quiz/ultimate-quiz.html
Think you know all about sharks and how dangerous they are? Test your knowledge with this interactive quiz.

Please note: Every effort has been made to ensure that these websites are suitable, and that their addresses are up-to-date at the time of going to print. Website content is constantly updated, as are website addresses – therefore, it is highly recommended that a responsible adult should visit and check each website before allowing access to a child.

MAMMALS

THE VARIETY OF MAMMAL SPECIES IS
AMAZING. Mammals share features in
common – they are vertebrates, and they
feed their young on milk produced by the
mother – but beyond that, they range from
tiny bats and shrews to the mighty blue
whale. They can be found in all habitats,
on land, in water, and in the air. Altogether
there are 5,488 recognised mammal species.

WHAT IS A MAMMAL?

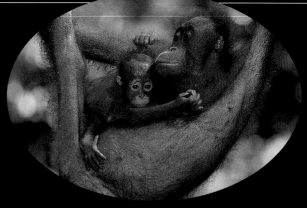

SIXTY-FIVE MILLION YEARS AGO, a gigantic comet slammed into Earth and wrecked the planet's climate. It was a catastrophe for the dinosaurs – they were wiped out entirely – but it cleared the way for another class of animals to take over. The mammals (class Mammalia) were little more than small, nervous creatures of the night at that time, but they had already evolved some of the features that were to help them succeed, such as hair, warm blood, and milk glands. With the dinosaurs out of the way, the mammals entered a new phase in their evolution. They exploded into thousands of new forms, conquering land, sea, and air to become the biggest and most spectacular animals on Earth.

MILK AND MOTHERS

The defining feature of mammals is that they feed their young on the milk they produce. The very word mammal comes from the Latin word mamma, meaning breast. In addition, for many species, the period of parental care is a time for their young to learn vital survival skills. The cleverest mammals, such as humans and orang-utans, have the most to learn and so spend the longest with their mothers.

A VERY STRANGE MAMMAL

Humans are mammals. Our species, *Homo sapiens*, belongs to the great ape family, along with chimps, orang-utans, and gorillas. In some ways we are very peculiar mammals. Our brains are abnormally large, and we have lost most of our hair. We are the only mammal species that walks on two legs, and we are possibly the only one with a complex language.

Mammals are warm-blooded, a feature they share with birds.

KEY FEATURES

Mammals have various unique features that set them apart from the rest of the animal kingdom. They have mammary glands that produce milk, and hair to keep them warm (though whales have lost their hair). Mammals also differ from other animals in aspects of their teeth, jawbones, ears, internal organs, and blood cells.

Mammalian skin often has scent glands and sweat glands.

Legs are directly below the body to carry the weight.

GETTING AROUND

The first true mammals were probably four-legged animals that scuttled about like shrews. After the dinosaurs perished, the mammals diversified and found new ways of getting around. Some grew wings and took to the air. Others adapted to life in water, their limbs turning into flippers. Thousands remained four-legged, but today they vary from silent stalkers prowling along the ground to agile climbers in the treetops.

Mammals have larger brains than other animals and are cleverer.

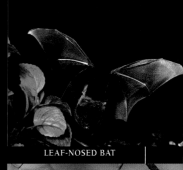
LEAF-NOSED BAT

JAGUAR

BROWN CAPUCHIN MONKEY

BOTTLENOSE DOLPHIN

SCENTS AND SMELLS

Smell is very important to mammals because most use body odours to communicate. When a rhino sprays the ground with urine, it leaves a unique scent as a message for other rhinos, telling its age, sex, social status, and whether it wants to breed.

Many mammals have outer ears to funnel sound waves.

Whiskers and eyelashes are special types of hair.

Mammalian teeth mesh together precisely and come in distinct varieties, such as canines, incisors, and molars.

BAT WING

The lower jaw consists of a single bone, hinged directly to the skull.

The arm bones in a dolphin's flipper are short and stubby.

Mammals are the only animals with a covering of hair.

DOLPHIN FLIPPER

The wing of a bat is supported by extended finger bones.

Five finger bones

Forearm bones (radius and ulna)

Upper arm bone (humerus)

MONKEY ARM

THE BARE BONES

Mammals look very different externally, but strip away the flesh and they all have the same basic skeleton. Evolution has simply changed the size of various bones to create the diversity of shapes that exists today. Birds, reptiles, fish, and amphibians also have this kind of skeleton. Scientists call all these animals vertebrates – animals with backbones.

Mammals have a skeletal plan with four limbs, each ending in five digits, on average.

TEMPERATURE CONTROL

MAMMALS ARE WARM-BLOODED (endothermic), which means their bodies generate heat from within to keep them continuously warm. In contrast, animals such as lizards and frogs are cold-blooded (ectothermic) – their body temperature goes up and down depending on outside climate conditions. Most mammals have a constant internal temperature, but this varies from species to species. Humans have a body temperature of 37°C (99°F), but rabbits and cats are warmer at 39°C (102°F), and armadillos are cooler at 32°C (90°F). Being warm-blooded allows mammals to stay active at night and survive in places where reptiles and frogs would freeze, but mammals pay a high price for their on-board heating system. To survive, they need about ten times as much food as cold-blooded animals. About 90 percent of their food is burned up just for keeping themselves warm.

COOLING OFF

Cold-blooded animals simply let their body temperature rise in hot weather, but mammals have to keep a constant temperature. Hippos cool off by wallowing in mud and water. Walruses blush to lose heat, dogs pant, and cats sweat (though only through the soles of their feet). Kangaroos lick their arms and hold them out to dry. Elephants flap their ears or hose themselves with water.

LIFE IN THE FAST LANE

Keeping warm is a problem for small mammals, like the southern flying squirrel. They lose heat faster than large mammals because the ratio between the body's surface area and volume is greater (peas get cold more quickly than potatoes for the same reason). So, to stay warm, small animals lead fast, furious lives. They spend most of their time frantically searching for food, and they grow old and die in just a few years.

Sleeping bats can go into a state called torpor, letting their body temperature fall.

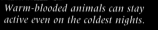

Warm-blooded animals can stay active even on the coldest nights.

WARM- OR COLD-BLOODED?

Some bats are so small that they can't get enough food to keep constantly warm. Instead of wasting energy generating heat while they rest, they let their body temperature plummet to that of their surroundings. Hibernating mammals do this in winter, but certain bat species can do it every day. When they wake up, they have to exercise vigorously until they become warm enough to fly again.

FUELING THE BODY

Some cold-blooded animals can get by with only one meal a year, but mammals need to eat far more often. Carnivores, such as polar bears, get all their energy from meat, while herbivores like the proboscis monkey make do with leaves. Shrews are omnivores – they eat both animals and plant foods. All mammals have teeth and digestive systems specialized to extract as much energy as possible from their food.

The bushy tail doubles as a blanket to wrap around the body.

The snow leopard has woolly underfur up to 12 cm (5 in) thick.

FUR COATS

Fur coats are vital for keeping warm. Only the largest sea mammals do without them, but they have an insulating layer of blubber below the skin. Fur usually has two layers: an outer layer of long, bristly "guard hairs" for protection, and an inner layer of soft underfur for warmth.

REPRODUCTION

SCIENTISTS SPLIT MAMMALS into three major groups depending on how they reproduce. Monotremes are unusual mammals that lay eggs; only three species exist. Marsupials carry their babies in a pouch. Placental mammals – the most common type of mammal – carry babies inside the body, where they feed through an organ called a placenta. Some mammals produce only one baby at a time, caring for it to give it a good chance of survival. Others have lots of babies and provide them with little but milk. The majority perish, but a few make it to adulthood.

A pair of guanacos strike a dance-like pose during their courtship.

BABY FOOD

Although male mammals have nipples, only the females produce milk (with one bizarre exception: the male Dayak fruit bat). Milk is a mixture of water and nutrients, including protein, fat, carbohydrate, and vitamins. It also contains antibodies, which protect babies from disease. Its content varies enormously between species. Sea lion milk is about 50 percent fat, allowing baby sea lions to double their weight in days, but human milk is only four percent fat. Lion milk is very sugary, providing lion cubs with the instant energy they need for playing.

Lion cubs depend on their mother's milk until they are about three months old.

THE MATING GAME

The first stage of reproduction is courtship, when mammals try to attract a partner. In most species the females make the choice, so the males have to work hard to impress them. Often the males try to prove themselves by fighting rivals or winning a territory. Mating may occur at a certain time of year – the breeding season – so that young are born when food is plentiful.

Female tenrecs give birth by the dozen. The young start breeding when only a month old.

FAST BREEDERS

The common tenrec – a Madagascan animal a bit like a hedgehog – has the most nipples (29) and the largest litters (up to 32) of any mammal. In theory, a single tenrec could produce a population of millions in one year if all its offspring bred at the maximum rate.

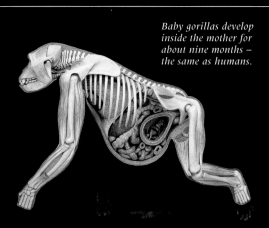

Baby gorillas develop inside the mother for about nine months – the same as humans.

PLACENTAL MAMMALS

Placental mammals give their young a head start in life by letting them develop to an advanced stage in the mother's body. Baby elephants spend 20 months inside the mother, and are born so well-developed that they can run within minutes of birth. Before birth, placental mammals are nourished by a placenta, a complex organ in which the baby's blood and the mother's blood flow past each other without mixing.

MONOTREMES

Echidnas and platypuses are the only mammals that lay eggs. Echidnas carry their eggs in a pouch, but the platypus puts them in a nest. Monotremes have no nipples – the mother's milk oozes into her fur like sweat.

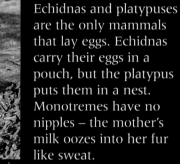

Echidnas have spiny bodies like hedgehogs.

MARSUPIALS

Marsupials give birth to wormlike babies far tinier than the young of placental mammals. Newborn kangaroos are the size of beans and don't even have hind legs. After birth, they wriggle through the mother's fur and into a pouch, where they stay for up to a year. A young kangaroo is called a joey.

GROWING UP

MOST ANIMALS SIMPLY ABANDON THEIR YOUNG to fate after giving birth or laying eggs, but mammals are different. Mammals feed and care for their offspring during the perilous early days of life. This period of parental care frees the young from the need to fend for themselves and gives them time to learn valuable survival skills. Baby turtles rely on instinct alone when they hatch, but mammals are free to play, explore, and copy their parents – all vital parts of the learning process. Parental care, coupled with large brains, is one of the features that makes mammals so successful and adaptable. It is most important in primates and especially so in humans – we have the longest childhood of any animal.

Female elephants suckle their young with a pair of breasts between the front legs.

CHANGING SHAPE
A fox cub is born helpless and blind, but it grows quickly on its mother's milk and soon starts to change shape. By two weeks, its eyes are open, and at four weeks, it starts to leave the den and explore. Its snout, ears, and legs get steadily longer, and the rolls of insulating puppy fat on its body gradually disappear.

By ten weeks, a fox cub has developed its adult colours.

NEWBORN FOX CUB   2 WEEKS   4 WEEKS   8 WEEKS   10 WEEKS

HITCHING A RIDE
Baby anteaters spend their first year or so riding on their mother's back. This is especially important for tree-dwelling anteaters, such as tamanduas, which live in the forests of South and Central America. The mother tamandua provides a safe perch for her baby until it is old enough to risk climbing on its own.

Tamandua's raid treetop ants' nests and eat up to 9,000 ants a day.

PROTECTIVE PARENTS

An elephant takes about 17 years to grow up. The calf and mother form a very strong bond and spend the first ten years close together, using their trunks to maintain physical contact. Elephants live in all-female herds and are fiercely protective of all the young in the herd, not just their own. If a person or animal gets too close, the leader of the herd spreads her ears and charges while bellowing thunderously through her trunk.

Young elephants hide under their mother's legs for protection.

KILLER INSTINCTS

Cats sometimes give their youngsters live prey to play with. Though it seems cruel to us, this is an important way to develop the skills they need to hunt. Cheetah cubs practise killing baby gazelles, learning how to trip them up as they try to race away.

WATCH WITH MOTHER

Cracking open a nut with rocks is one of the trickiest skills for a chimpanzee to master. Young chimps spend years watching their mothers doing it and slowly acquire the skill themselves by patient trial and error.

MAKING SNOWBALLS

Young mammals are very playful by nature. Play teaches them about their surroundings and hones essential survival skills, such as how to fight, hunt, or escape from attackers. But sometimes mammals seem to play just for the fun of it.

In winter, Japanese macaques make large snowballs by rolling them along the ground, in the same way as children make heads for snowmen.

171

PRIMITIVE PRIMATES

Grasping hands, large brains, and forward-facing eyes are the hallmarks of primates – the branch of the mammal family tree to which our own species belongs. Primates live throughout the world's tropical forests, and most are tree-dwellers. Apes and monkeys are the most famous primates, but there are many other, smaller species that are less well known. While apes and monkeys tend to be active by day, their smaller cousins are mostly secretive animals of the night, with big eyes for seeing in the dark and long, moist snouts for smelling their way around. Scientists call these mammals the prosimians, or primitive primates.

TWIGGY FINGER
The aye aye is a type of lemur with a middle finger that looks like a dead twig. After gnawing a hole in a tree trunk, the aye aye pokes in its finger and hooks beetle grubs on a sharp claw. This unique finger also makes a handy scoop for reaching into coconuts and eggs.

LEAPING LEMURS
The island of Madagascar near Africa is home to a group of primates found nowhere else: the lemurs. The sifaka is a type of lemur that moves about by leaping. It jumps from trees and lands upright on vertical boughs, which it grabs with colossal thumbs on its feet. Its arms are so short that when on the ground it has to bounce as if on a trampoline with its arms held high for balance.

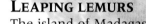

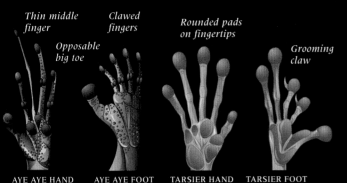

Thin middle finger *Clawed fingers* *Rounded pads on fingertips* *Grooming claw*

Opposable big toe

AYE AYE HAND AYE AYE FOOT TARSIER HAND TARSIER FOOT

HANDS AND FEET

The hands and feet of primitive primates remind us of our own. They have opposable thumbs and opposable big toes – these move the opposite way to the rest and so allow primates to grip branches as they climb. Primates tend to have nails rather than claws, giving improved grip and touch. For extra grip, tarsiers have huge round fingertip pads.

3-D VISION

The eyes of primates both face forward – quite unlike the sideways-facing eyes of rabbits or deer, for instance. Forward-facing eyes see the world twice, but they create two slightly different pictures. By combining these images, the primate brain produces a single, 3-D image of the world. Seeing in 3-D allows primates to judge distances.

The lorises of Asia have especially big eyes for seeing in the dark.

BOUNCING BABIES

The bushbabies of Africa can cover great distances in seconds by making a quick succession of leaps. Rather like sifakas, they use massive hind legs to spring from trees and then hold their bodies upright as they fly and land. These tiny nocturnal animals have astonishingly quick reflexes, and can even snatch passing moths from the air in mid-leap.

To mark their territory, bushbabies urinate on their feet and leave a trail of smelly footprints.

Ring-tailed lemurs like to sunbathe. They bask in sunlight sitting down, with their arms spread out.

STINK FIGHTS

Most primitive primates are nocturnal loners, but ring-tailed lemurs live in large groups and are active during the day. When rival groups clash, they have a "stink fight". The males rub their tails between scent glands on their wrists and then march towards each other, flicking their tails angrily to waft the scent. This battle of odours allows them to settle their differences without coming to blows.

THE APES

PEOPLE TEND TO CONFUSE APES with monkeys, but there are important differences. Apes are more upright and have no tails. They climb in a different way, using their huge arms to haul themselves up trees and hang from branches. Apes have bigger brains and are cleverer. They can manipulate and deceive each other, recognize themselves in mirrors, and learn to use all sorts of tools.

BEG FOR FOOD

INTENSE FEAR OR EXCITEMENT

FEAR GRIN

CONTEMPLATING

MAKING FACES

Although none of the apes has language anything like as complex as ours, they can communicate in sophisticated ways. Africa's chimps make at least 30 different calls and sometimes kick the giant roots of rainforest trees to make booming noises that carry far away. They also communicate with facial expressions more varied than any other animal's. Some are the opposite of our own – for instance, baring the teeth in a grin is a sign of fear to a chimp.

GENTLE GIANTS

Gorillas are the biggest primates and can weigh up to 210 kg (33 stone). Despite their great bulk and fearsome image, they are placid herbivores that spend all day chomping leaves in the mountains and rainforests of Central Africa. They move about as they forage, taking only a few leaves from each plant so as not to destroy their food supply.

CHIMP TOOL KITS

The ability of chimps to use tools is a reminder that these clever apes are our close cousins. They use sticks to fish for termites, rocks to crack open nuts, leaves as sponges and tissues, and all sorts of plants as herbal medicines. One captive chimp even learned how to light a barbecue and cook his own sausages.

All large apes walk on the soles of their hind feet and the knuckles of their hands.

Gorilla social groups are dominated by huge, silvery haired males called silverbacks, which mate with all the females.

SINGING SWINGERS

Gibbons swing through trees with breathtaking agility, using their hands as hooks. Their wrists and shoulders are so flexible that they can turn through 360 degrees, while hanging from one hand. Males and females live in monogamous pairs, like humans. Some species sing haunting duets to declare their bond.

GROWING UP SLOWLY

Young orang-utans spend up to ten years with their mothers. Like other apes, they grow up slowly as they need to learn many complex skills to survive. These gentle animals live in the steamy rainforests of Borneo and Sumatra and are threatened by deforestation.

BRAIN POWER

THERE IS A GOOD REASON why mammals make the best pets – they are cleverer than other animals. While pet snakes and birds have to be caged for their own good, cats and dogs are smart enough to wander freely. Mammals, in general, have larger brains than other animals (though there are several small-brained exceptions). They have sharper memories, are quicker to learn, and can adapt their behaviour to new situations. The cleverest mammals even show hints of abilities once thought to be uniquely human, including tool use and the beginnings of language.

LEARNING THE ROPES

As anyone with a birdfeeder knows, squirrels are ingenious as well as acrobatic. They can get past almost any obstacle in their quest for food, even if it means scurrying along a clothes-line upside down. They also have amazing memory skills. In autumn, grey squirrels hoard thousands of nuts for the winter, burying each one individually and memorizing its location.

FINDING THE WAY

Like many mammals, rats find their way about by memorizing the position of landmarks. They are so good at this that they can quickly learn the route through a maze and remember it perfectly. In the wild, rats use smell as well as vision to build up a map of landmarks. Their regular foraging routes become so ingrained that a rat will continue to leap over a remembered obstacle even after it has been removed.

BRAINY DOLPHINS

Dolphins have brains almost as large and complex as ours, but scientists are not sure what they use them for. With no hands, dolphins can't make tools, though they sometimes pick up sponges to protect their noses while foraging. Dolphins whistle and click to each other, but do their calls mean that they have a language? Captive dolphins can learn to understand sign language, and wild dolphins have personalized whistles that they use as names. But as yet there is no clear evidence that dolphins can string sounds together into sentences – an essential feature of human language.

The diet of a sea otter includes clams, sea urchins, crabs, and abalone from the sea bed.

TOOL USERS

Using tools was once thought to be the sole preserve of our own species, but we now know that many other animals are tool-users. The sea otter uses a rock as an anvil. It dives to the sea bed for shellfish and returns to the surface to eat them. Floating on its back, it places the rock on its belly and smashes the shellfish against it to break them open.

TOOL MAKERS

Orang-utans and chimpanzees not only use tools, but make them too. Both use specially prepared twigs to "fish" for ants and termites, and both are expert nest-makers, building a treetop sleeping platform every night by folding branches together. If it's raining, orang-utans add a roof to their nest or use giant leaves as umbrellas.

TALKING APES

Apes will never be able to speak to us because their voice boxes can't produce human sounds, but could they talk in other ways? Scientists have tried teaching our closest relatives – chimpanzees and bonobos – to communicate with sign language and symbols. So far, the most successful ape was a young bonobo called Kanzi, who picked up several hundred "words" by watching his adoptive mother being trained to use symbols. Kanzi went on to construct his own short sentences, but he only progressed to a two-year-old child's level.

Kanzi the bonobo talks to his trainer by pointing at symbols on a chart.

Bottlenose dolphins are curious and playful animals. They sometimes play with human divers or leap out of the water for fun.

ON THE HOOF

A HOOF IS NOTHING MORE THAN A TOENAIL, though a very big one. Long ago, the ancestors of hoofed mammals had feet much like ours. Over time, nails evolved into hooves, the heel travelled halfway up the leg, and these animals ended up walking gracefully on their toe tips. In some species, all but the middle toe withered away. The changes gave hoofed mammals a vital ability – speed, which was essential for running from meat eaters. Today, these endurance runners make up one of the biggest and most successful groups of mammals on Earth.

BATTLING MALES

Hoofed mammals are mostly plant eaters, but they can be just as violent and aggressive as any meat eater. Battles between males are common, especially when the prize is the right to mate with a whole herd of females. African plains zebras live in harems – groups of females owned by a single stallion. In the breeding season, the male faces challenges from rivals determined to steal his harem. The frenzy of bites and kicks can leave either contender mortally wounded.

With their lips drawn back, fighting zebras tear at each other with their teeth.

PLANT EATERS

Most hoofed mammals are either grazers or browsers. Grazers eat low plants like grass, while browsers nibble trees and shrubs, often specializing in food at a particular height. Gerenuks can stand on their hind legs to reach higher than most antelopes, though they are no match for giraffes.

BIRTH ON THE HOOF

A dangerous moment in a wildebeest's life comes immediately after birth, when the youngster is easy prey for predators. However, newborns can stagger to their feet within minutes of birth and can run with the herd within an hour. For added safety, all the females in a herd give birth during the same three-week period, ensuring there are far too many babies for the predators to kill.

The mother gives birth standing up. She eats the afterbirth and licks the baby to rouse it. During this critically dangerous period, wildebeest mothers are fiercely protective and will charge angrily at any curious onlookers.

A mouthful of grass takes about 80 hours to pass through the body of a ruminant, such as this highland cow.

ODD AND EVEN

Scientists split the hoofed mammals into two major groups, depending on whether they have an odd or even number of toes. In odd-toed animals, such as rhinos and horses, the weight rests on the central or single toe. In even-toed animals, such as camels, a pair of toes carries most of the weight.

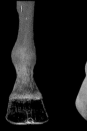 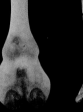

HORSE   CAMEL   RHINOCEROS

CHEWING THE CUD

Plant food is difficult to digest, so some hoofed mammals eat it twice. The first time they swallow a mouthful of grass, it goes into a special stomach chamber called a rumen. Later, the animal regurgitates the partly-digested grass, or cud, for a second chewing and swallows it again. This type of digestion, called rumination, is slow but efficient.

The ridges on horns prevent them from slipping in a sparring match.

The impala is one of the most common grazing animals in Africa. Only the male has horns.

A well-aimed kick from a zebra can cripple an opponent and leave it defenceless against lions or hyenas.

HORNS AND ANTLERS

Horns or antlers allow hoofed mammals to settle disputes without resorting to bloodshed. By locking their horns or antlers together and pushing (sparring), a pair can quickly work out who is strongest, while preventing injury.

CAT FAMILY

Cats are nature's most specialized carnivores, built to live on a diet consisting mostly of meat. All 38 species are ruthless killing machines, bristling with natural weapons and programmed by instinct to hunt with stealth and cunning. Domestic cats and their wild cousins have more in common than you might suppose. They share the same retractable claws, night vision, and vicious canine teeth. Like domestic cats, wild cats can pounce silently, land on four feet when they fall, and purr when content.

CLAWS FOR CLIMBING

Like nearly all cats, leopards have razor-sharp claws that serve both as weapons and as hooks for climbing. To keep them sharp, they are withdrawn into sheaths. Most cats live in forests and are good climbers, though up is easier than down! Patterned coats camouflage them in the dappled forest light.

A POWERFUL BUILD

Cats are ambush predators, built to stalk in silence and then attack with a burst of power. Unlike dogs, which are tall and athletic for long-distance running, cats have a sturdier, more powerful frame, yet they are also lithe and agile. Their muscular legs are built for pouncing and climbing. Their snouts are shorter than dogs', and their jaws are massive to accommodate muscles that inflict a fatal bite.

TIGER'S SKELETON

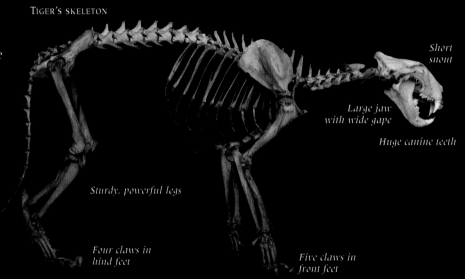

Short snout

Large jaw with wide gape

Huge canine teeth

Long tail for balance

Sturdy, powerful legs

A typical cat's litter has two to three infants.

Four claws in hind feet

Five claws in front feet

BABY CARE

Female cats are attentive mothers. They will hide their young in a den while away and call to greet them on returning. If the den proves unsafe, the mother quickly finds a new site and carries the infants there, one by one, by the scruff of the neck.

NIGHT VISION

DAY VISION

A lion cub becomes limp when picked up by the neck.

A lion's eyes glow at night because they contain a reflective layer called a tapetum.

NIGHT VISION

Cats are creatures of the night. Though they can't see as much colour as we can, their eyes are six times more sensitive in the dark. To catch as much light as possible, their eyes contain a reflective layer at the back. Depending on the species, cats' pupils shrink to dots or slits in daylight, but open to huge black discs at night.

SOCIABLE CATS

Cats are renowned for being loners, but some are more friendly than others. Male cheetahs often form small groups, probably because this helps them to take over other cheetahs' territories. Lions live in large groups called prides, and even stray domestic cats can be sociable. They sometimes rear their young in communal dens, the mothers taking turns to suckle all the young at once.

All cats have rough tongues to clean their fur and keep it fluffy. Grooming also serves to strengthen social bonds.

POUNCING PUMA

Cats are agile pouncers, able to spring off their haunches and sail gracefully through the air. Pouncing is handy for surprising prey or for jumping up trees. Domestic cats can slip up fences with gravity-defying ease.

SOFT LANDING

A superb sense of balance allows cats to land on all fours when they fall. First the neck twists until the head is level. Then the rest of the body swings quickly around. The front legs stretch out and absorb the impact of landing.

The head twists around first.

The rest of the body quickly follows.

The front legs touch down before the back legs.

181

SOCIAL LIVES

FOR MANY MAMMALS, life is easier if they gang together. Living in a social group is often a good form of defence – predators find it very difficult to sneak up unseen when there are dozens of eyes on the lookout for danger. Pack hunters, like dogs, hyenas, and lions, can take on bigger prey by pooling their strength and working as a team. They also find it easier to steal from rivals, defend their territory, and raise and protect their young. Some mammals have very fluid social groups that split up easily, but other groups are more tight-knit. Often the core of the group consists of closely related females, who stick together for life. Sometimes, completely unrelated species form a partnership, such as coyotes and American badgers, who team up to dig prairie dogs out of their burrows.

Musk oxen have the longest fur of any animal.

SAFETY IN NUMBERS

Small herbivores usually bolt at the first sign of danger, but bigger animals tend to stand their ground. When musk oxen face attack from wolves or polar bears, they draw together in a tight circle, with the youngsters in the middle behind a formidable wall of horns. Musk oxen live in northern Canada, where they have to brave subzero temperatures and ferocious winds.

FEMALES RULE

Spotted hyenas live in a society dominated by a strict female hierarchy. Even the highest-ranking male has a lower status than the lowest female. Hyena clans cooperate to defend a collective territory, though clan members frequently break up into smaller groups to hunt. At night, they communicate by making blood-curdling "woo-up" calls and cackling – hence the nickname "laughing hyenas".

Spotted hyenas raise their young in communal dens. The youngsters learn their place in the pecking order by fighting with each other from the moment they are born.

Meerkats watch for danger by standing on their hind legs, often on the top of a termite mound or a bush.

PACK HUNTERS

Dolphins live in groups called pods and have a very fluid society, with members leaving and joining all the time. Sometimes pods aggregate in groups of several hundred to cooperate in the hunting of shoaling fish, such as anchovy. By circling the fish and swimming below them, the dolphins drive them into an ever tighter formation and force them to the surface, making them easy to snatch.

Like many social animals, coatis cement the bonds between them by grooming each other.

SEPARATE SEXES

Scientists once thought that male and female coatis were different species. The large males are solitary, but the smaller females live in tight-knit groups. They tolerate the presence of males only in the breeding season and banish them afterwards.

MEERKATS UNITED

Meerkats take turns to keep a lookout while most of the group snuffle about on the ground for grubs. If the sentry sees an eagle, it makes an alarm call that sends the group sprinting in terror for the nearest hole. If the predator is a land animal, a different kind of call sends the meerkats dashing less urgently into any available hiding place.

SMALL AND WILY

THE WORD "CARNIVORE" CONJURES UP IMAGES of lions and tigers, but most of the 230 or so species in the carnivore branch of the mammal family tree (the order Carnivora) are small, wily animals like weasels, skunks, mongooses, and raccoons. These tiny terrors make up for their small size with cunning, agility, and determination. They are clever enough to outsmart prey ten times their size and swift enough to disarm animals as dangerous as cobras. Many of the small carnivores have a lithe and slender build for darting up and down trees or slipping through the narrowest of spaces in their relentless pursuit of prey. The least weasel – the smallest carnivore of all – can even chase mice and voles deep into their burrows.

PORCUPINE KILLER
The fisher of North America is one of the only predators that can kill a porcupine. It attacks from the front, delivering a series of deep bites to the porcupine's face. Each time the porcupine turns around to present its quills, the fisher darts around it like lightning and strikes the face again. After about half an hour, the wounded porcupine collapses from exhaustion and the fisher begins feasting on its unprotected belly.

Wolverines have amazingly powerful jaws to break spines and crunch frozen meat. Their wide feet act like snowshoes, spreading their weight and supporting them on soft snow.

THE GLUTTON
The wolverine is only the size of a small dog, yet it kills reindeer by chasing them into snowdrifts and inflicting a crippling bite to the neck as they flounder. This ferocious animal has a huge appetite, but even a wolverine can't eat a whole reindeer. It hides the leftovers in snow to freeze for eating later.

Despite its name, the fisher eats very few fish. It much prefers small mammals, eggs, and insects.

Snakes make up a small part of mongooses' diet. They mainly eat tiny animals like insects and spiders.

Stoats are immensely strong for their size. They can kill rabbits ten times their weight and haul them back to the den.

RABBIT CHARMER

The stoat charms its prey by leaping up and down in a bewitching dance. Rabbits become transfixed by this performance and sit still to watch it, unaware that the cunning stoat is inching slowly closer. When near enough, the stoat springs on the rabbit and bites into the victim's neck.

THE FASCINATING FOSSA

If you're ever lucky enough to see a fossa scampering down a tree, you might think you're watching a mutant cat with double-jointed legs. While cats struggle down tree trunks backwards, Madagascar's fossas can run headfirst by twisting their back feet round. Their agility allows them to race through the treetops while chasing Madagascar's other unique tree-dwellers, the lemurs.

FAST AND AGILE

Speed and agility are what save mongooses from a deadly bite when they hunt venomous snakes, such as the Indian cobra. By taunting the snake and darting from side to side, the mongoose eventually gets close enough to snatch it by the neck and crush its spine. Mongooses are not immune to snake venom, but they can survive a dose that would kill many other animals. As well as tackling poisonous snakes, they eat scorpions after biting off their stings.

CHEMICAL WEAPONS

Skunks are among the few mammals that defend themselves with chemical weapons. If a skunk fails to scare off an attacker by charging, stamping its feet, or performing a handstand, it plays its trump card: it turns round, lifts its tail, and fires a blast of foul-smelling liquid from nozzles flanking the anus. Skunks have a surprisingly good aim and can hit an enemy directly in the eye, causing intense pain and temporary blindness. People can smell the potent odour from up to 1 km (0.5 miles) away.

HOMES AND SHELTERS

SMALL MAMMALS FACE LOTS OF CHALLENGES, but two of the greatest are keeping warm and not being eaten. A neat way of dealing with both is to build a snug shelter in which to hide, raise young, and sleep. An underground burrow is the most obvious solution, but some mammals are even more inventive. Bamboo bats squeeze into hollow bamboo stems, and North American flying squirrels make edible nests out of lichen. Beavers even build their own private island. In winter, when finding food gets especially difficult, some mammals stay in their hideaways for months on end, entering a kind of deep sleep called hibernation.

A BEAVER'S LODGE

Beavers live in an artificial island called a lodge, made from a mound of mud and sticks close to a dam. Inside the lodge is a spacious living chamber above the level of the water. Underwater tunnels allow the beaver to come and go without being seen, even when the pond freezes over. In winter, the beaver feeds on a stash of leafy branches gathered earlier in the year and kept chilled in the bottom of the pond.

A beaver's lodge is always upstream from a dam, which creates a pool around the lodge.

A beaver's lodge is a safe haven from predators.

DAM BUILDERS

Beavers create artificial ponds and lakes by building dams across streams. Using their chisel-like teeth to cut trees to pieces, they pile thousands of stick and logs across the stream until it forms a watertight dam up to 90 m (300 ft) long, sealed with mud and rocks. Beavers slowly enlarge their dams year after year.

TEMPORARILY DEAD

A hibernating dormouse is so cold and motionless in winter that it seems to be temporarily dead. Its body temperature plummets to just one degree above freezing, and its heartbeat and breathing slow to less than a tenth of the usual rate. Dormice can stay like this for seven months.

Tent-making bats sleep under leaves during the day and wake up to feed at night.

TENT-MAKING BATS

Home for a tent-making bat is a folded leaf. These bats bite through the ribs of giant leaves to make them fold into a tent shape. Then they fly underneath and hang upside-down, protected from the rain and the eyes of predators. There are several species of tent-making bat in the rainforests of South and Central America, but the Honduran white bat is the only one with fur as white as snow.

During their long hibernation, dormice occasionally wake up for a few minutes.

UNDERGROUND CITIES

Prairie dogs live in vast burrow systems called towns, with interconnected tunnels providing a maze of routes to escape from predators. One of the biggest ever towns was reported to have 400 million residents and covered nearly a tenth of the state of Texas. Prairie dogs have now been exterminated in much of the American prairies because their burrows used to trip up horses and cattle, and break their legs.

WORM HUNTER

The European mole finds food by scurrying along its tunnels and catching any worms that fall in. When it finds a worm, it paralyses it with a venomous bite, squeezes the soil out of the worm's gut, and eats it. Moles can crawl forwards as well as backwards, and have whiskers at both ends for feeling in the dark.

Spare worms are stored in an underground larder.

Moles collect straw from above ground to build a warm nest.

A mole has gigantic forelimbs for digging but tiny, almost useless eyes.

A single mole can build hundreds of metres of tunnels during its four-year life. Most of the tunnels run horizontally, but occasionally the mole digs a vertical shaft to get rid of the soil, pushing it out and creating a molehill.

ENDURANCE

THERE ARE FEW PLACES ON EARTH that mammals have failed to conquer, from the peaks of the highest mountains to the depths of the oceans. For mountain dwellers and polar animals, subzero temperatures are not the only hardship they have to endure. They also have to contend with air so thin that it would kill humans, or winters so harsh that food is impossible to find. In deserts, stifling heat and lack of water add to the challenge of finding scarce food. Ocean mammals face a very different endurance test: holding their breath. For, like all mammals, they have to breathe air, which they can only do at the surface.

SNOW MONKEYS

To beat the winter blues, Japanese macaques relax in a hot bath. The hot volcanic springs provide a welcome relief from winter temperatures as low as –15°C (5°F), though the monkeys can get a nasty chill when they climb out again and wait for their wet fur to dry out. Japanese macaques are the ultimate endurance monkeys and survive further north than any other monkeys, thanks partly to their luxuriously thick fur. In winter, when food is hard to find, they make do on a diet of bark and tree buds.

LIFE IN THIN AIR

High in the Andes, the air is so thin that mountaineers without oxygen tanks risk a deadly condition called altitude sickness. Yet vicuñas live comfortably at 4,000 m (13,000 ft). They survive in the thin air because they have unusually small, oval-shaped blood cells that efficiently absorb sufficient oxygen.

Sperm whales slow their hearts down and store oxygen in their muscles during their record-breaking dives.

DEEP-SEA DIVER

As well as having the largest brain known to science, the sperm whale makes the deepest dives of any creature. It holds its breath for more than an hour as it plummets up to 3.2 km (2 miles) down to search for squid (in pitch darkness).

Camels can lose up to half their body weight after a long spell without food or water.

SHIP OF THE DESERT

Camels can go for up to ten months in the desert without water, but how do they do it? Firstly, they can release water from food or from the store of fat in their hump. Secondly, when they do drink they can take in up to 136 litres (30 gallons) in one go, which is about a whole bathful, or a quarter of a camel's body weight. Thirdly, camels waste very little water in their sweat, urine, or faeces. Their droppings are so dry that desert people use them as firewood.

KEEPING YOUR COOL

Staying cool in the Sahara isn't easy. The fennec fox hides in its burrow during the heat of the day and keeps cool by panting up to 700 times a minute. Its enormous ears work like cooling radiators, helping it shed excess heat without having to sweat. Like many other desert animals, the fennec gets all its moisture from food and never has to drink.

The fennec's ears not only keep it cool, but also help it hear the faint sounds of its prey as it hunts at night.

INSECT EATERS

INSECTS CAN MAKE A RICH DIET – but only if you catch enough of them. While many mammals eat the odd grub, some have turned catching insects into a way of life. They come from a range of mammal families, but have evolved some striking parallels. The biggest specialize in raiding ant and termite nests. They have powerful claws for digging and long, sticky tongues. Smaller insect eaters, like shrews and tarsiers, use a different strategy. They have keen senses and lightning reflexes to catch their prey one at a time.

THE GIANT ANTEATER

The element of surprise is vital to South America's giant anteater. It can only steal about 100 ants and grubs from a nest before the colony's biting soldiers flood out. After tearing a hole with its huge claws, the anteater inserts its 60-cm- (2-ft-) long, sticky tongue, which darts in and out 150 times a minute, hooking prey with tiny, backward-pointing spikes. Giant anteaters visit up to 200 ants' nests a day, but they do very little damage to any of them.

Giant anteaters have been known to crush jaguars with their immensely powerful arms.

DIGGING FOR DINNER

With ears like a rabbit's and a snout like a pig's, the aardvark is one of the oddest animals in Africa. At night, it snuffles about in grasslands, sucking up soil into its snout and feeling for ants or termites. When it finds them, it digs into the nest and gathers ants with a tongue as sticky as flypaper. Aardvarks dig so quickly that they can disappear underground in just five minutes.

MAKING TRACKS

The elephant shrew has a miniature version of an elephant's trunk – a long and flexible snout, which it uses to sniff out ants, termites, beetles, and centipedes in Africa's savanna. It finds insects while darting nervously about a system of trails as complex as London's roads. It spends about a third of each day meticulously cleaning its trails, removing any twig or leaf that might trip it up when it needs to flee from danger.

ARMOUR PLATING

Pangolins have a long, sticky tongue to feed from ant and termite nests in the same way as anteaters. Sometimes they raise their scaly armour and let the angry ants scurry over their skin. The ants rid the skin of fleas and ticks that pangolins can't scratch.

A three-banded armadillo rolls up to leave no openings for a predator to get to its soft parts.

Tarsiers' eyes are bigger than their brains. They have the biggest eyes, relative to body size, of any mammal.

Moths and flies are snatched from mid-air.

HAVING A BALL

Self-defence is important for armadillos because they often attract attention while rummaging about noisily for insects. Rolling into an armour-plated ball is the usual technique, but some can also escape danger by walking into rivers and holding their breath on the riverbed. Ants, termites, and beetles make up most of the diet. One species also burrows under rotting carcasses to gorge itself on maggots.

SLEIGHT OF HAND

With huge hands and quick reflexes, the tarsiers of Southeast Asia can snatch flying insects from mid-air. These nocturnal hunters can't move their eyeballs, so instead they swivel their heads right round, like owls. Moths, grasshoppers, beetles, and cicadas are their favourite food, but they also hunt lizards and baby birds. Sometimes they leap through the canopy to pounce on victims.

ON THE WING

WHILE BIRDS RULE THE SKIES DURING THE DAY, flying mammals take over at night. Various mammals have taken to the air, but the most famous and the most common are the bats. Though seldom seen, they make up a quarter of all mammal species and live all over the world. They are true fliers, with beating wings to keep themselves aloft. Other "flying" mammals are merely gliders. They leap off trees, stretch out their legs, and cruise through the air on a parachute of skin.

FLYING SQUIRRELS

America's flying squirrels can cruise 100 m (330 ft) between trees by gliding on flaps of skin between their legs. They steer by adjusting their feet and tails, and they brake by swinging the body upright. They lose height as they glide, so they have to scamper back up a tree before flying off again.

LIVING KITE

The colugo of Southeast Asia looks like a kite as it glides. Its furry gliding membrane stretches from the tips of its fingers to the tip of its tail. It is so huge and floppy that the animal is clumsy on its feet and almost helpless on the ground.

Babies cling tightly to the mother's stomach, while the mother's furry cloak forms a warm hammock for the baby.

For extra protection from predators, the colugos' fur is speckled for camouflage on lichen-covered branches.

Colugos are also called flying lemurs, though they aren't lemurs and they can't truly fly.

FRUIT BATS

Fruit and nectar make up the diet of the fruit bats – large bats that live in the rainforests of Africa, Asia, and Australia. They search for food at night, but unlike insect-eating bats, they have big eyes and find food by sight. They can cover 65 km (40 miles) in a night and island-hop their way across the vast Indian Ocean.

Fruit bats are also called flying foxes because of their fox-like faces.

Fruit bats roost together in treetops, squabbling noisily and fanning themselves to keep cool.

SEEING WITH SOUND

Many bats have the amazing ability to "see" with sound (echolocation). They fire a stream of clicks into the air up to 200 times a second and analyse the echoes to create a kind of picture. A bat can pluck flying insects out of the air in total darkness thanks to this ability.

A horseshoe bat preys on a flying moth.

Forearm (radius)

Second finger

Thumb

Upper arm (humerus)

Third finger

Fourth finger

Fifth finger

Bats can "see" flying insects by listening for echoes of their own calls.

The bat sends out an ultrasound pulse.

The ultrasound pulse bounces off the moth and the echo is picked up by the bat.

RECORD BREAKER

The world's smallest mammal is the Kitti's hog-nosed bat. At only 1.5 g (a twentieth of an ounce), it is not much bigger than a bumblebee. This tiny bat is found in the rainforests of Thailand, and eats tiny midges and spiders.

VAMPIRE BAT

The blood-sucking vampire bat not only attacks livestock but also feeds on sleeping humans, and its bite can transmit rabies. To avoid waking a victim, it lands nearby and crawls silently onto the body. It has razor sharp teeth to slit open the skin and pain-killing saliva, so the victim is unaware of the attack.

Nasal outgrowth focuses the sound waves.

Large, sensitive ears collect echoes and can even hear an insect's footsteps.

NOSE AND EARS

Many bats have ugly nasal outgrowths to focus their echolocation calls. The sounds are too high-pitched for us to hear, but to them the sound can be deafening. So, to protect themselves, some bats shut their ears with each call. Others are "whisperers" – they make faint calls so as not to disturb prey.

LIFE IN WATER

WHILE MANY MAMMALS go for an occasional swim to forage for food or bathe, others take to water on a more regular basis. These amphibious mammals lead double lives, split between land and water. Hippos, for instance, come onto land only to feed, and return to water to rest. Seals and sea lions do the opposite. Over thousands of years, species that spend a great deal of time in water evolve bodies suited to their aquatic habitat. Their shape becomes streamlined, their fur becomes dense and velvety, and their legs eventually turn into flippers.

Sea lions twist and turn through the water with remarkable ease as they chase fish, or play with each other.

RIVER OTTERS
River otters have only partly evolved into aquatic animals. Their lithe and slender bodies, typical of the weasel family, give them amazing agility in the water, yet they can still scamper about and hunt on land. To keep them warm in water, otters have dense fur that traps a layer of insulating air.

Each square centimetre of an otter's coat contains 70,000 hairs.

SEA LIONS
Sea lions have gone further than otters in adapting to life in water. Their legs have become flippers, though they can still use them to support their weight and "walk" on land. Like otters, sea lions have dense velvety fur, but they also have a layer of blubber under the skin for extra insulation.

Sea lions use their sensitive whiskers to find the way in murky water.

Male elephant seals have a large inflatable snout to impress females.

ELEPHANT SEAL
Seals are even more aquatic than sea lions. Their outer ears have disappeared to make them more streamlined, and their flippers are almost useless on land – instead of walking they have to shuffle on their bellies. The elephant seal is the champion diver of the seal world. It can hold its breath for two hours and dive 1.5 km (1 mile) deep.

WATER SHREW
The water shrew holds its breath for more than 30 seconds as it dives for insects, frogs, and fish. Its long toes have a fringe of stiff hairs to give extra force to its kicks when it swims. This system works so well that the shrew can even run across the surface of the water for several metres without falling in. Its fine fur does the same job as an otter's, trapping a layer of air to keep the animal warm.

AQUATIC ACROBAT

Though slow and clumsy on land, seals and sea lions become swift and graceful as soon as they get in the water. Their swimming techniques are quite different. Sea lions propel themselves with powerful strokes of their strong front flippers, while using the hind flippers to steer. In contrast, seals swing their hind flippers sideways for propulsion and use the front flippers to steer.

SWIMMING TRUNKS

With their trunks serving as snorkels, elephants make such good swimmers that some scientists think they must have passed through an aquatic phase in their evolution. While African elephants only immerse themselves to bathe, Asian elephants are much more ambitious. In the Indian Ocean, working elephants sometimes swim for miles between the Andaman Islands, with their owners riding on their backs. A captive elephant once swam 64 km (40 miles) after falling off a boat en route to a zoo in the USA.

BLUSHING WALRUSES

Walruses have so much blubber that they risk overheating when they come out of the water to rest. So to shed excess heat, they blush – blood rushes to the surface of the skin and makes them turn pink. Walruses live around the edge of the Arctic Ocean, and have enormous, blubbery bodies for coping with the chilly water. They feed on the sea floor, grubbing around like pigs for crabs and shellfish hidden in the mud.

OCEAN GIANTS

WHALES, DOLPHINS, AND SEA COWS are the most aquatic mammals of all. Their four-legged ancestors left the land to live in water maybe 50 million years ago, beginning a process that changed them beyond recognition. Over time, evolution turned forelimbs into flippers, added a wide fluke to the tail, and made the hind limbs and fur wither away to nothing. With water to support their weight, some of these animals grew to monstrous proportions. All now spend their whole lives in water, though they come to the surface to breathe air. They eat, sleep, mate, give birth, and suckle their young entirely in water. If they ever leave the water, they risk crushing themselves to death.

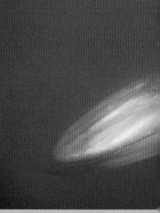

Blue whales seem to find their way through the oceans by making deep booming noises and listening to the echoes that rebound off continents and the sea floor.

HUMPBACK WHALE

Leaping out of the water and letting its 30-tonne (27-ton) body crash back in is one of the ways that humpback whales communicate. To the highly sensitive ears of other whales, the splash must sound like a deafening explosion. Hearing is the most important sense for whales and dolphins. They use sound to locate food, to find their way, and to sing to each other over great distances.

Male humpback whales leap from the water and fall back on their sides. This spectacular display is called breaching.

BLUE WHALE

At 27 m (90 ft) long and 150 tonnes (136 tons) in weight, the blue whale is the largest animal ever to have existed. It is 33 times the weight of an elephant and one-and-a-half times heavier than the biggest dinosaur. Its tongue alone is the size of a car. Even in the coldest water, a blue whale's sheer size helps it retain heat.

TOOTHED WHALES

Scientists divide whales and dolphins into two major categories: toothed whales and baleen whales. The toothed whales include dolphins, porpoises, killer whales, and several other types of whale. All of them are intelligent predators, with sharp, peg-like teeth for snatching slippery prey like fish and squid. Killer whales even leap onto beaches to grab sea lions.

BALEEN WHALES

The largest whales are baleen whales. Instead of teeth, their mouths contain hundreds of bristle-covered "baleen plates" that hang from the upper jaw, forming an enormous curtain. Baleen whales feed by taking in a huge mouthful of water and forcing it through the baleen plates with the tongue. In each gulp, small animals like krill are sieved out of the water by the million.

Dolphins live in social groups called pods. They often swim in formation and leap out of the water together.

DOLPHINS

With a sleek, streamlined build, dolphins are built for speed in water. Though playful and friendly, dolphins also have a vicious streak – the males especially are often covered with the scars of battle. Like other toothed whales, dolphins hunt by echolocation. They make a stream of high-pitched sounds and their brains decipher the echoes to create a kind of picture.

KRILL

Dugongs grub about on the sea floor for the roots of an aquatic plant called sea grass.

SEA COWS

Dugong and manatees are sometimes called sea cows because they are large, docile herbivores. They live in shallow water in the tropics – manatees in rivers and coasts around the Atlantic, and dugongs around the coast of the Indian and Pacific Oceans. Scientists think dugongs and manatees evolved from a land animal related to elephants. Whales and dolphins, on the other hand, probably evolved from a relative of the hippopotamus.

Marsupials

WHEN EXPLORERS brought the first opossum to Europe in the 16th century, the king of Spain in wonder put his finger in its pouch. Scholars called the pouch a "marsupium", meaning purse, and so this mammal group became known as the marsupials. In fact, not all marsupials have a pouch, but most do give birth to tiny babies that develop outside the mother's body. Most marsupials live on the islands of Australia, New Guinea, and Tasmania, but around 70 species of opossums live in the Americas.

LARGE LITTERS

Opossums can give birth to dozens of babies at once. The mouse opossum has no pouch, so its babies have to cling tightly to the mother, with their tails coiled around hers. At birth they are no bigger than rice grains. They quickly latch onto the mother's nipples, which fit in their mouths like plugs to hold them in place. If there are more babies than nipples, the spare ones drop off and die.

TINY TERRORS

Mulgaras look like cute mice, but in fact are vicious little carnivores. They eat house mice – from head to tail – peeling back the skin like a banana as they devour the flesh. They also like insects, centipedes, lizards, and birds.

BOXING KANGAROOS

In the mating season, male kangaroos battle for the right to mate. Standing upright, they lock their arms together and try to push their opponent over, or kick them in the belly. A lot is at stake in these fights – the victor gets to mate with all the females in the area, while the loser has to wait at least another year for a chance to mate.

During a fight, their immensely powerful hind legs slash at each other's belly.

MARSUPIAL MOLE

Some marsupials have evolved into counterparts of their nonmarsupial cousins, a process known as convergent evolution. The marsupial mole looks just like an ordinary mole, with huge claws for digging, a shovel-shaped head, and tiny, useless eyes. Unlike true moles, however, it doesn't dig proper burrows – instead it "swims" through sandy soil, which caves in behind it. Its pouch opens backward to prevent it filling with soil.

REPRODUCTION

The main difference between marsupials and placental mammals is the way they reproduce. Marsupials give birth to a tiny, underdeveloped baby that usually completes its development in a pouch. In placental mammals, the baby stays inside the uterus (womb) for much longer, attached to the mother by a placenta. While placental mammals have a single uterus and vagina, marsupials have a double system.

STRANGE DIETS

When a baby koala is old enough to stop suckling, its first meal is a mouthful of faeces from its mother's anus. The faeces contain vital bacteria, which live inside the koala's intestine and help it digest its normal food: eucalyptus leaves. Koalas are the only mammals that can live off eucalyptus leaves. The leaves are so low in nutrients and difficult to digest that koalas have to spend about 19 hours a day sleeping.

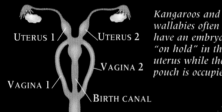

UTERUS 1   UTERUS 2

VAGINA 2

VAGINA 1

BIRTH CANAL

Kangaroos and wallabies often have an embryo "on hold" in the uterus while the pouch is occupied.

The nipple fills the mouth of a newborn kangaroo and holds it in place. This baby red kangaroo is about four weeks old.

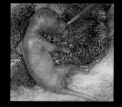

RED KANGAROO

RED-NECKED WALLABY

The ears of Tasmanian devils turn bright red when they are angry.

Tasmanian devils have a very sharp sense of smell for sniffing out carrion.

TASMANIAN DEVIL

Though little bigger than a domestic cat, the Tasmanian devil is the world's biggest marsupial carnivore. It has immensely powerful jaws for crushing bones – which it then swallows. Tasmanian devils eat every scrap of a carcass including bones, fur, and feet. They also attack farm animals and are hated by Tasmania's farmers.

TAMING THE BEAST

ANIMALS THAT ARE BOTH CLEVER AND SOCIABLE – as many mammals are – can easily learn to live with humans. For thousands of years, people have domesticated all sorts of mammals, carefully breeding them to make them tamer and more useful: horses became taller and faster than their wild ancestors, dogs shrank and grew friendlier, while pigs, cattle, and sheep got fatter, more docile, and more stupid. Domestication also transformed our own species, triggering the beginnings of agriculture, city life, and civilization. Today, the mammals we keep have countless uses – we eat them, milk them, ride them, make clothing from them, train them to hunt and work for us, and keep them as pets.

NORTH AMERICA

Guinea pig (3,000 years ago)

SOUTH AMERICA

Llama (7,000 years ago)

MAN'S BEST FRIEND

The ancestor of the domestic dog was the grey wolf. Today, most dog breeds look very different from wolves, but their behaviour gives them away. Just like wolves, they are pack animals that form strong social bonds. Well-trained dogs see humans as the leader of the pack, which is why dogs are so friendly and obedient. Dogs are useful in lots of ways: as pets, hunting companions, guards, sniffer dogs, and for pulling sleds across snow.

Huskies still bear a strong resemblance to grey wolves, their distant ancestors.

Herding cattle is an important way of life in tropical grasslands, where the weather is too harsh for crops.

MEAT, MILK, AND BLOOD

Cattle are descended from a wild animal called the aurochs, which is now extinct. People once hunted herds of aurochs, but over time they learnt to lead and drive the animals. Today, cattle are kept for milk as well as meat. The Masai people of Africa also drink the blood, taking a little at a time from a vein in the cow's neck.

LIVING TRACTORS

In Asia, people use water buffaloes instead of tractors to plough marshy fields before sowing rice. Like their wild, swamp-dwelling ancestors, domestic water buffaloes have splayed feet for walking on mud, and they often spend the heat of the day wallowing in water. When the animals reach the end of their working lives, their owners eat them.

The map shows approximately where and when people began to keep various domestic mammals. Many of the dates and locations are uncertain.

Cattle (8,000 years ago)

Horse (6,000 years ago)

Goat (9,000 years ago)

EUROPE

ASIA

Dog (15,000 years ago)

Pig (8,000 years ago)

Camel (5,000 years ago)

Cat (5,000 years ago)

AFRICA

AUSTRALIA

ANTARCTICA

DOMESTICATION DATES

The first mammal to be domesticated was probably the dog, perhaps as early as 15,000 years ago in China. Between 9,000 and 6,000 years ago, the people of Western Asia invented agriculture and domesticated many of the farm animals that we keep to this day. South America's people invented agriculture separately and domesticated a range of very different mammals.

BEAST OF BURDEN

Llamas and alpacas are domestic versions of the wild guanacos and vicuñas that live in the high Andes mountains of South America. They are valued as much for their thick wool as for their strength as beasts of burden. They are close relatives of camels, and, like their cousins in Africa, they can withstand extreme environments, such as deserts and mountains.

WORKING ELEPHANTS

Elephants are among the few animals able to fell whole trees, an ability that made them invaluable to Asia's timber industry. In recent times the timber industry has gone into decline, but working elephants are still to be seen carrying tourists around wildlife reserves, or taking part in religious festivals.

Working elephants use their trunks to move heavy logs. A mahout – the elephant's owner and driver – sits on its neck.

MAMMAL DATA

EVOLUTION OF MAMMALS

Scientists have identified more than 4,680 species of mammals. Together they make up the class Mammalia. Over 200 million years ago the class separated into the mammals that laid eggs (monotremes) and those that gave birth to live young (subclass Theria). Later, there was a further split of subclass Theria into marsupials and placental mammals.

Rodents (order Rodentia) 1,999 species

Rabbits, hares, pikas (order Lagomorpha) 87 species

Tree shrews (order Scandentia) 18 species

Shrews, moles, hedgehogs (order Eulipotyphla part of order Insectivora) 399 species

Colugos (order Dermoptera) 2 species

Primates (order Primates) 256 species

Pangolins (order Pholidota) 7 species

Carnivores (orders Carnivora and Pinnipedia) 264 species

Odd-toed ungulates (order Perissodactyla) 16 species

Even-toed ungulates (order Artiodactyla) 196 species

Whales and dolphins (order Cetacea) 88 species

Bats (order Chiroptera) 977 species

Anteaters, sloths, armadillos (order Xenarthra) 29 species

Tenrecs and golden moles (order Afrosoricida part of order Insectivora) 45 species

Elephant shrews (order Macroscelidea) 15 species

Aardvark (order Tubulidentata) 1 species

Hyraxes (order Hyracoidea) 11 species

Dugong and manatees (order Sirenia) 4 species

Elephants (order Proboscidea) 3 species

Marsupials (7 orders) 289 species

Monotremes (order Monotremata) 3 species

205   144   millions of years   65 55   34 24   5 1.8

CRITICALLY ENDANGERED MAMMALS

The *2002 ICUN (International Union for the Conservation of Nature and Natural Resources) Red List of Threatened Species* names 181 mammals as critically endangered in the wild. This list includes:

Abyssinian wolf currently found in Ethiopia
Baiji (changjiang dolphin) currently found in Yangzte River, China
Black-faced lion tamarin currently found in Brazil
Cochito (vaquita porpoise) currently found in Gulf of California
Garrido's hutia currently found in Cuba
Kouprey (grey ox) currently found in Cambodia
Iberian lynx currently found in Portugal and Spain
Javan rhinoceros currently found in Indonesia and Vietnam

Malabar civet currently found in India
Mediterranean monk seal currently found in Atlantic Ocean, Mediterranean Sea, and Black Sea
Northern hairy-nosed wombat currently found in Australia
Pygmy hog currently found in India
Seychelles sheath-tailed bat currently found in Seychelles
Sumatran rhinoceros currently found in Indonesia, Malaysia, Myanmar, Thailand, and Vietnam
Tamaraw (dwarf water buffalo) currently found in Philippines
Tonkin snub-nosed monkey currently found in Vietnam
Yellow-tailed woolly monkey currently found in Peru

GROWING OLD

The mammal with the shortest life span is the pygmy shrew, which lives a maximum of 13 months. Humans hold the record for the longest life span, of 120 years. Life spans are affected by lifestyles and the level of threat from predators.

MAXIMUM LIFE SPANS

Mouse 6 yrs	Rabbit 13 yrs	Dog 20 yrs	Tiger 26 yrs	Cow 30 yrs	Polar bear 38 yrs	Bison 40 yrs

THE BIG FIVE

By weight, the top five biggest land animals are adult males of the species shown here. Males are usually bigger than females because they have to fight each other to win mates. Even the lightest of these animals – the giraffe – weighs as much as 30 men.

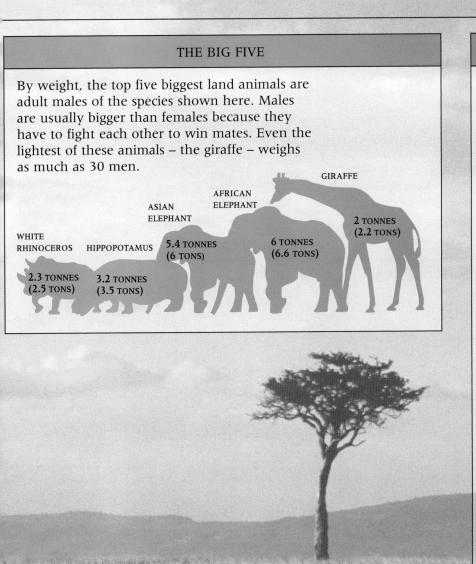

GIRAFFE

AFRICAN ELEPHANT

ASIAN ELEPHANT

WHITE RHINOCEROS

HIPPOPOTAMUS

5.4 TONNES (6 TONS)

6 TONNES (6.6 TONS)

2 TONNES (2.2 TONS)

2.3 TONNES (2.5 TONS)

3.2 TONNES (3.5 TONS)

MAMMAL RECORDS

Biggest marine mammal Blue whale. Largest recorded length: 33.5 m (110 ft). Largest recorded weight: 196 tonnes (193 tons). Bigger examples may exist.

Biggest land mammal African elephant. Largest recorded length: 7.3 m (24 ft); height: 4 m (13 ft); weight: 14.9 tonnes (13.5 tons).

Tallest mammal Giraffe. Tallest recorded length: 6 m (20 ft).

Smallest mammal Bumblebee (Kitti's hog-nosed) bat. Head and body length: 27.9–33 mm (1.1–1.3 in).

Fastest land mammal Cheetah. Fastest speed recorded: 105 kph (65 mph).

Slowest land mammal Three-toed sloth. Speed in trees: 0.27 kph (0.17 mph).

Largest litter Common tenrec. Largest number recorded: 32 (30 survived), although normal litter size is 15.

Longest gestation period Indian elephant. Average period of 609 days (over 20 months) with a maximum period of 760 days (22 months).

Shortest gestation period American opossum (Virginian opossum) and rare water opossum (yapok). Average period of 12–13 days.

Longest migration (swimming) Grey whale. A round trip of 20,000 km (12,400 miles).

Deepest diver Sperm whale. Can probably reach depths of at least 3.2 km (2 miles).

Highest altitude Yak. Can climb to about 6,000 m (20,000 ft).

Loudest land mammal Howler monkey. Sound can be heard 4.8 km (3 miles) away.

Loudest sound produced Some baleen whales produce sounds that can travel all the way across entire oceans. The sound of blue whales and fin whales have been recorded at 188 decibels.

Smelliest mammal Striped skunk. Its smell contains seven major volatile and foul-smelling chemicals.

MAMMAL WEBSITES

http://www.bbc.co.uk/nature/animals
The BBC's online guide to information, features, and games about mammals.

http://www.animaldiversity.ummz.umich.edu/
Find out about the characteristics of individual mammal species, their classification and distribution.

http://www.animalinfo.org
Detailed information about rare, threatened, and endangered mammals summarising their biological features, history, and threats, as well as links to other websites and organizations about mammals.

http://www.worldwildlife.org
Learn more about endangered species and conservation projects on the World Wildlife Fund website.

http://nmml.afsc.noaa.gov/education
Accessible information about marine mammals from the National Marine Mammal Laboratory.

http://lynx.uio.no/catfolk/cat-spcl.htm
A comprehensive list of all cat species with additional details including description, behaviour, and vulnerability. A must for wild cat enthusiasts.

http://www.primate.wisc.edu/pin/factsheets
Find out about the wide variety of primates from the Wisconsin Primate Research Center website.

http://www.ultimateungulate.com
An informative guide about the hoofed mammals of the world.

http://www.lioncrusher.com
Detailed facts about the families within the order Carnivora.

http://www.abdn.ac.uk
The Mammal Society website includes a fun zone of activities and quizzes.

http://www.biosonar.bris.ac.uk/
Fascinating details about the echolocation process used by bats and dolphins including sound effects.

Please note: Every effort has been made to ensure that these websites are suitable, and that their addresses are up-to-date at the time of going to print. Website content is constantly updated, as are website addresses – therefore, it is highly recommended that a responsible adult should visit and check each website before allowing access to a child.

| Rhino 50 yrs | Chimp 53 yrs | Hippo 54 yrs | Dolphin 65 yrs | Indian elephant 77 yrs |

BIRDS

FROM BIRDS OF PREY TO SCAVENGERS, from incredible nests to elaborate courtship rituals, birds provide endless fascination. Some live their lives in one tiny area, others travel across continents in spectacular annual journeys. From early beginnings among dinosaurs, with the fossilized *Archaeopteryx*, to the incredible variety of birds today, enter a wonderfully colourful world.

WHAT IS A BIRD?

BIRDS ARE THE MOST SUCCESSFUL flying animals that have ever existed. They make up the scientific class *Aves*, distinguished from other animals by one feature: feathers. Birds almost certainly evolved from small, predatory dinosaurs called theropods more than 150 million years ago. Over time, the theropods' scales were transformed into feathers, their front legs stretched and became wings, their bony tails withered away, and their snouts and teeth were replaced by lightweight bills. Evolution made them masters of the sky, and they soon spread across the planet.

A COAT OF FEATHERS

Birds are the only animals with feathers. These are not just for flight – they also provide a warm coat to trap heat in the body. Birds are warm blooded, which means they maintain a constant internal temperature, rather than warming up and cooling down with the surroundings, as happens in reptiles.

FIRST BIRDS

The oldest bird fossil is that of *Archaeopteryx*, which lived about 150 million years ago and was a curious mixture of dinosaur and bird. *Archaeopteryx* had feathers like a modern bird, but teeth, a bony tail, and front claws like those of a *Velociraptor*.

FITTING THE BILL

Bills (or beaks) evolved because they are lighter than toothed jaws and so make flying easier. They are also simpler than jaws, consisting merely of thin bone coated with the tough protein that forms human fingernails. As a result, evolution can change their shape relatively easily, giving each species a design adapted to its way of life. Flesh-eaters, for example, have hooked bills for tearing flesh.

IBIS

VULTURE

PARROT

TOUCAN

Primary flight feathers produce the power for flying and are used for steering.

Secondary flight feathers provide lift.

Tertiary feathers shape the wing.

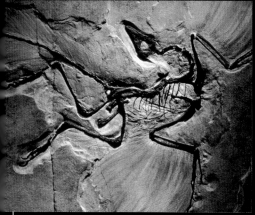

PROVENTRICULUS

OESOPHAGUS

LARGE INTESTINE

CROP

CLOACA

SMALL INTESTINE

GIZZARD

DIGESTIVE SYSTEM

Since they have no teeth, birds must break up food inside their bodies. They have a special stomach chamber called a gizzard, with powerful muscular walls that squeeze and grind the food. Less frequent flyers swallow grit or stones to help the gizzard do its job. Many birds also have a food storage chamber, or crop, in the throat. This helps them to wolf down food quickly and then bring it up again later to feed their chicks or to lose weight when fleeing danger.

Boneless tail.

Warm blooded: body temperature 41-44°C (106-111°F).

SENSES

Vision is the most important sense in birds. Many can see colours invisible to our eyes or tiny details that we would need a telescope to notice. When they sleep, birds can keep one eye open and half the brain stays awake, wary for danger. Most birds have a poor sense of smell but excellent hearing. What sounds to us like a single note of birdsong might be heard by a bird as 10 separate notes.

Powerful breast muscles to operate the wings.

No projecting ears or nose.

Large eyes and sharp vision.

Lightweight bill without teeth.

Compact, streamlined shape.

Downy feathers cover skin.

Thin legs with scaly skin.

Most birds have three forward-facing toes and one backward-facing toe.

REPRODUCTION

While mammals carry babies inside the body, birds lay eggs, like their reptilian ancestors. But, unlike most reptiles, which simply abandon their eggs, birds care for both eggs and chicks. Usually both parents cooperate to keep the young warm, and to protect and feed them.

GLOBAL DOMINATION

Flight has allowed birds to colonize almost every environment, from deserts and cities to remote islands, mountain peaks, and the freezing wastes of Antarctica. Birds can endure colder weather and thinner air than any other animals. The only habitat they haven't conquered is the deep sea.

RAINFOREST

WETLANDS

DESERT

MOUNTAINS

ARCTIC

TOWNS AND CITIES

SMALL PERCHERS

Passerines, or perching birds, account for some 5,700 of the world's 9,700 bird species. Most of the birds that we see around our homes and gardens belong to this group.

Passerines such as this blue tit have thin, grasping toes for perching on twigs.

BUILT FOR FLIGHT

Almost every part of a bird's body has been shaped by evolution to meet the demands of flight. Wings and feathers are the most obvious features – they provide the "lift" to overcome gravity. Most birds also have a streamlined shape with weight concentrated in the middle for balance. The bones are riddled with hollow spaces to save on weight, and many are rigidly fused together to reduce the need for heavy joints or unnecessary muscles. The flight muscles are huge and powerful, but they need plenty of oxygen, so birds have special lungs to extract as much oxygen as possible from the air.

FEATHER LIGHT

Feathers are made of fine, lightweight fibres of keratin, the protein that coats bills. Flight feathers have a stiff central shaft, called a quill, with hundreds of side branches called barbs. The barbs bear thousands of tiny branches called barbules, which lock together to form a flat, streamlined surface.

Outer vane (windward edge of feather)

Notch for reducing turbulence

Inner vane (leeward edge of feather)

This magnified view shows the feather's central shaft, with barbs branching off the shaft and barbules branching off the barbs.

Quill

THE BARE BONES

A bird's skeleton has the same basic plan as a human skeleton, but the details are very different. Birds have only three "fingers" (digits), and these are fused to form a strut supporting the wing. The wing pivots at the shoulder, and the elbow and wrist can bend only horizontally to fold or extend the wing. The tail bones are fused into a stump, and sidebars on the ribs overlap to form a solid cage. An enormous bone called the keel provides an anchor for the powerful flight muscles.

ON THE WING

A bird's most important feathers are its flight feathers, found on the wings and tail. Most of the lift required for flight is generated by the primary and secondary flight feathers in the outer part of the wing. There are usually 9–12 of these on each wing. Other parts of the body are covered with small "contour feathers", which give the bird a streamlined surface, or fluffy down feathers, which keep the bird warm.

Secondary flight feathers

Primary flight feathers

Tertiary flight feathers

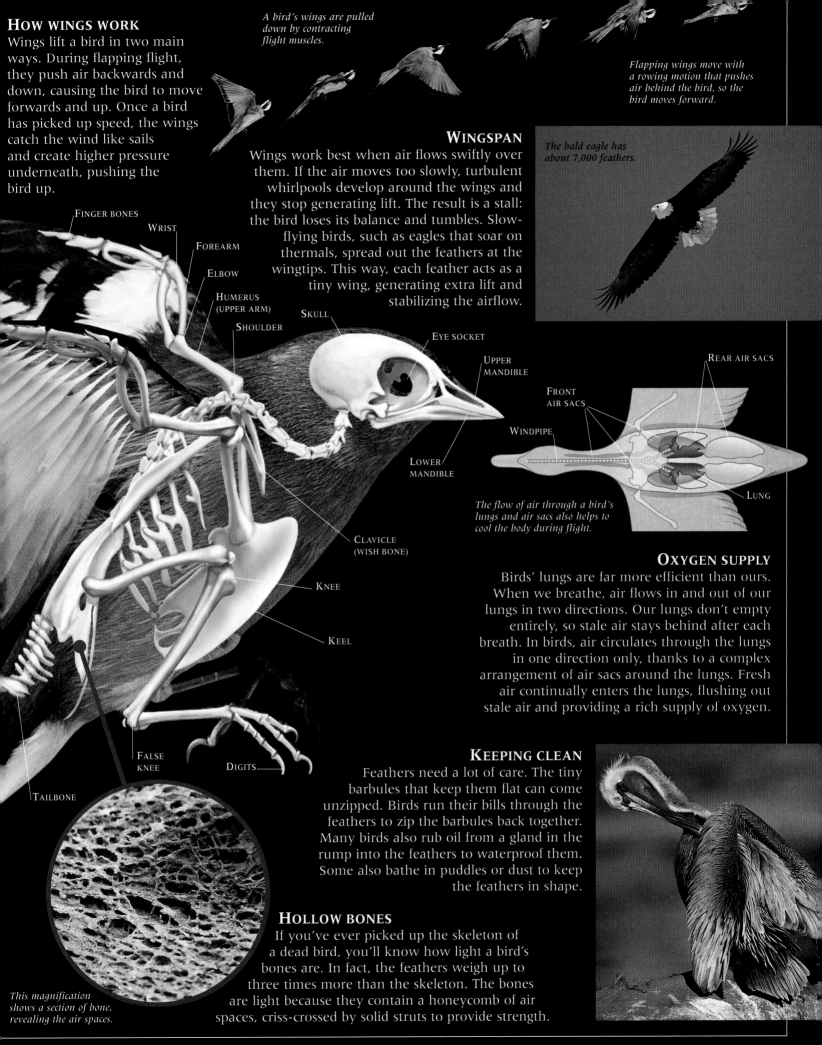

HOW WINGS WORK

Wings lift a bird in two main ways. During flapping flight, they push air backwards and down, causing the bird to move forwards and up. Once a bird has picked up speed, the wings catch the wind like sails and create higher pressure underneath, pushing the bird up.

A bird's wings are pulled down by contracting flight muscles.

Flapping wings move with a rowing motion that pushes air behind the bird, so the bird moves forward.

WINGSPAN

Wings work best when air flows swiftly over them. If the air moves too slowly, turbulent whirlpools develop around the wings and they stop generating lift. The result is a stall: the bird loses its balance and tumbles. Slow-flying birds, such as eagles that soar on thermals, spread out the feathers at the wingtips. This way, each feather acts as a tiny wing, generating extra lift and stabilizing the airflow.

The bald eagle has about 7,000 feathers.

FINGER BONES
WRIST
FOREARM
ELBOW
HUMERUS (UPPER ARM)
SHOULDER
SKULL
EYE SOCKET
UPPER MANDIBLE
LOWER MANDIBLE
CLAVICLE (WISH BONE)
KNEE
KEEL
FALSE KNEE
DIGITS
TAILBONE

REAR AIR SACS
FRONT AIR SACS
WINDPIPE
LUNG

The flow of air through a bird's lungs and air sacs also helps to cool the body during flight.

OXYGEN SUPPLY

Birds' lungs are far more efficient than ours. When we breathe, air flows in and out of our lungs in two directions. Our lungs don't empty entirely, so stale air stays behind after each breath. In birds, air circulates through the lungs in one direction only, thanks to a complex arrangement of air sacs around the lungs. Fresh air continually enters the lungs, flushing out stale air and providing a rich supply of oxygen.

KEEPING CLEAN

Feathers need a lot of care. The tiny barbules that keep them flat can come unzipped. Birds run their bills through the feathers to zip the barbules back together. Many birds also rub oil from a gland in the rump into the feathers to waterproof them. Some also bathe in puddles or dust to keep the feathers in shape.

HOLLOW BONES

If you've ever picked up the skeleton of a dead bird, you'll know how light a bird's bones are. In fact, the feathers weigh up to three times more than the skeleton. The bones are light because they contain a honeycomb of air spaces, criss-crossed by solid struts to provide strength.

This magnification shows a section of bone, revealing the air spaces.

UP AND AWAY

B IRDS MOVE THROUGH THE AIR with such grace that flying looks effortless to our eyes. But it takes tremendous effort to overcome the force of gravity and travel on nothing but air. For most birds, getting off the ground is the hardest part. Wings work best when air is blowing over them, so until a bird has built up speed it relies on muscle power alone. Once they get going, birds can conserve energy by catching the wind, gliding on air currents, or taking brief rests.

A buzzard rides on a thermal, its wings outstretched to catch the rising air.

HITCHING A LIFT

Birds of prey and vultures soar to great heights by riding on upwellings of warm air called thermals. To stay in a thermal they have to keep turning, which is why they are often seen circling. After reaching the top of a thermal, they can glide for miles without having to flap.

Puffins' short wings are better suited to swimming than flying, but they can take off with relative ease by jumping off cliffs.

JUMP START

Puffins get airborne by throwing themselves off cliffs. As they fall they pick up speed and their short wings begin to generate lift. They find it much harder taking off from the sea after diving for fish, however. To do so they must run across the water and beat their stubby wings as fast as they possibly can.

FLIGHT PATTERNS

Birds differ a great deal in their style of flight. Small birds tend to flap intermittently and close their wings for barely perceptible rests. As a result, their flight paths move up and down. Ducks and geese are non-stop flappers. They are fast and have enormous stamina, but they use up energy quickly. Long-winged birds like vultures and albatrosses are gliders. They conserve energy by riding on thermals or catching the wind.

Small birds such as finches have an up-and-down flight path because they shut their wings intermittently.

FINCH FLIGHT PATTERN

Ducks and geese flap their wings continuously and fly in a straight line.

WATERFOWL FLIGHT PATTERN

Birds of prey glide in circles on thermals to climb without wasting energy.

WHITE TAILED EAGLE

FLOCKING TOGETHER

Flying in a flock has several advantages. If each bird flies slightly to the side of the bird in front, it gets a lift from currents blowing off the leading bird's wings. This is why ducks and geese fly in V-formations. Flocks also make finding food easier and give protection from predators. Starlings sometimes flock by the thousand, forming dark clouds that twist and pulse as the birds swoop past each other in perfect co-ordination.

LANDING

Landing takes less effort than taking off, but it requires skill – especially in birds that land on a small perch. To lose speed, birds bring their wings into a more vertical position and lower their tails. Many birds have a special tuft of feathers (the alula) on the bend of the wing that helps stabilize airflow over the wings as they slow down, keeping them balanced.

GETTING AIRBORNE

It takes tremendous effort for a swan to get into the air. Its wings, like the wings of an aircraft, only generate sufficient lift when a fast stream of air is flowing past them. So to overcome gravity, the swan must sprint with all its strength, using the surface of the water as a runway. Facing the wind helps, but in still air a heavy swan has to reach about 48 kph (30 mph) to take off.

The alula helps keep the bird stable as it slows down.

Water birds use their feet as brakes when they land.

The tail is lowered to act as a brake.

AERIAL ACROBATS

SWIFTS AND HUMMINGBIRDS SHARE A SPECIAL TYPE OF WING that makes them the most acrobatic of birds. Their "wrist" and "elbow" joints are very close to the body and their wings rotate at the shoulder. This gives superb flexibility and a very rapid wing beat. Swifts are among the fastest birds in level flight and can stay airborne for years. Hummingbirds can hover motionless and fly backwards or even upside down. To fuel their aerial stunts, these birds need a lot of food. Swifts trawl the air with their mouths agape to catch tiny midges; hummingbirds use their long bills to suck nectar from flowers.

EUROPEAN SWIFT

The European swift is the world's most aerial animal and can stay airborne for two years at a time. It eats, drinks, sleeps, mates, and gathers nest material entirely on the wing. Its tiny legs are so feeble that it cannot walk, but it can cling to vertical surfaces.

The swift's streamlined shape helps it catch insects in mid-air.

BEHIND THE WATERFALL

South America's great dusky swift builds its nest behind a waterfall and can fly straight through the raging torrent to reach it. Swifts can't land to gather nest material, so they build nests from a mixture of sticky spit and fluffy materials caught in the air. The nests of certain swifts are considered a delicacy in China and are boiled to make soup.

A LIFE ON THE WING

Swallows and martins are not close relatives of swifts, but they are a similar shape and they also feed during flight. Their pointed wings and forked tails help them twist and turn with breathtaking agility as they chase flying insects one by one. They also drink on the wing, swooping low over ponds to take mouthfuls of water.

TINY NESTS

Hummingbirds build tiny but deep cup-shaped nests from moss and spider's silk. The outside may be decorated with lichen for camouflage and the inside is lined with soft fibres. The bee hummingbird's nest is the size of a thimble.

SMALLEST BIRD

The male bee hummingbird of Cuba is only 5.7 cm (2.2 in) long from bill to tail, making it the world's smallest bird. To stay airborne it must beat its wings an amazing 200 times a second, which produces a buzzing sound like a bee.

Bee hummingbirds are so small and light that they often get trapped in spider's webs and die.

Hummingbirds' wings move so fast that they normally appear as a blur.

The long bill is used to reach nectar deep in the flower.

HOVERING HUMMER

Hummingbirds fly in a different way to other birds, twisting their wings back and forth in a figure-of-eight pattern rather than flapping them up and down. This motion allows a hummingbird to hover and stay perfectly still before pulling out of a flower. But the wings are short and must beat very quickly, which uses a great deal of energy.

Hummingbirds have only about 1,000 feathers each – the fewest of any bird.

The sword-billed hummingbird's bill is nearly twice the length of its body.

FUELLED BY NECTAR

Hummingbirds use energy so quickly that they must visit up to 2,000 flowers a day. In doing so they unwittingly spread pollen between flowers and so help plants to reproduce. At night, hummingbirds go into a kind of hibernation to conserve energy.

BIRDS OF PREY

FLESH IS THE MOST NUTRITIOUS type of food, but it is exceptionally hard to obtain. Nevertheless, the birds of prey, or raptors, have made killing and scavenging their way of life. There are around 300 species, and nearly all share the specialized features needed to hunt and butcher: superb vision, a vicious set of talons for killing their prey, and – as raptors cannot swallow prey whole as owls can – a hooked bill for stripping flesh.

DADDY WITH DINNER

As with most birds of prey, the female red-tailed hawk guards the eggs and the young, and the father, who is smaller, does most of the hunting. The chicks spend about 48 days in the nest. In the last week they learn to use their wings by standing on the edge of the nest and flapping while facing the wind.

Powerful, hooked bill for tearing flesh.

EAGLE EYE

Huge eyes give goshawks razor-sharp vision. A ridge over the eye protects it and gives the bird a mean, glowering expression.

A special pit in the back of each eye provides birds of prey with telephoto vision so sensitive they can spot the twitch of a rabbit's ears from up to 2 miles away. Our eyes focus on one point at a time, so we have to keep moving them to look around. Raptors have eyes that can focus on three zones at once: the horizon on each side and a single, magnified spot straight ahead.

Huge, incurved talons for seizing prey. In many raptors, the rear talon is the strongest and deadliest.

BALD EAGLE

Eagles are among the largest
and most powerful raptors, built
to overpower animals as big as
sheep or even reindeer. Like owls,
they often tear their victims' heads
off before dismembering them.
The bald eagle is truly a colossal
bird with a wingspan greater
than a man's height, but it feeds
mainly on fish such as salmon.

FIVE FAMILIES

Experts can't agree how
to classify the raptors, but
most authorities split the
307 species into five families,
shown below. Owls are not
usually classed as birds of
prey, but vultures are.

ANDEAN CONDOR

*American vultures and condors
consist of seven species (Cathartidae)
and include some of the largest flying birds.*

SECRETARY BIRD

*Africa's peculiar secretary bird is classified
in a family of its own (Saggitaridae).
It looks a bit like an eagle on stilts.*

BALD EAGLE

*Eagles, hawks, kites, harriers, and Old
World vultures make up a family of
over 200 species (Accipitridae).*

OSPREY

*The osprey is classed in a family of its own
(Pandionidae) because it has an unusual
reversible outer toe.*

FALCON

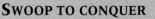

*About 60 species belong to this family
(Falconidae). They have a kind of tooth
on the upper bill and pointed wings.*

SWOOP TO CONQUER

The peregrine falcon performs a stunning
dive. It turns its body into a dart and plunges
at up to 200 kph (124 mph), making it the
fastest bird on Earth. As it closes in for the kill
it leaves the dive, swings its feet forward, and
shreds open the victim's back with an
enlarged rear talon – the "killer claw".

*Peregrine falcons
are successful on
less than 1 in 10
of their dives.*

SCAVENGERS

MANY BIRDS WILL HAPPILY TUCK into a
corpse, but the best-known scavengers
of the bird world are the vultures. Circling
high on thermals, they scan the ground
for signs of death. They are attracted to
the sick, the injured, and the commotion
caused by hunting. They also spy on each
other – so when one finds a carcass, others
soon follow from miles around.

TOO FULL TO FLY
White-backed vultures are the most common
vultures in Africa and often the first to locate a
carcass. They cram so much food into their crops that
they can barely fly. After eating, they flap awkwardly
into a tree and rest while the meal is digested.

MARABOU STORK
The marabou stork of Africa is a wading
bird that has turned to scavenging. As well
as muscling in on flocks of vultures, it lingers
near fires to catch animals fleeing the heat.
Its legs are stained white by excrement, which
it squirts on itself to keep cool. The fine white
feathers lining its tail used to be much in
demand to decorate hats.

FEEDING FRENZY
African vultures can strip an antelope to the bone in
as little as 20 minutes. Small griffon or white-backed
vultures are usually first on the scene and quickly cover
the body in a scrum, squabbling noisily as they shove
past each other. Larger marabou storks and lappet-faced
vultures arrive later but take priority because they are
stronger. Any bones left afterwards are crushed and
eaten by hyenas.

STRONG STOMACH

The lammergeier prefers bones to flesh. Strong acid in its stomach dissolves the hard, outer part of a bone and releases the rich marrow inside. If the bones are too big to swallow, the lammergeier drops them onto rocks to smash them open. It can drop the same bone several times if it does not break on the first attempt.

SINISTER AND SILENT

The turkey vulture is unusual in finding food by smell rather than sight – a distinct advantage in the dense forests of the Amazon, where bodies are hidden from view. It is one of the few birds that has no syrinx (voicebox) and so cannot sing. Between meals, flocks roost together in dead trees in sinister silence.

RAVENOUS RAVENS

Ravens scavenge mainly in winter, when other animals succumb to the cold and lack of food. People have long seen ravens and their relatives – crows and magpies – as symbols of evil, but they are intelligent and inquisitive birds. Unlike vultures, ravens cooperate and seem to tell each other where to find food.

Like other birds of prey, most vultures have a hooked bill for tearing flesh.

EGG CRACKERS

The Egyptian vulture is not just a scavenger, but an egg thief. It knows how to crack even the thick-shelled eggs of ostriches by gripping a heavy stone in its beak and hurling it against the egg. Ravens and crows use a different technique, carrying eggs to a height and dropping them.

BALD AND UGLY

Most vultures have bald heads and necks so that they can push their way deep inside a carcass without soiling their plumage. Baldness is also useful when living in a hot climate, as heat trapped by body feathers escapes through the bare skin.

FISHER KINGS

To catch a fish you need patience, a sharp eye, and lightning reactions. But most of all you need the element of surprise. For some birds, this means standing motionless in water until a fish blunders into range. Others attack from the air, performing a spectacular plunge-dive and striking before the victim has time to react.

FISH SCOOP

The brown pelican uses two tricks to catch fish. First, it plunge-dives into the water, dropping from a height of 10 m (30 ft) and hitting the surface with a terrific splash. Then it uses an enormous throat pouch to scoop up fish. The pouch also takes in lots of water, so the pelican must rest on the surface afterwards to let the water out before swallowing its catch.

SKIMMING THE SURFACE

Skimmers fly very close to the surface of lakes, rivers, and lagoons keeping their specially enlarged lower bill wide open in the water. If anything touches the bill – a fish, for example – it snaps shut automatically.

Fish get sucked into the pouch with a rush of seawater. The edges of the pouch then close and trap the fish inside.

The pouch holds three times as much as the pelican's stomach.

KINGFISHER

The European kingfisher sits by a river as patiently as a fisherman, watching for prey to swim into striking range. At the sight of a small fish, it springs off its perch, hovers for a few seconds, and plunges into the water to snatch the fish with split-second precision. A powerful beat of the wings lifts it clear of the water again, firmly gripping its prey. A kingfisher may need to catch up to 50 fish a day to feed its young.

Darters' feathers become waterlogged in water, helping them sink below the surface.

SPRING-LOADED NECK

Indian darters impale fish on their pointed beaks. Their necks are normally folded back in a z-shape but can straighten out with explosive speed to drive the tip of the beak straight through a fish. The darter tosses off the fish with a flick of the head and swallows it whole. Darters are also known as "snakebirds" thanks to their habit of swimming with only a long snake-like neck visible above the water.

FISHERMAN'S UMBRELLA

Herons also use spring-loaded necks to hunt, but they strike from above the water. The black heron spreads its wings into an umbrella to cast a shadow over the water. This habit is called "mantling". Fish are naturally drawn into the shade, and the lack of reflection probably helps the heron peer through the surface and see its prey.

PATIENT FISHER

The extraordinary shoebill stork catches fish and frogs in muddy African swamps. It can stand still for hours on end waiting for something edible to come into view, at which point it gets very excited and hurls itself at the animal. The enormous bill chops up the prey like a giant pair of scissors.

DIVE BOMBER

Gannets and boobies hit the water like missiles. They dive from amazing heights, accelerating as they plunge and folding their wings right back at the very last moment to form a streamlined torpedo. They strike the water at up to 95 kph (60 mph) and often shoot straight past the shoal they are targetting. When that happens, they simply turn around and swim back up, snapping at fish on the way.

The bill's hooked tip is used to pull animals out of mud.

BESIDE THE SEA

L IVING BY THE SEA HAS GREAT ADVANTAGES for a bird. Most of
the Earth is covered in water, and it is full of rich pickings.
It is also true that craggy coastlines and islands provide a safe
haven from the predators – human and animal – that are
common inland. Some seabirds always stay close to the shore,
searching for worms, shellfish, and other invertebrates in the
shallow water and sand. Others make epic voyages to hunt
the open ocean for fish. Kept aloft by the strong sea breezes,
they can spend months on the wing, only alighting on land
for short periods to breed or feed their chicks.

*A frigate bird attempts
to steal food from a
brown booby.*

PIRATES OF THE AIR

Frigate birds are the
pirates of the world's
tropical oceans. In the
air they are as swift
and agile as any bird of
prey, yet their plumage
is not waterproof and
they cannot swim. So
instead of diving for
fish themselves, they
attack other birds
returning from fishing
trips and force them to
regurgitate and give up
their catch.

ALBATROSS

At 3.5 m (11.5 ft) across –
twice the height of a man
– the wandering albatross
has the greatest wingspan
of any bird. Wings spread
out to catch the wind,
it glides effortlessly for
miles, even sleeping on
the wing. It can fly
around the world on
a single fishing trip.

SEABIRD CITIES

Many seabirds nest in
noisy, smelly colonies,
like this horde of Cape
gannets in South
Africa. Thousands of
birds come here every
year to breed and raise
a single chick. When
the breeding season
ends, the gannets
disperse and the
colony disappears.

GULL GATHERING

Seagulls have an uncanny knack of finding fish in miles of apparently empty water. Their secret lies in being nosy: when one spots a shoal of fish and begins feeding, nosy neighbours are sure to follow. Many seagulls scavenge for food as well as hunting. In some seaside towns in England, the local gulls have learnt to dive-bomb people and snatch food from their hands.

A shoal of fish driven to the surface by underwater predators attracts a frenzy of activity as seagulls arrive from miles around to pick them off.

BLACK OYSTERCATCHER

SANDERLING

AMERICAN AVOCET

TURNSTONE

LIFE'S A BEACH

Shorebirds generally have stilt-like legs for wading and long beaks for probing, but each species feeds in its own way. Oystercatchers pull up mussels and smash or split them by pecking. Sanderlings scamper back and forth over breaking waves, picking out tiny animals that get stranded. Avocets swing their curved beaks in muddy water and feel for shrimps, and turnstones flip pebbles over to find small crabs.

ATLANTIC PUFFIN

With their sad eyes and seemingly painted faces, Atlantic puffins look rather like clowns. Their stubby wings beat with a whirring, propellor motion that seems clumsy in the air, but they double as highly effective flippers underwater, enabling these amphibious birds to dive to depths of up to 60 m (200 ft). The large bill is particularly colourful during the mating season. It has spiny edges and can hold as many as 60 fish at once.

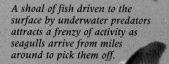

WADERS AND FLOATERS

VISIT A WETLAND OR A LAKE and you're sure to see lots of birds poking around in the shallows or swimming on the surface. Unlike mammals, birds have been very successful in adapting to freshwater habitats. While beavers and otters have to submerge completely to travel and hunt in water, birds keep themselves warm and dry by wading on stilt-like legs, floating on the surface, or probing the water only with their long beaks or necks. And when food gets hard to find, water birds can simply fly away and make a new home elsewhere.

Flamingos get their colour from pigments in their food.

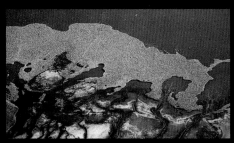

FLAMINGO FIESTA

Millions of flamingos congregate on the salt lakes of east Africa, forming vast pink slicks that are visible from the sky. In the breeding season their courtship dances are a breathtaking spectacle as thousands of birds nod and bow in unison.

A flamingo's false knee bends backwards.

FILTER FEEDERS

Flamingos use their unusual bills to collect microscopic organisms from water. They place their heads upside down in the lake and use the tongue to pump water across a sieve inside the bill. Shrimp, algae, and bacteria are filtered out of the water and swallowed. This way of feeding allows flamingos to live in salty lakes where no other animals can survive.

LONG LEGS

The stilt is the bird with the longest legs in relation to its body size. It can search for food in much deeper water than other small waders, but in shallow water it has to bend awkwardly to reach the mud. Its legs are too long to be tucked away in flight, so the stilt flies with them trailing elegantly behind it.

FEEDING BY TOUCH

In murky water, the best way to find food is not by sight, but by touch. Spoonbills sweep their broad bills from side to side and snap them shut if anything enters. Sometimes they advance in a line and herd fish into a corner. Ibises poke their longer bills into mud and feel for worms and crabs.

FOOD COLOURING

Scarlet ibises and pink flamingos get their colour from chemicals called carotenoids, which are also found in carrots. Carotenoids are made by algae in the water. The algae are either swallowed directly by the birds, or passed on inside via shrimps and worms that eat them.

WATERPROOF COAT

Birds that float rather than wade, such as swans, ducks and geese, have boat-shaped bodies and webbed feet for swimming. To protect their feathers from water they smear them with waterproof oil from a gland on the rump. This "preen oil" makes water slide off in shiny pearls.

Many ducks hunt by dabbling (upending) – heads go into the water, and tails up in the air.

SMOOTH OPERATOR

Though clumsy on land, some water birds become as nimble as otters when they disappear underwater. The goosander can catch salmon and trout – which is why fishermen hate it. Loons also dive for fish and can spend minutes underwater and reach 30 m (100 ft) deep. They are so well adapted to life on water that they cannot walk on land.

BIRD FOOD

Rich, easily digested food makes up the bulk of most birds' food. Because they need lots of energy, but have to keep their weight down for flight, very few birds eat bulky plant food such as grass or leaves. The majority are omnivores, taking a mix of seeds, fruit, and small animals including insects. Without teeth to grind and chew, birds must make do with their bills and their muscular stomachs. And they must digest their meals as quickly as possible to get rid of any excess weight.

A blue tit enjoys a snack provided by a thoughtful bird-lover.

INSATIABLE APPETITE

Small birds burn energy at an amazing rate and must eat vast amounts just to stay warm, let alone fly. In winter, a blue tit can spend 90 per cent of its waking hours feeding to stay alive. Hummingbirds use up fuel at 10 times the rate humans do.

A herring gull drops a mussel onto a rocky beach.

DROPPED FROM A HEIGHT

Foods encased in a shell can be problematic when a bird's bill lacks the power to crack them. One solution is to drop them from a height. This tactic is used by herring gulls on mussels, by lammergeiers to break bones, and by crows to smash eggs.

A collared dove chick takes crop milk from its mother's throat.

Jays bury acorns in autumn to provide a supply of food in winter.

A jay can't swallow a whole acorn. Instead it wedges the acorn in a hole and pecks at it to split the shell.

FEAT OF MEMORY

Food is hard to find in winter, so some birds build up a secret stash during the autumn glut. Jays bury thousands of acorns, hiding each one in a different part of the forest and memorizing its location. Nutcrackers bury up to 100,000 nuts and seeds each year and can remember their locations nine months later.

PIGEON MILK

Pigeons and doves are unique among birds in that they produce a kind of milk from the crop to feed their young. Crop milk, a thick soup of protein and fat, is made for the first three weeks of the chicks' lives. After that the mother weans them onto solid food by swallowing mouthfuls of seeds and storing them in the crop, where they soak in the milk to form porridge.

A golden eagle feeds on a mountain hare it has killed.

BIG EATER

The golden eagle tackles the largest prey of any bird. In Scandinavia, it is said to kill reindeer up to 35 kg (77 lbs) in weight – about the size of a 10-year-old child. It kills by grasping the head with one set of talons and puncturing vital organs with the other.

SPIKED BY A SHRIKE

Birds can't store as much body fat as mammals can because they need to keep their weight down for flight. A better way to store excess food is to hoard it, and this is what shrikes do. They keep a grisly larder of dead bodies impaled on thorns or barbed wire. Most shrikes collect insects, but this red-backed shrike has captured a lizard, and the great grey shrike also has mice and even birds in its larder.

QUICK DIGESTION

An average meal takes half an hour to pass through a bird's body (compared to 24 hours in humans). A turkey vulture, for instance, can digest a whole snake in 90 minutes; the reverse process (a snake digesting a turkey vulture) takes weeks.

Droppings are a mixture of white uric acid (concentrated urine) and black faeces.

EAT DIRT

Small birds hull their seeds to avoid carrying extra weight, but bigger seed-eaters such as farmyard chickens swallow seeds, husks and all. They grind up their meals in the gizzard, a muscular stomach that contains swallowed grit and stones to mash the food. A wood duck's gizzard can puree walnuts, and an eiderduck's can crush mussel shells. Turkeys are said to be able to grind

BIRDS IN THE WOODS

WOODLAND BIRDS CAN FIND EVERYTHING THEY NEED in trees: safety from predators, shelter from the weather, holes to nest in, and an endless supply of food – provided they know where to look. Unsurprisingly, many birds have made forests their permanent home. The most specialized tree-dwellers are the woodpeckers, whose feet can grip vertical trunks and whose amazing, chisel-like bills can drill into wood to hollow out nests, chase wood-boring grubs, and send rattling calls echoing through the trees.

TREE CREEPERS

European tree creepers hop their way up tree trunks using their bills as tweezers to pull insects out of crevices. To perch on vertical surfaces they cling tightly to the bark using their stiff tail as a prop just like woodpeckers do. Tree creepers can even walk upside down on the bottom of branches.

The sheath wraps tightly around the skull to push the tongue out.

The sheath moves away from the skull to pull the tongue in.

TONGUE ACTION

Woodpeckers pull insects out of holes with a sticky tongue that extends to up to four times the length of the bill. The tongue's base connects to a flexible sheath that circles the skull. In some species this curls right round to an anchor point under the nostrils. A muscle pulls the sheath tight against the skull to push the tongue out.

TREE VAMPIRES

The sapsucker is a kind of tree vampire. It drills shallow pits in the bark of trees and uses a feathery tongue to soak up the sap that oozes out. If the pits fully encircle the trunk, they can eventually cut off the tree's food supply and kill it.

AT HOME IN A HOLE

Holes drilled in trees make the perfect place to raise chicks – they are warm, dry, and safe from any predator too big to crawl inside. Green woodpeckers use the same hole for up to 10 years.

HAMMER HEAD

A woodpecker's beak can strike wood at 40 kph (25 mph). Such a blow would knock another bird unconscious but woodpeckers can hammer away 20 times a second and 10,000 times a day. Their brains are protected by a very thick skull and shock-absorbing muscles, and the rigid bill locks shut to stop it crumpling.

ACORN LARDER

Acorn woodpeckers accurately drill different sized holes in a tree and hammer an acorn firmly into each one. Together, a family – consisting of up to 15 members of different generations – can build up a larder of 50,000 acorns in a single tree, providing enough food to see them through winter. The larder needs constant upkeep because the acorns slowly dry out, shrink, and have to be moved to smaller holes to stop them falling out.

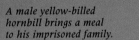

A male yellow-billed hornbill brings a meal to his imprisoned family.

TOCO TOUCAN

Toucans are close relatives of woodpeckers, but live only in the tropics. Their outsized bills look heavy, but are actually hollow and light. The toco toucan uses its bill to reach for fruits on the tips of twigs or to pull chicks out of nest holes. To get food into its throat, it tosses its head back and catches the food with its tongue.

IMPRISONED IN A TREE

Female hornbills seal themselves inside their nest holes by blocking the entrance with mud, leaving only a narrow slit for the male to pass in food. The female spends about three months imprisoned in her home before breaking out to help gather food for the chicks

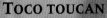

FEATHERS AND FINERY

Feathers are not just for flying – they are also for attracting attention. In the breeding season birds, unlike drably coloured mammals, flaunt brilliant colours, oversized tails, and all manner of decorations to impress the opposite sex. The showiest birds of all are males that mate with lots of partners. They contribute little to raising families, and devote all their energy to showing off. Their glossy colours and elaborate displays perform a vital function, advertising the excellence of their genes.

A quetzal is about the size of a large pigeon, not including its tail.

The wild birds have black heads and purple breasts, but captive Gouldians are more colourful.

COAT OF MANY COLOURS

The vivid colours of the Gouldian finch have made this Australian bird irresistible to trappers and breeders. Only a few thousand remain in the wild today.

A LENGTHY TAIL

Central America's resplendent quetzal has tail streamers more than a metre (3 ft) long and a coat of brilliant, metallic green. The Aztecs worshipped quetzals and made it a capital offence to kill them. Today the quetzal is the national bird of Guatemala.

At the tip of each tail feather is a black eyespot ringed with blue and bronze. Eyespots attract attention because animals find them startling.

A PUZZLING TAIL

Scientists don't know why the peacock's large and cumbersome tail evolved. It is a serious handicap, hampering flight and making males conspicuous to predators, yet females love it! One explanation is that glossy plumage is a sign of health and therefore of good genes. Another theory is that females choose large-tailed males so their sons will be equally well-endowed.

PEACOCK   ROYAL FLYCATCHER   AMERICAN KING VULTURE

ACE FACES

Sensational wings and tails are not always enough to impress a mate. Peacocks complement their tails with a blue head-crest, while royal flycatchers have a crest that retracts when they need to hide. American king vultures have featherless heads but startling eye rings, luridly coloured skin, and a fleshy orange flap over the bill.

SEDUCTIVE SONG

The superb lyrebird of Australia displays his gauzy tail by draping it over his head to form a canopy. Then he begins a complex song in which he mimics everything from kookaburras and car alarms to mobile phones and chainsaws.

IRIDESCENT PLUMAGE

Like many birds, ocellated turkeys have feathers that glint and change colour as they move. The feathers are "iridescent" – they reflect and split white light into different colours like soap bubbles and CDs do.

Male Cabot's tragopan in full, startling display.

WHAT A WATTLE!

This colourful wattle – a flap of skin on the neck – is normally folded away. The male Cabot's tragopan exposes it with his head vibrating and his two blue horns erect to impress a nearby female.

PRETTY PLUMES

Great egrets of both sexes grow ornamental plumes to impress each other in the breeding season. In the 19th century, hats sporting egret feathers were the height of fashion, and egrets were hunted almost to extinction. The hats have since gone out of fashion, and egrets have returned to the southern USA.

THE MATING GAME

Birds, like all animals, are driven by the urge to reproduce. Choosing the right partner is of vital importance, so birds have evolved rituals and displays that help them assess the opposite sex. Usually the female gets to choose and the male strives to impress her. She has to choose a partner of the same species, and this is why most birds, especially males, have distinctive calls and markings. Next, the male must prove he is a good catch using every trick in the book, from bringing gifts to singing love songs, dancing, or battling with his rivals.

DANCING COUPLES

When courting herons meet, they perform a dance-like ritual, bending and straightening their necks and clashing their beaks together. Such behaviour looks odd to us, but it is full of signals that only the herons can understand. It helps them overcome their wariness of strangers, and strengthens the bond between them. Like most birds, herons are monogamous, which means that couples stay together to raise a family.

FIGHTING FIT

Male birds don't win mates simply by looking beautiful – they have to prove their superiority over rivals, even if it means a fight to the death. Male golden pheasants slash at each other with the vicious spurs on the feet, but they usually settle their disputes without serious injury.

BUILDING A BOWER

As a substitute for showy feathers, bowerbirds collect colourful objects and arrange them around a stack of twigs. Satin bowerbirds are particularly choosy, collecting only blue objects. Females mate with the males who produce the most artistic displays.

LOOK AT ME!

Frigate birds attract attention from females by inflating a scarlet neck pouch until it is as big as a person's head and looks sure to burst. On some tropical islands the males congregate on trees, clustered like enormous ripe fruits. When females fly past, the males clack their bills, wave their wings about wildly, and make a strange gobbling noise.

COURTSHIP CLOTHES

The male Count Raggi's bird of paradise has a fountain of gauzy red tail feathers that he fluffs and shakes while rolling around a branch and hanging upside down. But who is he trying to impress? Although females take a great interest in the display, it may actually be directed at other males. Groups of males gather and display together in the same tree, and in this way, seem to establish a ranking system. Visiting females always head straight to the top male.

Gifts of food are a key part of the common tern's courtship. If the courtship is successful, the birds will probably stay together for life.

GIFT GIVING

Some male birds give presents to prospective mates. Male herons bring nest material, offered with much ceremonial bowing, and snowy owls offer freshly killed lemmings. Gifts of food are of more than symbolic value. They allow the female to assess how well her partner will feed future offspring, and they provide her with the valuable nutrients she needs to produce eggs.

Blue-cheeked bee eaters, like many other birds, mate in a matter of seconds.

A BRIEF AFFAIR

Courtship is often a long and complex affair, but mating itself is usually very brief. The male flutters onto the female's back and the two birds press their genital openings together, allowing sperm to pass from male to female.

MASTER BUILDERS

With only instinct to guide them and only bills to serve as tools, birds construct nests of amazing complexity. A nest may take weeks to build and involve thousands of flights in search of suitable material. Some birds use whatever comes to hand – even string, nails, plastic bags, or old clothes. Others are much fussier. Hummingbirds build nests from spider's silk one strand at a time, while swallows collect a certain kind of mud from the edge of puddles.

Lichen is used for camouflage.

CUP NEST

Most birds use a sequence of movements to create a cup-shaped nest with a snug hollow in the middle. First, they roughly organize the material, with softer items like feathers on the inside. Then they sit in the nest, and turning round and round, push themselves against it to form a perfectly sized cup.

Straw and stiff fibres hold the nest together.

Feathers provide warmth.

COMMUNAL LIVING

In the deserts of southern Africa, sociable weaver birds build gigantic straw nests that house up to 100 families. From a distance they look like haystacks dropped on trees, but close inspection reveals a gallery of entrance tunnels on the underside. The nests can last for 100 years, and they provide both a cool refuge from midday heat and a warm shelter on chilly nights.

Telegraph poles provide an alternative to trees in barren parts of the desert.

WOVEN HOME

Usually females do most of the nest-building, but in weaver birds the males do the work and females choose mates by inspecting their craftsmanship. Weavers are superb nest-builders and can tie knots by using their beaks and feet together. Like all birds, they work entirely from instinct, which means they know exactly how to construct a nest without ever being shown.

TREE HOUSES

Woodpeckers make their homes by drilling holes in trees with their chisel-like bills. Boring through solid wood is hard work, so males and females work together, taking up to a month to complete the task. Instead of lining the nest with soft feathers or leaves, they finely chip the inner wall to make a cushion of sawdust.

A male great spotted woodpecker delivers food to his family.

Birds that nest in colonies keep a careful distance from their neighbours.

LESS IS MORE

For many seabirds, a nest is little more than a scrape in the ground or a rocky ledge on a cliff. Gentoo penguins build simple mounds of pebbles, sticks, and grass. To impress their mates, the males collect pebbles of the same size and colour and arrange them in a neat ring around the nest.

A tightly woven hem around the entrance stops this nest from unravelling.

MALLEE FOWL   BARN SWALLOW   BEE EATER

OUT OF HARM'S WAY

Many birds go to great lengths to keep their nests out of predators' reach. Mallee fowl bury their eggs under an enormous mound of rotting leaves, which not only hides the eggs, but keeps them warm. Barn swallows nest high under the eaves of buildings in a cup of mud and straw lined with grass and feathers. Carmine bee eaters burrow their way into sandy river banks and live in large colonies, where many eyes and ears can remain on the alert for danger.

Mud nests are built one mouthful at a time and left to dry in the sun.

MUD HUT

Providing it stays dry, mud is an excellent nesting material. Ovenbirds use a mixture of mud, dung, and straw that sets rock hard under the sun, keeping out all but the strongest egg thieves. Their dome-shaped huts always face away from the wind and have an ingenious barrier inside the entrance to block draughts.

The grosbeak weaver uses tough fibres torn from a particular type of grass. It weaves them into a wickerwork ball, slung between two plant stems.

EGGS

ALL BIRDS LAY EGGS rather than giving birth to live young as mammals do. This is because birds need to keep their weight down in order to fly, so mothers must get rid of their offspring as soon as they can. An egg, therefore, serves as an external womb, containing all the nutrients that a chick will need to develop. Parents simply keep their eggs warm, protect them from predators, and wait for them to hatch. We think of eggs as fragile, but in fact they are surprisingly tough: ostrich eggs are strong enough to stand on.

HUMMINGBIRD EGG

Tiny as it looks, this egg is pretty hefty in proportion to the adult bird.

EXTRAORDINARY EGGS

Eggs are surprisingly varied and many are very different from the chicken eggs we eat. They range in size from hummingbird eggs the size of your little fingernail, to ostrich eggs, which are bigger than pineapples. Shapes range from cones to spheres (spherical eggs are strongest), and textures vary from rough and chalky to smooth and shiny. Many eggs are coloured or speckled, either for camouflage or so that the mother can tell her own eggs from impostors, which other birds may have sneaked into her nest.

INSIDE AN EGG

A freshly laid egg consists of little but egg white and yolk. At first the chick is a tiny pink speck on the yolk, called a germ spot or embryo. Drawing on the food in the yolk and the water in the egg white, the embryo grows and a recognizable chick begins to take shape.

The shell is semi-permeable, meaning that air and moisture can pass through it.

The yolk sac provides food for the embryo. It shrinks as the embryo matures

The chorion encloses the growing chick and all the structures supporting it.

The waste sac collects the embryo's urine.

The embryo floats in a sac of fluid called the amnion.

Albumen (egg white) is a jelly-like fluid that cushions the embryo and provides a store of water.

ELEPHANT BIRD EGG

The air bubble grows as the chick matures.

The embryo also needs warmth to grow.

Ground-nesting birds like kiwis lay larger eggs than birds that nest in trees. As a result, their chicks develop to a more advanced state and can run about soon after hatching.

CASSOWARY EGG

STORK EGG

EGYPTIAN VULTURE EGG

CUCKOO EGG

BOUBOU SHRIKE EGG

A DIFFICULT LAY

Although the largest birds lay the largest eggs, small birds lay big eggs in proportion to their body size. An ostrich's egg is a hundredth of its weight, but a hummingbird's is more than a tenth of its weight. Kiwis lay proportionately the biggest eggs, a a quarter of the adult bird's weight

HOT SEAT

Birds appear to be doing little while sitting on their eggs, but they are expending up to 25 per cent of their energy just keeping the eggs warm. Incubating eggs is especially important for birds in cold places, such as snowy owls. Their bellies have a special patch of almost bare skin which they press against the eggs to keep them warm.

This inhospitable-looking cliff face is a good spot for a nest as it is out of the reach of many predators.

BELLY BLANKET

Male emperor penguins balance an egg on their feet and tuck a paunchy flap of belly over the top to keep it from contact with the icy ground or air. They can go for months without eating while the mothers are away looking for food.

EGGS THAT ROLL BACK

Guillemots lay their single eggs on rocky cliffs without nests to hold them. The eggs are cone-shaped so that they roll in a circle when bumped, which stops them falling off the cliff and smashing. Other shorebirds, such as plovers, lay groups of pointed eggs. The pointed ends fit neatly together in the middle so the plover can sit on them all at once.

When mallee fowl chicks hatch, they climb out of the mound and scamper away, without ever meeting their parents. Chicks can fly within hours of hatching.

HOME SMELLY HOME

The mallee fowl of Australia builds an incubator. It lays its eggs in a huge mound of rotting vegetation that generates heat just as a garden compost heap does. Parents adjust the temperature of the mound by adding or removing material, but have no contact with their eggs or chicks.

Mallee fowls' mounds can reach more than 10 m (33 ft) across and are built by the males, who spend up to 11 months of the year guarding and maintaining them.

HATCHING OUT

Breaking out of an egg is such hard work that it takes hours or even days. To make the first crack, the chick pushes its "egg tooth" – a hard spike on its beak that it loses after hatching – against the shell with all its might.

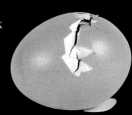

The chick extends the crack around the egg to make a trap door.

The blunt end of the shell is shoved off and the chick falls out.

Damp feathers soon dry and fluff up. Young chickens can walk within minutes of hatching.

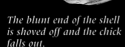

CHICK

235

FAMILY LIFE

IN SOME WAYS, THE FAMILY LIVES OF BIRDS are much like our own. More than 90 per cent of bird species are "monogamous", which means that males and females form stable couples that work together to raise a family. In some species, such as swans, couples may stay together for life. But despite the appearance of stability and harmony, family life among birds is full of hardship, deceit, and even cruelty. Birds almost always lay more eggs than will reach adulthood, and from the moment they hatch, chicks face a struggle to survive that only the strongest can win.

DIVORCE RATE
Family life in birds can be as complicated as in humans. Swans might appear to be a model of the perfect family, but DNA tests reveal that parents often cheat on their partners and lay eggs "out of wedlock". And if a couple has problems breeding, they may get "divorced" so each can try mating with a different partner.

GROWING UP
Young birds fall into two main types. Ground-nesting birds such as ducks and geese have "precocial" young, which are downy and can walk and feed themselves within hours of hatching. In contrast, tree-nesting birds have "altricial" young, which are tiny, naked, and helpless. Their parents face the exhausting challenge of feeding the young until they can leave the nest.

Newly hatched blue tits are blind and naked.

Feathers are forming five days after hatching.

At 2 weeks old, the chicks look almost adult.

STAY-AT-HOME DAD
In jacanas, traditional sex roles are reversed. These three chicks will be cared for entirely by their father, while their mother (who may have up to three "husbands") battles with other females for control of her territory. If a jacana family wanders into the wrong area, the resident female will kill the chicks and lay new eggs for the father to rear.

IMPRINTING
Newly hatched ducklings follow their mother, whose voice and appearance become permanently "imprinted" in their brains. If the mother isn't present, ducklings imprint on whatever else they can follow.

PROGRAMMED TO KILL
Young birds learn some survival skills from their parents, but most knowledge is instinctive. A cuckoo never meets its parents, yet it knows how to kill the other chicks in the nest within hours of hatching.

SIBLING RIVALRY

Birds of prey often have more chicks than can survive. The parents give most of the food to the strongest chick and turn a blind eye when it begins to bully the others. Often the well-fed chick ends up killing and eating its brothers and sisters, but sometimes the parents eat the weakest or most sickly chicks themselves.

INSATIABLE APPETITE

Birds that feed their young work non-stop to meet their chicks' needs. A wren may make 1,000 feeding trips in a single day, and a swift may fly 1,000 km (600 miles) daily to gather enough food. Black terns spend three or four weeks flying to and from their nests, which are hidden on rafts of floating vegetation in lakes.

A black tern returns to its chicks with a fish.

237

SONGBIRDS

ABOUT 60 PER CENT of the world's bird species belong to a group called the passerines, or perching birds. These small, compact birds typically live in trees or bushes and are distinguished by their unique feet, which enable them to perch securely on twigs and branches. Most perching birds are also known as songbirds. They use an organ called a syrinx to produce highly complex songs, usually to declare their ownership of a territory or to attract a mate. Most commonly it is the male that sings, but in some species males and females sing duets.

DAWN CHORUS

Dawn is the noisiest time for songbirds, especially in the forests of Europe and North America during spring. Robins and redstarts usually start the singing, with finches and sparrows joining last. But why sing at dawn? One reason might be that the cool, still air helps sound to travel, making the songs more effective. Another reason may be that birds wake up before it is warm enough to hunt for insects, so they concentrate on singing instead.

The song of the great reed warbler consists of up to 40 different phrases.

TAKING A BATH

Songbirds love to bathe, even in the middle of winter. They wash with a careful sequence of actions. First they wade into the water and dunk their heads. Then they crouch and flutter their wings to splash water across their feathers. After the bath they fly to a safe perch and preen the feathers with their beak.

STEREO SOUND

A bird's voicebox, or "syrinx", creates noise as air passes over a membrane, causing it to vibrate. It is located deep down in the bird's throat, where the windpipe splits into two tubes going into the lungs. This arrangement gives birds two chambers for making sound, which means they can sing two distinct notes at the same time.

THE SYRINX

WINDPIPE

Birds use these muscles to control the sound the syrinx makes.

MEMBRANE

TUBES TO LUNGS

The bare-throated bellbird perches at the very top of the tree so that its call will travel further.

The European robin stays in its territory all year and sings all year round as well.

RAINFOREST RACKET

Birdsong is not always pleasant to the ear. The bare-throated bellbird of Brazil has such a loud, jarring call that people call it the brain-fever bird. The African tinkerbird's maddening "song" sounds like a hammer bashing metal. Compared to the melodious songs of northern songbirds, the calls of tropical songbirds are simple, loud, and repetitive to carry through the dense rainforest canopy and remain audible over the background din of insects.

ROWDY ROBIN

The European robin is a very noisy little bird. It is the first bird to start singing in the morning, the last to stop singing in the evening, and the most likely to be caught singing in the middle of the night, especially in places where streetlights or floodlights have confused it. Males and females both sing, but the males are noisiest.

Songbirds' long claws can wrap around anything from thin twigs to stout branches.

The dipper's preen gland is larger than that of any other songbird.

DIPPING IN

Perching feet are not just useful for gripping branches. The dipper uses them to hold on to pebbles and so walk into fast-flowing streams where it immerses itself completely to look for aquatic insects. Its dives last about three seconds each, and it stays dry by smearing itself with water-repellent preen oil.

PERCHING FEET

Songbirds have three forward-facing toes and one backward-facing toe, all of which are long and slender for gripping twigs of various sizes. When the legs bend, a special locking mechanism closes the claws to give a very firm grip, even when the bird is sleeping.

HOUSE CALLS

House wrens, found in the Americas, know over 130 songs. They sing while building nests, to defend their territory, and for courting. Males can sing for 10 minutes to attract females, while those with mates sing quietly so as not to attract rival males.

SAMPLING AND MIXING

Many songbirds improve their singing ability by stealing tunes from other species. Marsh warblers not only mimic other songs, but combine them into new compositions. They pick up hundreds of songs both from their winter feeding grounds in Africa and their European breeding territories. When the male sings, he weaves samples of many songs together to make a beautiful, fluid stream of sound.

The European marsh warbler can mimic the songs of 99 European bird species and 113 African species.

KEEP AWAY!

WHEN YOU'RE UNDER ATTACK, the best form of self-defence is usually to make a quick exit. We humans rely on our legs, but birds have the advantage of flight. Once airborne, nothing can catch a bird except another bird. But there are some situations when a quick getaway is not the best solution. Eggs and chicks can't take to the wing – their parents must hide them or drive attackers away. And if a predator can follow its victim into the air, a bird may have no option but to fight.

The frogmouth's bright pink mouth and yellow eyes can startle a predator and make it back off.

SAFETY IN NUMBERS

For many birds, flocking together is the first line of defence, and reduces the risk of attack for each individual bird. Predators rely on the element of surprise, but they stand little chance of getting close if there are hundreds of eyes on the lookout. In some British estuaries, red knots form flocks of more than 10,000. Birdwatchers travel hundreds of miles to see these vast flocks carpeting the mudflats and whirling around like smoke when the birds collectively take flight.

These crows have ganged up to drive an eagle away.

MOBBING

Some birds gang together to "mob" predators and drive them off. They fly around the intruder, shrieking angrily and taking turns to swoop close, sometimes even making physical contact. Birds of prey, cats, and humans all regularly get mobbed.

CAMOUFLAGE

Potoos and frogmouths stay out of sight by impersonating tree stumps. Perched bolt upright, they raise their heads, close their eyes, and let camouflaged feathers do the rest. If anything gets too close, the frogmouth opens its cavernous mouth and startles the attacker with sudden, vivid flash of colour.

A fieldfare splatters a blackbird with a volley of excrement.

DEATH BY DEFECATION

Fieldfares not only mob attackers but defecate on them – and with great accuracy. A flock of fieldfares can cover a predator with so much excrement that its feathers become too soiled for flight and it falls to the ground. There are even reports of birds dying after fieldfare faeces have ruined the insulating properties of their plumage.

The trumpet-shaped entrance tube makes the nest completely snake-proof.

SNAKEPROOF NESTS

Weaver birds have to protect their nests from marauding snakes. The openings are on the underside, where they are difficult to reach, and the nests are often suspended from long branches over water, providing a trap for any snake that loses its grip.

FEIGNING INJURY

Birds that nest on the ground are at great risk from predators. The parents' only option is to make sure predators don't find the eggs. Plovers lure foxes away from their nests by pretending to have broken wings and scampering away just slowly enough for the fox to follow. Once the fox has been led astray, the plover stages a miraculous recovery and flies off.

HIDING IN THE REEDS

The bittern is almost impossible to see when it wants to hide. With its head upright, the markings on its throat blend in perfectly with the reeds around it. It will even sway gently in a breeze to match the swaying reeds. The bittern's other notable feature is the male's extraordinary booming call, which sounds like a foghorn and is said to be audible from as far away as 5 km (3 miles).

SPOT THE EGG

Plovers' eggs are superbly camouflaged, and the type of camouflage varies enormously, even within the same plover species. Birds that nest on sand or gravel tend to lay speckled eggs; those that nest on bare earth lay mottled eggs; and those that nest in moorland lay eggs with dark spots and blotches.

EPIC JOURNEYS

IN THE 1950s, researchers captured a Manx shearwater on an island off the coast of Wales. They took it to the city of Boston, USA, and released it. Twelve days later it was back in Wales. Many birds share this extraordinary knack of finding their way, even when it entails flying for thousands of miles across featureless ocean. It is an ability that around 10 billion individual birds put to use twice every year, when they set off on their epic migrations.

MIGRATION AND NAVIGATION

The long journeys that birds make in autumn and spring are called migrations. Most migrating birds fly between cold and warm places, partly to avoid the winter. Their trips are exhausting and dangerous - fewer than half of first-time migrants make it back the next year. Small birds tend to fly at night, stopping during the day to rest and refuel. Birds of prey migrate by riding on thermals, so they must stay over land and travel by day.

Migrating Canada geese in California use the Sun to tell which way is south.

KEY TO ROUTES

RUBY-THROATED HUMMINGBIRD
Flies 3,000 km (1,900 miles) from Central America to Canada in search of food.

ARCTIC TERN
The longest route of any bird: 15,000 km (9,300 miles) from the Arctic Circle to Antarctica.

COMMON CRANE
Young common cranes learn the routes to their winter sites in Asia and Africa by flying with their parents.

WHITE STORK
By flying over Spain or the Middle East, European white storks avoid the long journey over sea, where they cannot stop to rest.

SNOW GOOSE
These birds made their way to Canada at the end of the Ice Age. Where the ice had melted, the land provided plenty of food.

NORTH AMERICA

GULF OF MEXICO

ATLANTIC OCEAN

SOUTH AMERICA

PACIFIC OCEAN

HOMING IN

Experiments with homing pigeons reveal that some birds have a built-in magnetic compass. This enables pigeons to find the way home from hundreds of miles away even when blindfolded. But when tiny magnets are attached to their heads to confuse them, they get lost.

ACROSS THE GULF

The tiny ruby-throated hummingbird has to make a 20-hour, non-stop flight across the Gulf of Mexico during its treacherous trip from North to Central America. It will perish at sea if bad weather blows it off course.

ARCTIC OCEAN

EUROPE

ASIA

AFRICA

*Arctic terns experience more
hours of daylight than any
other creature because their
migrations allow them
to enjoy the extremely
long summer days
at both poles.*

PACIFIC
OCEAN

INDIAN
OCEAN

AUSTRALASIA

SOUTHERN OCEAN

FOLLOW THE SUN
Birds that migrate by day use
the Sun as a compass. They also have
an internal clock, to help compensate for
the Sun's movement across the sky as the
day progresses. Snow geese are prompted
to migrate by the Sun; when days grow
longer, a hormone within the snow goose
kicks in, making it restless and inclined
to set off on the long journey.

*Sandhill cranes fly 6,400 km
(4,000) miles from Alaska and
eastern Siberia to the southern
United States.*

LANDMARKS
Some migrating birds seem
to have a genetic map that
tells them where to go.
Cuckoos, for example, can
find the way without being
shown. Other birds learn
the route by following a flock
and memorizing landmarks,
such as mountains and
rivers. Landmarks based on
smell and sound – such as
the scent of a pine forest or
the sound of crashing waves
– may also help.

FLIGHTLESS BIRDS

FLYING IS A GREAT WAY OF FLEEING FROM DANGER and finding food, but it quickly burns through a bird's energy reserves. So, if a bird can find food and keep out of danger without having to fly, it pays to stay on the ground. Over thousands of years, many ground-dwelling birds have lost the power of flight altogether, their wings becoming withered and useless or adapted for other uses. Freed from the need to stay small and lightweight, some species evolved into the biggest birds on Earth.

MALE MOTHER

Emus are the Australian equivalent of ostriches. As with ostriches, the males are devoted parents, incubating the eggs without getting up to eat, drink, or even defecate, and guarding the chicks for months with no help from the mother.

The feathers are shaggy because the barbules don't zip up neatly like those of flying birds.

Enormous muscles power the long legs.

RECORD BREAKERS

Africa's ostriches don't need to fly because they can run from danger. They are the fastest birds on land and can top 72 kph (45 mph), which is twice as fast as the best Olympic sprinters. They are also the world's largest birds, with the heaviest eggs, the longest necks, the biggest eyes, and one of the longest life spans (up to 68 years). Contrary to popular belief, they never bury their heads in the sand.

Ostriches' eyes are bigger than their brains.

A flightless cormorant holds its stunted wings out to dry after diving for fish.

ISLAND LIFE

On remote islands with no mammals, birds had few enemies and many became flightless. When explorers reached these islands, the birds proved an easy catch. The dodo of Mauritius, the Hawaiian giant goose, and New Zealand's moas were hunted to extinction. One of the few survivors is the Galapagos flightless cormorant.

THE CURIOUS KIWI

Over time the kiwi's wings and tail have all but disappeared and its feathers have turned to fur. It lives like a badger, snuffling around forests at night and hiding in a burrow during the day. Its nostrils are at the end of a long bill, which it uses to probe the ground for worms.

Ostriches would have to reach a ground speed of 160 kph (100 mph) to get airborne.

Ostriches are the only birds with just two toes, a feature that helps them sprint.

WINGS AS OTHER THINGS

The flightless wings of penguins, far from becoming weak with disuse, have evolved to perform a different function: instead of beating against air, they beat against water. Large wings would be slow to swim with, so they have become short, flat, and paddle-shaped. This adaptation has made penguins the fastest and most agile swimmers of any birds.

STRANGE BUT TRUE

Birds sometimes do the most peculiar things. Magpies and jays are famous for their strange habit of hoarding shiny trinkets such as coins and jewellery in their nests, but nobody knows why they do it. And some birds seem to do things just for fun. In Iceland, eider ducks have been seen white-water rafting down rivers and then waddling back to the start point to do it again, and Adelie penguins sometimes sledge down ice slides for a thrill. But for the most part, the way birds behave has a perfectly rational explanation, however weird and wonderful it might seem.

ROAD RUNNER
It seems odd that a flying bird should choose to get around by running, but that's what roadrunners do, expertly. They sprint at 24 kph (15 mph) as they chase after prey, using their tails as rudders to make sharp turns without slowing down, and flipping them up in order to brake.

KORI BUSTARD
The male Kori bustard of Africa has a few tricks for attracting mates. First he inflates his neck, then he drags his wings along the ground in a mating dance, sometimes bowing to the female. Some males will puff up all their feathers, making them look like a big, white ball. Finally, in case the females still have not noticed him, he will call with a loud booming sound across the African plains.

The Kori bustard is one of the world's largest flying birds. The males can weigh up to 19 kg (42 lb), twice the weight of the females.

Hoatzin chicks have tiny claws on their elbows.

HANGER ON

Hoatzin chicks are strange in having claws on their wings, which they use for climbing. The claws are a throwback to the distant, evolutionary past, when the dinosaur ancestors of birds had clawed front legs.

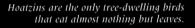

Hoatzins are the only tree-dwelling birds that eat almost nothing but leaves.

HORNBILL

Hornbills have spectacularly large bills topped by a helmet called a casque. The casque is usually hollow, but in one species it is solid ivory. Quite why such huge, cumbersome bills should evolve is a puzzle, but the bright colours suggest they may be decorations to impress potential mates.

Blue-footed booby eggs are laid within a circle of booby droppings, which is how the birds mark out their territory – the only sign of a nest.

PROJECTILE VOMIT

Birds can't produce venom, but the next best thing is toxic vomit. Fulmar chicks squirt vomit at unwelcome guests like eagles or seagulls, and can hit anything within a 1.5 m (5 ft) radius. It contains acid and fish oil, which ruin seabirds' waterproofed feathers, leaving them at risk of drowning.

BLUE-FOOTED BOOBY

This bird's ridiculous feet serve an important function. Blue-footed boobies nest on the same Pacific islands as red-footed and masked boobies, and females need to be able to tell them apart for mating. So, when a blue-footed booby is courting, he parades back and forth, stamping his blue feet to prove he belongs to the correct species.

THE CASSOWARY'S KICK

As well as its bizarre appearance, the cassowary is also remarkable for being one of the only birds that can kill an adult human (the other is the ostrich). The dagger-like claws on its feet can disembowel a person with a single kick. The most recent fatality was in 1926, when an Australian man was kicked in the throat.

BIRD DATA

BIRD ORDERS

Birds make up the class *Aves*, one of the five main groups of backboned animals (vertebrates). There are around 9,700 species of birds, and closely-related species are grouped together into orders. There are 27 orders – although some experts use fewer or more orders – listed below by common name.

Ostrich (order Struthioniformes) 1 species

Rheas (order Rheiformes) 2 species

Cassowaries and emus (order Casuariiformes) 4 species

Kiwis (order Apterygiformes) 3 species

Penguins (order Sphenisciformes) 17 species

Divers (order Gaviiformes) 5 species

Grebes (order Podicipediformes) 22 species

Albatrosses and petrels (order Procellariiformes) 108 species

Herons and relatives (order Pelecaniformes) 65 species

Flamingos (order Phoenicopteriformes) 5 species

Waterfowl (order Anseriformes) 149 species

Birds of prey (order Falconiformes) 307 species

Game birds (order Galliformes) 281 species

Cranes and relatives (order Gruiformes) 204 species

Waders, gulls, and auks (order Charadriiformes) 343 species

Pigeons (order Columbiformes) 309 species

Sandgrouse (order Pteroclidiformes) 16 species

Parrots (order Psittaciformes) 353 species

Cuckoos and turacos (order Cuculiformes) 160 species

Owls (order Strigiformes) 205 species

Nightjars and frogmouths (order Caprimulgiformes) 118 species

Hummingbirds and swifts (order Apodiformes) 424 species

Mousebirds (order Coliiformes) 6 species

Trogons (order Trogoniformes) 35 species

Kingfishers and relatives (order Coraciiformes) 191 species

Woodpeckers and toucans (order Piciformes) 380 species

Passerines (order Passeriformes) over 5,200 species

BIRD WEBSITES

www.rspb.org.uk
The website of the Royal Society for the Protection of Birds, Europe's largest wildlife conservation charity.

www.birdlife.net
The BirdLife Partnership looks at the welfare and conservation of birds across the world. The website includes news reports and project updates.

www.math.sunysb.edu/~tony/birds/
Hear birds' songs through your computer speakers by clicking on the birds. Use the map to link through to more birds across the world.

http://birds.cornell.edu
From the Cornell Lab of Ornithology, this site looks at bird research and provides a useful "all about birds" educational section.

www.earthlife.net/birds/intro.html
An introduction to many bird-related topics, such as migration and anatomy, with easy explanations and fun facts.

www.birdsofbritain.co.uk/
Birdwatching site for the UK including a bird guide, quizzes, and gallery.

Please note: Every effort has been made to ensure that these websites are suitable, and that their addresses are up-to-date at the time of going to print. Website content is constantly updated, as are website addresses – therefore, it is highly recommended that a responsible adult should visit and check each website before allowing access to a child.

RECORDS

Tallest bird Male North African ostrich. Tallest recorded height: 2.74 m (9 ft).

Tallest extinct bird Giant moa of New Zealand. Height: 3.7 m (12 ft)

Smallest bird Male bee hummingbird. Body length: 5.7cm (2.25 in), half of which is bill and tail.

Largest wingspan Wandering albatross. Largest recorded wingspan: 3.63 m (11 ft 11 in).

Largest bill Australian pelican. Largest recorded size: 43 cm (18.5 in).

Heaviest flying bird Great bustard. Heaviest recorded weight: 21 kg (46 lb).

Most feathers Whistling swan (25,216).

Fewest feathers Ruby-throated hummingbird (940).

Longest feathers Onagadori. In this breed of domestic chicken the cocks have tails up to 10.59 m (34.75 ft).

Longest legs Ostrich.

Shortest legs Swifts. Legs are almost nonexistent in swifts.

Fastest bird on land Ostrich. Speed: 72 kph (45 mph).

Fastest flying bird in a dive Peregrine falcon. Speed: 200 kph (124 mph).

Fastest flying bird on a level flight Both the spine-tailed swift and red-breasted merganser have been recorded flying at 161 kph (100 mph).

Slowest flying bird American woodcock and Eurasian woodcock. Speed: 8 kph (5 mph) without stalling.

Fastest wingbeat Hummingbirds (90 beat per second).

Slowest wingbeat Vultures (1 beat per second).

Fastest swimmer Gentoo penguin. Capable of reaching 36 kph or 22 mph underwater.

Deepest diver Emperor penguin. Can reach a depth of 540 m (1770 ft) and hold its breath for 18 minutes underwater.

Highest flight Ruppell's griffon vulture. Highest recorded flight: 11,277 m (37,000 ft).

Longest recorded migration Common tern. Total distance: 26,000 km (16,210 miles).

Largest nest Mallee fowl build incubation mounds of up to 4.57 m (15 ft) high and 10.6 m (35 ft) across. The amount of material in the mound would weigh about 300 tonnes.

Largest tree nest Bald eagle. Florida bald eagles construct nests 6 m (20 ft) deep, 3 m (10 ft) wide, and almost 3 tonnes in weight.

Smallest nest Vervain hummingbirds' nests are the size of half a walnut shell, and bee hummingbirds have thimble-sized nests.

Largest egg Ostrich. Average size: 150–200 mm (6-8 in) long and 100-150 mm (4-6 in) in diameter. Average weight: 1–1.78 kg (2 lb 3 oz to 3 lb).

Smallest egg Vervain hummingbird. Smallest recorded size: 10 mm (0.4 in) long.

Largest clutch Bobwhite quail. Lays up to 28 eggs in a nest.

Smallest clutch Albatross. Lays only one egg every two years.

Largest tongue Flamingo.

Loudest song Male kakapo. The song can be heard 7 km (4.4 miles) away.

Most varied singer Marsh warbler. Can perform up to 84 different songs.

Largest eye Ostrich. Eyeball is 5 cm (2 in) wide.

Best sense of smell Kiwi.

Best sense of hearing Barn owl.

Most intelligent bird African gray parrot or Caledonian crow.

Best weightlifter Bald eagle. Can lift a 6.8 kg (15 lb) deer into the air with its talons.

Longest lifespan in the wild Royal albatross (58 years).

Longest lifespan in captivity Sulfur-crested cockatoo (80 years).

CRITICALLY ENDANGERED BIRDS

The 2009 IUCN (International Union for the Conservation of Nature and Natural Resources) Red List of Threatened Species names 192 birds as critically endangered in the wild. The three biggest causes are habitat loss (HL), harvesting (hunted by humans; HV), and invasive alien species (AS). These are just a few of the birds on the Red List.

Beck's petrel Papua New Guinea; forest and sea; AS
Blue-fronted lorikeet Indonesia; forest; HL
California condor Mexico, USA; forest, savanna, shrubland; HV
Forest little owl India; forest; HL
Fuertes's parrot Colombia; forest; HL
Giant ibis Cambodia; forest, arable land, wetland; HL, HV
Gorgeted puffleg Southwest Colombia; HL
Himalayan quail India; shrubland, grassland; HL
Kakapo New Zealand; forest; AS
Little blue macaw Brazil; forest; HL, AS, HV. Possibly extinct in the wild.
Mangrove finch Ecuador; forest; AS
Medium tree-finch Floreana Island, Galápagos; AS
Noguchi's woodpecker Japan; forest; HL
Siberian crane western Asia; wetland; HL
Slender-billed vulture eastern Asia; forest; pollution

EVERYTHING ON EARTH

GLOSSARY

Abyssal plain Broad, flat areas of the ocean basin floor, usually below 3,650 m (12,000 ft).

Acid rain Rain made more acidic by some types of air pollution.

Algae A group of plants that includes seaweeds and single-celled, floating plankton.

Alula A tuft of feathers on the leading edge of a bird's wing that it raises to prevent it from stalling as it slows down.

Aquatic Living in water.

Asteroid Small body of rock, orbiting the Sun, left over from the birth of the Solar System.

Atmosphere Gas-rich layer around Earth.

Atoll Ring of coral that forms on the site of a sunken volcanic island.

Barbs Tiny side branches off a feather shaft that make up a bird's feather vane.

Black smoker Chimney of deposits on the sea floor through which a black jet of superheated, chemical-rich water gushes.

Blubber A thick layer of insulating fat that forms the skin of sea mammals and polar bears.

Camouflage A pattern, colour, or body shape that helps an animal hide by blending in with its surroundings.

Carbon dioxide A gas breathed out by living organisms. Also a by-product of burning fossil fuels, such as petrol (in cars).

Carnivore An animal that eats flesh. Also, a member of the mammalian order Carnivora.

Chalk Soft limestone made up mostly of the skeletons of dead, microscopic algae called coccolithophorids.

Climate Weather conditions in a particular area averaged over 30 years or more.

Colony A large group of birds that lives together in one place to breed or roost, or the place in which they live.

Comet A mass of ice and rock hurtling through near Space. Sunlight melts some of the ice, producing a comet's tail.

Condensation The process by which warm air cools, turning its water vapour into liquid water. Condensation causes breath to become misty on a cold day.

Contour feathers Also called body feathers, these are the small, overlapping feathers on a bird's head that give it a streamlined shape.

Copepods Tiny, shrimp-like animals that are part of the ocean's plankton.

Core Dense, hot iron-rich centre of the Earth

Crop A bag-like extension of a bird's gullet used to store food. It is often used to carry food back to the nest.

Crust Outer rocky layer of the Earth, varying between 5–80 km (3–50 miles) in thickness.

Dinoflagellates A group of single-celled organisms that form part of plankton. Some produce poisons that kill sea creatures.

Down feathers Very soft, fine feathers that trap air close to a bird's body and help to keep it warm.

Earthquake Shaking of the Earth's crust caused when tectonic plates slide past or over each other.

Echinoderms A group of marine animals that includes starfish, brittlestars, sea urchins, sea cucumbers, and featherstars.

Echolocation Seeing by sound. Bats and dolphins echolocate by producing special sounds and analysing the echoes.

Egg tooth A small structure on the tip of a chick's upper bill, which it uses to crack open the eggshell when hatching. The egg tooth drops off soon after hatching.

El Niño This event happens every 5-7 years when a change in wind direction over the Pacific Ocean affects the ocean currents there, disrupting weather patterns.

Epicentre The place on Earth's surface that lies directly above the focus of an earthquake.

Epipelagic (sunlit) zone The top open water zone of the ocean, which runs from the surface down to about 200 m (650 ft).

Erosion The processes by which rock or soil are loosened and transported by agents such as glaciers, rivers, wind, and waves.

Evaporation The process by which water turns into an invisible gas, or vapour, when heated and mixes with air.

Extinction The process by which living things, such as the dodo, die out completely and no longer exist.

Fault Fracture in Earth's crust where one rock slides past another.

Flight feathers The long feathers that make up a bird's wings and are used to fly. They can be grouped into primary feathers (on the outer wing) and secondary feathers (on the inner wing).

Flock A group of birds, usually of the same species, flying or feeding together.

Fossils Remains or traces of living things preserved in Earth's rocks.

Geologist A scientist who studies the Earth's surface and rocks, and the processes by which they are created, transformed and broken down.

Gizzard The muscular chamber in a bird's stomach, where the food that it has eaten is ground to a pulp.

Glacier Mass of ice and snow flowing slowly downhill under its own weight.

Global warming Gradual increase in the average temperature across the world.

Greenhouse effect The trapping of infrared radiation from the Earth's surface by greenhouse gases in the atmosphere, producing a warming effect.

Habitat The type of environment where a bird is normally found, such as wetland, forest, or grassland.

Hatching The process by which a baby bird breaks out of its egg by chipping its way through the shell with the tiny egg tooth on its beak.

Herbivore An animal that mainly eats plants.

High pressure This weather system is caused by sinking cold air. This brings sunny weather as it keeps clouds away.

Hot spot Place in the Earth's mantle, well away from a plate boundary, where hot rock burns through the crust, creating volcanoes.

Hurricane A rapidly spinning mass of wind that begins over a tropical ocean and can cause immense damage if it hits land.

Hydrothermal vent A crack in the seabed where hot water gushes upwards, after being heated by volcanic activity.

Ice Age Cold period during Earth's geological history. During an Ice Age there are very cold periods (glacial maxima) when ice sheets and glaciers advance, and warmer periods (interglacials) when they retreat.

Igneous rock Rock formed by molten rock from the Earth's interior cooling and solidifying on the surface or underground.

Iridescent A glittering sheen seen on some birds' feathers, and other objects, that reflects light and splits it into colours, giving the appearance of a rainbow.

Jet stream A strong wind that blows high in the troposphere, and which pilots use when flying in certain directions to speed their journey time.

Larvae Young stages of an invertebrate animal (an animal without a backbone), usually completely different in shape and size from the adult. Many marine animals produce floating (planktonic) larvae.

Lava Hot, molten rock that emerges from volcanoes.

Limestone Sedimentary rock composed mainly of calcium carbonate (calcite).

Lithosphere The outer, surface part of the Earth, which includes the outer-most part of the planet's rigid crust.

Low pressure This weather system is caused by rising warm air. As the air rises, it cools and its water vapour condenses to create clouds. Low pressure usually means bad weather.

Magma Hot, molten rock below Earth's surface.

Mantle The deep layer of rock – part solid, part molten – that lies underneath Earth's crust.

Marsupial A type of mammal that gives birth to tiny young that develop further in a pouch, or attached to teats on the mother's belly.

Metamorphic rock Rock formed by the alteration of existing solid rock by heat or pressure.

Meteorite Rock, falling from space, that strikes the Earth.

Mid-ocean ridge Zig-zagging ridge on the sea floor at the boundary where two plates move apart.

Migration A long journey undertaken by animals to find food or a place to breed. Many animals migrate each year during certain seasons.

Mineral Naturally occurring chemical – either a single element or a combination of elements – found within rock.

Monotreme A type of mammal that lays eggs.

Moraine Debris deposited by a glacier, especially sand and gravel.

Nectar The sweet liquid produced by a flower that attracts birds and insects to feed from it, and so pollinate it at the same time.

Nocturnal Active at night.

Omnivore An animal that eats both plant foods and animals.

Ozone layer Gas layer, derived from the element oxygen, that forms high in Earth's atmosphere. It provides some protection against the Sun's ultraviolet radiation.

Pangaea Supercontinent which existed 225 million years ago, and broke apart, becoming the continents that exist today.

Placenta An internal organ that allows unborn mammals to absorb food and oxygen from the mother's bloodstream.

Planet A large mass that orbits a star. In our Solar System, eight planets, including Earth, orbit the Sun.

Plate tectonics Movement of Earth's tectonic plates.

Plumage A bird's feathers.

Polyps Tiny animals that resemble anemones. Corals consist of many polyps joined together in a colony.

Predator An animal that kills other animals for food.

Preening The way in which birds keep their feathers in good condition, drawing them through their beaks to clean and smooth them.

Prey An animal that is hunted and killed by another animal.

Primary feathers The long flight feathers on the outer half of a bird's wings that provide the power for flying.

Primate A type of mammal with grasping hands, forward-facing eyes, and a large brain.

Prosimian A type of primate that is only distantly related to monkeys and apes. Most are small nocturnal creatures.

Rainforest A type of forest that gets heavy rain all year round. Tropical rainforests occur in tropical parts of the world; temperate rainforests occur in cooler places.

Rock Large, solid mass exposed at Earth's surface and composed of one or more minerals.

Rock cycle Cycle summarizing the creation and transformation of rocks (igneous, metamorphic, and sedimentary).

Rumination Regurgitating food to chew it a second time. Ruminant animals have a special stomach containing bacteria that help them digest plant food.

Savanna Areas of grassland found in tropical regions.

Scavenger An animal, such as a vulture, that searches for dead animals to eat.

Secondary feathers The inner wing feathers that provide lift during flight.

Sediment Debris loosened and transported by weathering and erosion, and deposited elsewhere.

Sedimentary rock Rock formed from sediment.

Seismometer (seismograph) Instrument that detects and records vibrations in the ground such as those produced by an earthquake's shock waves.

Solar System The Sun and the bodies that orbit it, including planets, moons, and asteroids.

Species A group of similar animals that can breed together and produce fertile offspring.

Stalactite A hanging, icicle-like structure composed largely of calcium carbonate (calcite).

Stalagmite A rising, candle-like structure composed largely of calcium carbonate (calcite).

Strata Layers of sedimentary rock.

Subduction One tectonic plate descending below another.

Sublittoral zone The area of seabed from just below the seashore down to a depth of about 100 m (325 ft).

Symbiosis A very close relationship between two different species.

Talons The sharp, curved claws of a bird of prey, used for seizing prey.

Tectonic plate One of 20 or so giant slabs of rock that form the Earth's crust. They move slowly across Earth's surface.

Territory An area occupied by an animal.

Tertiary feathers A bird's innermost flight feathers, which shape the wing into the body to ensure a smooth flight.

Thermal A rising column of warm air, often at the edge of a cliff or hillside.

Tornado A rapidly whirling column of air.

Trench A deep depression in the sea floor where one tectonic plate is forced down below another.

Troposphere The layer of the atmosphere immediately above Earth's crust, from 0–10 km (0–6 miles).

Tsunami Large sea wave that travels across the ocean following an earthquake, volcanic eruption, or impact by a large mass.

Typhoon See Hurricane

Volcano Opening in Earth's crust from which lava escapes.

Warm-blooded Having a relatively constant internal body temperature.

Weather Day-to-day atmospheric conditions affecting a particular locality.

Weathering Physical, chemical, or biological breakdown of rocks on Earth's surface.

Wetlands Swamps, marshes, and other wet areas of land.

Zooplankton Tiny, floating animals. Some spend their whole lives floating, while others are the larvae of bottom-dwelling creatures such as snails and crabs.

Zooxanthellae Single-celled plants that live inside the bodies of corals – plus some sea anemones – and help to make extra food for them.

INDEX

A

Aa 18
aardvark 190
abyssopelagic zone 104
acid rain 92
Agulhas Current 107
air pressure
Alaska, USA 20, 35
albatrosses 220
algae 89, 125, 133
Amazon rainforest 53
ammonites 84, 146
anchovies 183
Andes Mountains 15
anemone 129, 138–139
anemonefish 138
angelfish 20
Antarctica 32–33, 36, 89, 132–133
anteater 170, 190
antlers 179
apes 172, 174–175, 177
Apollo 17 9
Apollo butterfly 88
Apostles, Australia 108
Arabian Gulf 102
archaeology 146–147
Arctic Ocean 32, 153
Arctic tern 135, 242, 243
armadillo 19
ash, volcanic 16
Atacama Desert 36
Atlantis 90
atmosphere 8, 11, 12–13, 50
    ozone layer 88, 92
atolls, coral 116, 155
auroras 12, 62
Australia 38, 85, 109, 116, 142
avalanches 64

B

bacteria 43
badlands 37
bald eagle 214–215
balloons:
    hot-air 50
    weather 94
Bangladesh 91
Bardsey Island, UK
112
bathypelagic zone 104
bats 29, 167, 193
    wings 165
Bay of Fundy, Canada 106
beak, see bill
Beaufort scale 98, 161
beaver 186
beeches 41
bee hummingbird 213
Big Bang 6–7
bill
    birds of prey 214–215
    fish-eaters 218–219, 220–221
    hornbill 227, 247
    parrots 206
    toucans 227
    woodpeckers 226
bioluminescence 126
biomes 40–41
birds
birds of paradise 35, 58
birds of prey 210, 214–215
    killing techniques 215
birdsong 238–239
birth 179
black smokers 125
black tern 237
blizzards 65
block mountains 22
blow holes 109
blue-footed booby 247
blue tit 224, 236
bombs 117
bones, see skeleton
Bonington, Sir Chris 23
Bonobo 177
boobies 219
boreal forest 41
Boutan, Louis 144
brain
    mammals 176–177
    primates 173
breeding, see reproduction
Brent Spar 158
browsers 179
burrows 140
bushbaby 173

C

cacti 36
California 39, 96
camel 179, 189
cameras, underwater 144
Canada 37, 85, 106
carbon dioxide 11, 28, 43, 88, 89, 93, 157
caribou 32
carnivores 180
    small 184–185
cassowaries 247
cattle 200
cats 180–181
    hunting 171
caves 28–29, 109
CFCs 88
cheetah 171, 181
Chesil Beach, Dorset (UK) 109
chickens 225
chicks
    care of 236–237
    defence of 236
    hatching 235
Chile 24, 30, 36
chimpanzee 174, 177
Chromis fish 102, 103
clams, giant 125
claws
    retractable 180
cleaner fish 138, 141
climate 52, 53
climbing 180
clouds 12, 48, 54–55, 56, 58, 66, 68–69
clownfish, see anemonefish
coal 30
coasts 108–109, 110–111, 112–113
coati 183
coconuts 20
cod 152
cold blooded 166
cold fronts 51
colour
    displays 228–229
colugo 192
Columbus, Christopher 13
comets 11
communication 104, 174, 176–177, 182
    see also language
condensation 50, 68
    clouds 14, 58
    dew 56
    mist and fog 56–57
condors 215

D

darters 219
deepsea zone 124–125
defences
    animal
    bird
deforestation 43
desertification 42
deserts 36–37, 53
    duststorms 72–73
    sand erosion 37
    spread of 37
dew 56
diamonds 31
diatoms 125
digestion 179
dinoflagellates 143
dinosaurs 10
dive bombing 215
divers 144–145
dodo 130 , 245
dogs
    domesticated 201
    hunting 200
    wild 200
doldrums 13
dolphins 157, 165, 197
    brain 176–177
    pods 183
domestic animals 200–201
dormouse 187
doves 224
drought 49, 72, 83
ducks 223, 236
dugong 197

cone shells 143
continents 14–15
continental drift 14, 15, 102–103
continental slope 124
Copernicus, Nicolaus 45
coral reefs 116–117, 118–119
    destruction of 89, 153
cormorants 245
courtship 230–231
Cousteau, Jacques 157
crabs
    coconut 131
    ghost 111
cranes 242, 242, 243
currents (water) 107
cyclones, see hurricanes

dunes 36, 82
dust-devil 72
duststorms 72–73

E

eagles 214–215
Earth 6, 8–9, 10–11, 48–49, 102
    axis 53
    magnetic field 62
    rotation 12–13, 78
earthquakes 9, 20, 24–25
    categories 44
    plate tectonics 14, 22, 24, 103
    shock waves 26–27
East Pacific Rise 103
echidna 169
echinoderms 104
ecosystem 40–41
eels 135, 140–141
eggs 130
    incubation 235
    protecting 235
    size 234
egrets 229
elephant
    working 201
    young 170–171
El Niño 39, 74–75, 157
emperor penguin 133
emus 244
endangered species 202, 249
energy 24, 68, 96
epiplagic zone 104
equator 53
erosion 22, 23, 84–85, 108–109
Everest, Mount 9, 22
evolution 202
European marsh warbler 239
European robin 239
eyes 126, 173, 181, 214

F

falcons 215
families 236–237
famine 49
fault lines
feathers 228–229
    displays 228
    down feathers 208
    flight feathers 208
feet 173

hoofed mammals 179
   prosimians 12, 13
Fernandina 21
Fiennes, Sir Ranulph 38
fieldfare 241
fires 25, 38–39
fish 122
   of Antarctic 132
   of coral reefs 118–119
   deepsea 28, 29
   midwater 126
   shoals 123
   survival methods 83
fish farming 150–151
fisher 184
fishing 43, 107, 117, 119, 150, 152, 154, 159
fjords 34
flamingos 222, 223
flightless birds 244–245
floods 42, 74, 90, 80–81
   monsoon 49, 81
Florida, USA 91
flying lemur, see colugo
flying mammals 167
flying squirrel 167, 192
fog 50, 56, 57, 61
fogbow 61
fold mountains 22
footprints 84
foreshocks 26
forest 41, 120
fossa 184
fossil fuels 157
fossils 102, 146
foxes 170
frigate bird 220, 230
frogmouths 240
fruit bat 192
fulgurites 70
fulmars 247
fumaroles 17
Fundy, Bay of, Canada 106
fur 167

G
Gaia 41
Galápagos Islands 19, 21, 130
gannets 131, 219

geese 243
gems 31
Genders, Sidney 134
gentoo penguin 233
gerenuk 179
ghost bats 29
giant kelp 121
gibbon 175
glaciers 34–35, 156
global warming 42, 88–89, 93, 156, 157
GLORIA sonar device 124
gold 30
golden eagle 225
Golden Gate Bridge 57
goosanders 223
gorilla 169, 175
Gouldian finch 228
Gozo, Malta 109
Grand Canyon, Arizona 85
grasslands 40
gravity 7
grazers 179
Great Barrier Reef, Australia 116
greenhouse gases 89
Greenwich Mean Time (GMT) 94
grizzly bear
grooming 181, 183
guillemots 122, 235
Gulf Stream 52, 103, 154
Gulf War 93
gulls 221

H
habitats 207
hail 66–67
hands 173
harems 178
harmattan 73
Hawaii 16, 18, 23, 106, 109, 110
hawks 214, 215
heliostats 97
Heng, Chang 27
herbivores 167
herds 200
herons 112, 219, 230, 231
high pressure 51
Himalayas 22
hippopotamus 166
hoatzin 247
Homo sapiens 164
hoodoos 84

hoofed mammals 178–179
horns 179
horse 179
hot weather 82–83
humans 9, 82, 166, 168
hummingbirds 212, 213, 242
hurricanes 4, 18, 30–33, 52, 62, 78–79
   categories 98
   eye 79
   tracking 78
hydrothermal vents 125
hyenas 182

I
ice 11
   cloud crystals 55, 61, 64, 67, 70
icebergs 33
icebows 49
ice caps 33, 156
ice core 33
icefish 132
impala 179
Indian Ocean 89, 90
Indonesia 39, 86, 117
insect eaters 190–191
intelligence mammals 176–177
islands 20–21, 130–131

J
jackfish 123, 139
Japan 17, 21, 25, 27
jaws 165
jay 224
jellyfish 139, 142
jet-stream 13
Jupiter 7

K
kangaroo 166, 169, 198
kelp 120–121, 137
kingfishers 219
kiwis 245
kites 97
koala 199
Kobe, Japan 25, 27
Komodo dragon 130
Komodo Island, Indonesia 130

Kori bustard 246
krill 133, 152

L
language 176
Larsen Ice Shelf 89
lava 18–19, 21
lemur 172, 173
life span 202–203
light effects 55, 60–61, 62–63
lightning 70–71
   ball 70
   bolt 70
   cloud-to-cloud 71
   cloud-to-ground 70
   sheet 71
   upward discharges 70
limestone 28, 29, 31, 84
lion 168
lionfish 105, 143
llama 201
lobsters 134–135
loris 173
Lovelock, James 43
low pressure 51
lumpsucker 113
lungfish 83
lyrebird 229

M
macaque 171
magma 15, 16, 18
Maldives 90
mallee fowl 235
mammatus 68
manatee 197
mangrove forests 114
mangroves 114–115
manta ray 137
marble 31
Mariana Trench 31, 62
marine reserves 61
marmoset 61
marram grass 111
marsupials 169, 198–199
Mary Rose 146
Mars 7
mating 168–169
medicines 150
Mediterranean Sea 90
meerkats 183
memory 176
Mercalli scale 24
Mercury 7

mesopelagic zone 104
meteorites 10
meteorology 94–95
Mexico 93
mid-ocean ridges 103
   Atlantic 15
migration
   marine 134–135
milk 164, 168
Mississippi River 80
mist 56, 57
moles 187
mongoose 184–185
monotremes 168, 169
monsoon 49, 81
Moon 106
mountains
   formation 8–9, 22–23
   submarine 23, 124
   tallest 22
Mount Everest 9, 22
Mount St Helens 18, 86, 87
mud flats 114
mudslides 75, 80, 81, 87
mudskippers 115
mulgara 198
musk ox 182
mussels 104, 113
mythology 45, 161

N
Namib Desert 36
natterjack toad 111
navigation 242
Neptune 7
nests 212, 214
Netherlands 91
New York City, USA 96
Niagra Falls, Canada 85
nocturnal mammals vision 180
noise 239

O
oceans 52, 103, 104–105, 122–123, 132–133
   depths 124–125, 128–129
ocean floor 124, 128
oceanography 154–155
octopus 142, 143
oil 30, 153

orang-utan 175, 177
Orion nebula 7
osprey 215
ostrich 234, 244, 245
Otto, Nikolaus 156
ozone hole 93
ozone layer 88, 92

P
Pacific Ocean 102, 124
pack ice 133
paddies 49
Pahoehoe 18
Pangaea 45, 102
pangolin 191
Panthalassa 102
parasites 138
parrotfish 140
parrots 206
passerines 205
peacock 228
pearl farming 151
pelican 218
penguins 33, 133
    adaptation 245
    eggs and nests 235
peregrine falcon 215
piddocks 108
pigeons 224, 242
Pinatubo, Mount 87
placental mammals 169
plankton 30, 122, 136, 143
plants 136
plastic litter 159
polar bear 32, 167
poles 32–33, 52, 53
pollution 31, 92–93, 152
porcupinefish 141
pouncing 181
prairie dog 187
predators 180
primates 172–173
prosimians 172–173
puffins 158, 210, 221

Q
quetzal 228

R
ragworms 111
rain 58–59
rainbows 60–61
rainforest 40, 43
rats 176

rays 141
records 44, 67, 98, 160, 203, 249
Red Sea 103, 118
reindeer 32
remora 139
Remotely Operated Vehicles (ROVs) 145
reproduction 168–169, 207
rhinoceros 179
rice 49
Richter scale 24, 45
rift valleys 22
rivers 115
roadrunners 246
rock pools 113
rogue waves 107

S
Sahara 72, 73
salmon 151, 215
salt marshes 115
San Andreas fault 24, 26
Sargasso Sea, Bermuda 123, 135
sapsuckers 226
satellites 78, 94, 95, 154
satellite tags 155
Saturn 7
savannah 40, 155
scent 165, 173
scuba diving 144–145
seabirds 131, 220–221, 233
seagull 221
sea cows (dugongs) 120
sea cucumbers 104, 128, 129
seahorses 120
sea lavender 115
sea levels 90–91
sea lion 194, 195
seals 110, 120, 133, 153, 194
sea otters 121, 177
sea pens 128–129
sea slugs 139
sea snails 123
sea snakes 142
seasons 52–53
sea spiders, giant 132
sea urchins 104, 137
seaweed 150–151
    see also kelp
secretary bird 215

seismic waves 22, 26
seismograph 26
seismometer 24
sharks 119, 120, 122, 127, 136, 155
    basking 136
    blue 135
    bluntnose six-gill 129
    hammerhead 141
    lemon 120
    megamouth 127
    reef 119
    whale 122
shellfish 108, 150
shells 143
shelters 186–187
shipwrecks 146–147
shoals 123, 154
shoebill stork 219
shrews 167
shrikes 225
shrimps 126
skeleton 180, 209
skunk 185
smog 88
snow 64–65
snow goose 242
snowflakes 64
social groups 182–183
    cats 181
    dogs 200
    primates 175
solar power 96
Solar System 6–7
solar wind 62
songbirds 238–239
sperm whale 189
sponges 150
spoonbill 223
squid 126
squirrel 176
stalactites 28
stalagmites 28
staphylococci 43
starfish 104, 132–133
stilt 223
stoat 185
stonefish 143
storks
    migration 242
submersibles 145
storms 48, 68–69, 70–71, 76, 78–79
Sun 7, 11, 48, 106
    light effects 62–63
    solar corona 61
surfing 106–107
Surtsey Island, Iceland 15, 20
surveys 57

swans 236
swifts 212

T
tags, satellite 155
talons 214
tamandua 170
tarsier 173, 191
Tasmanian devil 199
tectonic plates 14, 22, 24, 103
temperate forest 41
temperature 12, 154, 156–157
tenrec 169
thunderstorms 70–71, 68–69
tidal power 157
tides 106
toads 111
tool-users 174, 176
tornadoes 76–77
trade winds 13
tremors 24, 25, 26
tripodfish 128
tuberculosis (TB) 43
tube worms 136
tuna 154
tundra 41
turtles 121, 130, 135, 139, 158–159
typhoons, see hurricanes

U
ultraviolet radiation 88
United Nations 93
Uranus 7

V
vapour trails 55
Venice, Italy 90
Venus 7
vertebrates 165
Victoria, Australia 108
volcanoes 9, 14, 15, 16–17, 18–19, 20–21, 86–87
    eruptions 16, 86, 87
    mountains 22, 23
    plate tectonics 14, 15
volcanology 19
vultures 206, 216–217, 225
    bill 217

digestion 217
eggs 217

W
wallaby 55
walrus 195
warm blooded 166
warm fronts 51
water 8–9, 48, 58
water buffalo 201
water vapour 50, 54, 55, 56, 57
waves 106, 107
weather 46–99
    see meteorology
weaver birds 232
Wegener, Alfred 14, 45
whales
    blue 104, 197
    grey 134
    humpback 152–153, 196
    killer
    migration 134
    sperm 105, 189
whaling 152
whirlpools 107
wildebeest 179
wind 97
    Beaufort scale 98, 161
    global 13
wind farm 97, 157
windmills 97
wings
    flightless birds 244–245
wingspan 209
wolf 200
wolverine 184
woodland birds
woodpeckers 226, 227, 233
wrens 41, 45

Y
young 179
    parental care 180

Z
zebra 178–179

ACKNOWLEDGEMENTS

Dorling Kindersley would like to thank the following people for their help with this book:

Andrew O'Brien for original digital artworks (Mammals and Oceans); Mount Washington Observatory for their picture of rime frost (Weather), Bedrock Studios Ltd, and Firelight Productions for computer graphics (Weather), Ian Wittmeyer for tornado chasing; The Sea Shepherd Organisation, California, USA, for supplying visual reference on Turtle Exclusion Devices (TEDs) (Ocean).

Additional photography and illustration by Max Alexander, Luciano Corbella, Mike Dunning, Frank Greenaway, Colin Keates, John Lepine, Colin Rose, Colin Salmon, James Stevenson, Matthew Ward, Richard Ward, and Francesca York (all originially published in DK Guides Savage Earth).

Dorling Kindersley would like to thank the following for their kind permission to reproduce their photographs: (Key: a-above; b-below/bottom; c-centre; f-far; l-left; r-right; t-top)

1 Corbis: Momatiuk - Eastcott. 2-3 Science Photo Library: John Mead. 4-5 Corbis: Momatiuk - Eastcott. 5 Corbis: Douglas Peebles (fcrb). 6 Bruce Coleman Ltd: Astrofoto (bl). 6-7 Science Photo Library: Mehau Kulyk. 7 Bruce Coleman Ltd: Astrofoto (cr). Science Photo Library: Celestial Image Co. (tc); NASA (br). 8 NASA: (ca, b); NSSDC / GSFC (br, cra, tc, tr). Natural History Museum, London: fcl. 10 Photolibrary: Andrea Ghisotti (br). Science Photo Library: Julian Baum (bl); Pekka Pariainen (tr). 10-11 Science Photo Library: Mark Garlick (c). 11 Corbis: Marc Muench (bc). Science Photo Library: JISAS (tr). 12 DK Images: NASA (cra); British Airways (br). Getty Images: Wayne Eastep (bl). 12-13 Science Photo Library: NASA. 13 The Bridgeman Art Library: (cr). Science Photo Library: NASA (br). 14 Science Photo Library: Martin Land (br). 15 Corbis: (c). Science Photo Library: Simon Fraser (bl); David Parker (t). 16 Corbis: Roger Ressmeyer (cl). Science Photo Library: NASA (br). 17 Corbis: Roger Ressmeyer (cr); Michael S. Yamashita (t). Robert Harding Picture Library: Tomlinson (bl). 18 Corbis: Roger Ressmeyer (cl). Science Photo Library: Bernhard Edmaier (b). 18-19 Science Photo Library: Bernhard Edmaier. 19 Camera Press: Kaku Kurita (cl). Photolibrary: David B. Fleetham (c). 20 Corbis: Lloyd Cluff (bc). FLPA: S Jonasson (cl). naturepl.com: Jurgen Freund (clb). 20-21 naturepl.com: Pete Oxford. 21 AFP: (br). 22-23 Corbis: Wild Country. 23 Chris Bonington Picture Library: Doug Scott (br). Hutchison Library: A. Eames (tr). Chris and Helen Pellant: (cl). 24 Science Photo Library: David Parker (t). 24-25 PA Photos: EPA European Press Agency. 25 Getty Images: Paul Chesley (tl). PA Photos: EPA European Press Agency (tr). 26 Corbis: Charles O'Rear (cl); Craig Lovell (r). DK Images: San Francisco Public Library (bl). 27 Corbis: Owen Franken (br). DK Images: Science Museum (bl, cl). Rex Features: Oshihara (t). 28 Corbis: David Muench (br). Robert Harding Picture Library: Nigel Gomm (cl). 28-29 Corbis: Annie Griffiths Belt. 29 akg-images: (bl). Corbis: Eric and David Hosking (tr). Rex Features: (br). 30 NHPA / Photoshot: Daniel Heuclin (tr); Trevor McDonald (bl). Still Pictures: Julio Etchart / Reportage (cr). 31 Corbis: Dave G. Houser (tr). Still Pictures: Daniel Dancer (b); Mark Edwards (tl). 32 Corbis: Dan Guravich (br); Charles Mauzy (cr). Science Photo Library: Simon Fraser (bl). 33 Bruce Coleman Ltd: Hans Reinhard (bl). Science Photo Library: Doug Allan (t); J. G. Paren (br). 34 Photolibrary: Colin Monteath (cl). Robert Harding Picture Library: Gavin Hellier (bc).

34-35 Corbis: Tom Bean. 35 Science Photo Library: Bernhard Edmaier (tl); Dr. Peter Moore (tr). 36 Corbis: Jeremy Horner (cl). 36-37 Bruce Coleman Ltd: Davis Hughes. 37 NHPA / Photoshot: Rod Planck (tl). Robert Harding Picture Library: Simon Harris (tr); E. Simanor (br). Science Photo Library: David Nunuk (c). 38 Ardea: Jean-Paul Ferrero (br). Science Photo Library: Jerry Mason (cl). 38-39 Getty Images: David R Frazier. 39 Corbis: Christian Simonpietri (br). Science Photo Library: NASA (bl). 40 Science Photo Library: William Ervin (bc); Dr. Morley Read (tr). Still Pictures: Roland Seitre (bl). 41 NHPA / Photoshot: Alberto Nardi (bl); R. Sorensen & J. Olsen (c). Science Photo Library: Simon Fraser (br). Still Pictures: Patrick Bertrand (tl). 42 Corbis: Galen Rowell (cl). Science Photo Library: Tom McHugh (tr). Still Pictures: G. Griffiths - Christian Aid (br). 43 DK Images: NASA (br). Science Photo Library: Dr. Karl Lounatmaa (bl); Dr. Morley Read (tl). Still Pictures: Mark Edwards (cr). 44-45 Science Photo Library: Sinclair Stammers. 46-47 Science Photo Library: NOAA. 47 Getty Images: Stone / Gary Holscher (fcrb). PA Photos: AP / Agencia Estado (crb). 48 Science Photo Library: Fred K Smith (bl). 48-49 Photolibrary: NASA. 49 Colorific!: Raghub / R Singh (tl). FLPA: Robin Chittenden (crb). Getty Images: Theo Allots (br). Still Pictures: Julio Etcharit (cra). 50 Getty Images: Kennan Harvey (l); Paul Kenward. 51 Photolibrary: Muzz Murray (tc); Alastair Shay (ca). Science Photo Library: ESA (bl). 52 Science Photo Library: Tom van Sant (cl). 52-53 Getty Images: John Chard (b). Still Pictures: Anne Piantanida (ca). 53 Photolibrary: Ian West (c); Denis Bringard (br). Still Pictures: Dennis Bringard (cr, crb); Luiz C Marigo (cb). 55 Science Photo Library: Magrath / Folsom (tr); George Post (br); Frank Zullo (cr). 56 Still Pictures: Carl R Sang II (tc). 56-57 Getty Images: E D Pritchard. 57 Photolibrary: John Brown (tr); Stan Osolinski (tl); Daniel Valla (cr). 58-59 Getty Images: Marc Muench. 59 Ecoscene: (br); Sally Morgan (c). SuperStock: (tr). 60-61 Science Photo Library: David Nunuk. 61 FLPA: C Carvalho (cla). Science Photo Library: David Parker (ca); Pekka Parviainen (bl); Jerry Schad (br). 62 Science Photo Library: NASA (cr); Jack Finch (l). 63 Photolibrary: David M Dennis (tr). Science Photo Library: Michael Giannechi (br); Pekka Parviainen (cr, l, t). 64 Getty Images: Gerben Oppermans (tr). Science Photo Library: W. Bacon (bl). 64-65 Getty Images. 65 Getty Images: Jake Evans (tl). Stock Shot: Tony Harrington (tr). 66 Gene E. Moore: (bl). Photolibrary: Warren Faidley (cb). 66-67 Science Photo Library: George Post. 67 Science Photo Library: NCAR (bl, br). 68 NASA: (bl). Photolibrary: Martyn Chillmaid (tr). 69 Science Photo Library: Keith Kent. 70 Johnny Autry: (tr). Fortean Picture Library: Werner Burger (br). Planet Earth Pictures: Steve Bloom (cl). Science Photo Library: Peter Menzel (bl). 71 Science Photo Library: Keith Kent. 72 Corbis: (bl). Panos Pictures: Dominic Harcourt-Webster (br). 72-73 NOAA: George E Marshall Album. 73 Photolibrary: Bob Campbell, Survival Anglia (br). 74 Associated Press AP: Agencia Estado (bl). NASA: (c). 74-75 OSF: Warren Faidley. 75 Colorific!: Alon Reininger / Contact (bl). 76 Ian Wittmeyer: (fcla, cla). 76-77 Getty Images: Stone / Alan R Moller. 77 Camera Press: Hoflinger (br). Photolibrary: Oxford Scientific (OSF) / Warren Faidley (cra). Ian Wittmeyer: (tr). 79 Corbis: Walter Rawlings / Robert Harding World Imagery (br). 80 Camera Press: L. Mayer / Liaison (tr); Noel Quidu (b). Science Photo Library: Earth Satellite Corporation (cl). 81 Camera Press: Carlos Angel (cr). Magnum Photos: Steve McCurry (l). 82 FLPA: Tom and Pam Gardner (cr). Magnum Photos: Steve McCurry (b). SuperStock: (tr). 83 FLPA: W Wisniewski. Photolibrary: Joan Root (tl). 84 Science

Photo Library: Simon Fraser (bl); Sinclair Stammers (cl). 84-85 Bruce Coleman Ltd: Jules Cowan. 85 Bruce Coleman Ltd: Derek Croucher (tl); Granville Harris (c). Corbis: David Muench (crb). 86-87 Science Photo Library: David Weintraub. 87 Camera Press: (cr). Rex Features: (tl). SuperStock: (crb). 88 Corbis: Stephanie Maze (bl). DK Images: Natural History Museum (c). 88-89 Science Photo Library: NASA. 89 Bruce Coleman Ltd: Atlantide (bl). Environmental Images: Steve Morgan (tr). NHPA / Photoshot: B. Jones & M. Shimlock (br). Science Photo Library: UK Meteorological Office (tl). 90 Science Photo Library: David Hardy (tc). Still Pictures: Adrian Arbib (bl). 90-91 Bruce Coleman Ltd. 91 Getty Images: Philippe Hays (tl). NHPA / Photoshot: David Woodfall (tr). 92 Getty Images: Oliver Strewe (bl). 92-93 Science Photo Library: ESA (b). Still Pictures: Julio Etchert. 93 Corbis: (br). TopFoto.co.uk: Permdhai Vesmaporn (tr). 94 Camera Press: Patrick Aventurier (clb). Colorific!: Rich Frishman/ Picture Group (cl); Michael Melford (bc). 94-95 NASA. 95 NASA: (br). 96-97 Science Photo Library: John Mead (t); Hank Morgan. 97 Bruce Coleman Ltd: Thomas Buchholz (tr). Getty Images: Nadia Mackensie (c). Still Pictures: John Kiefler (br). 98-99 Science Photo Library: Pekka Parviainen. 99 Getty Images: Johan Elzenga (br). 100-101 Corbis: Mark A. Johnson. 101 FLPA: Mark Jones / Minden Pictures (fcrb). Still Pictures: Kelvin Aitkin (crb). 102-103 Still Pictures: Fred Bavendam. 103 Science Photo Library: Dr. Ken Macdonald (tr). 104 naturepl.com: Georgette Douwma (cl). 104-105 Ardea: Francois Gohier. 105 Dr Frances Dipper: (clb). NHPA / Photoshot: Trevor Macdonald (bl). Science Photo Library: Matthew Oldfield (crb). 106 FLPA: Skylight (fclb, clb). 106-107 FLPA: Bob Barbour / Minden Pictures. 107 Corbis: Bettmann / PH3 James Collins (cr). FLPA: Silvestris Fotoservice (tc). naturepl.com: Jurgen Freund (tr). Still Pictures: Dahlquist-UNEP (br). 108 Corbis: Tony Arruza (clb). Photoshot / Woodfall Wild Images: David Woodfall (bl). Science Photo Library: Graham Ewens (cla). 108-109 Photoshot / Woodfall Wild Images: Ted Mead. 109 Chris Gomersall Photography. Corbis: Robert Pickett (tr); Lawson Wood (crb). 112 naturepl.com: Dan Burton (clb). Sue Scott: (cla). 112-113 Photoshot / Woodfall Wild Images: David Woodfall. 113 Dr Frances Dipper: (tc). naturepl.com: Sue Daly (br); Jurgen Freund (cr). 114 naturepl.com: Jurgen Freund (br); Anup Shah (bl). NHPA / Photoshot: Alan Williams (cla). 114-115 naturepl.com: Jurgen Freund. 115 Chris Gomersall Photography. Corbis: NASA (cr). 116 naturepl.com: Florian Graner (bl). Science Photo Library: Douglas Faulkner (c). 116-117 NHPA / Photoshot: B Jones & M Shimlock (br). 117 SeaPics.com: Doug Perrine (cr). 118 naturepl.com: Jeff Rotman (tr). Science Photo Library: Andrew J Martinez (bl). 118-119 Science Photo Library: Nancy Sefton. 119 Dr. Frances Dipper: (tr, cra). NHPA / Photoshot: Agence Nature (bc). Still Pictures: Kelvin Aitken (bl). 122 Corbis: Amos Nachoum (bc). Photolibrary: Doug Allan (cl). 122-123 Science Photo Library: Matthew Oldfield. 123 naturepl.com: David Shale (tr). SeaPics.com: Dour Perrine (bl). 124 Science Photo Library: Institute of Oceanographic Sciences / NERC (tr). 125 Corbis: Ralph White (tl). Photolibrary: Scripps Inst. Oceanography / Kenneth L. Smith, Jr. (cl). Science Photo Library: Juergen Berger (cr); Andrew Syred (crb). 126 naturepl.com: DavidShale (clb); David Shale (c); Sinclair Stammers (br). SeaPics.com: Rudie Kuiter (cl). 127 SeaPics.com: Bruce Rasner. 128 NHPA / Photoshot: Norbert Wu (bl). Visuals Unlimited, Inc.: David Wrobel (bl). 128-129 Visuals Unlimited, Inc.: David Wrobel. 129 Corbis: Ralph White (cr). SeaPics.com: Saul Gonor (tr). Visuals Unlimited, Inc.: David Wrobel (br). 130 Ardea: Adrian Warren (clb). Dr. Frances Dipper: (cra). naturepl.com: Bristol City Museum (cla); Jurgen Freund (ca); Tom Vezo (ca). 130-131 Corbis: Paul A Souders. 131 naturepl.com: Nigel Bean (tc); Pete Oxford (tr).

Photoshot / Woodfall Wild Images: Nigel Bean (tl). **132 Corbis:** Rick Price (cl, clb). **132-133 NHPA / Photoshot:** Norbert Wu (tc). **133 DK Images:** Natural History Museum (crb). **naturepl.com:** Doug Allan (cr). **NHPA / Photoshot:** Norbert Wu (cra). **Photoshot / Woodfall Wild Images:** Inigo Everson (br). **134 Ardea:** Francois Gohier (c). **134-135 SeaPics.com:** Doug Perrine. **135 naturepl.com:** Tim Martin (cra, cla). **Science Photo Library:** Fred McConnaughey (ca). **136 naturepl.com:** Dan Burton (tr). **Science Photo Library:** Andrew Syred (bl). **136-137 Corbis:** Ralph White (b). **David Doubilet. 140 naturepl.com:** Constantinos Petrinos (tr). **140-141 naturepl.com:** Georgette Douwma. **141 FLPA:** M Jones / Minden Pictures (cr). **Getty Images:** Steven Hunt (tr). **naturepl.com:** Georgette Douwma (crb); Peter Scoones (cra). **144-145 naturepl.com:** Georgette Douwma. **145 Jules Undersea Lodge:** (br). **OceanWorks International Corporation:** (tc). **Science Photo Library:** Richard Folwell (c). **SeaPics.com:** Doug Perrine (cra). **146 Dr Frances Dipper:** (bl). **DK Images:** British Museum (bc); Mary Rose Trust (c); National Maritime Museum (cl). **The Mary Rose Trust:** (cla). **naturepl.com:** Michael Pitts (cra). **Phil Rosenberg:** (tr). **147 NHPA / Photoshot:** B Jones & M Shimlock. **148-149 Imagestate:** Pictor. **149 Corbis:** Bettmann (tc, cr). **Getty Images:** DigitalGlobe (fcrb, fbr). **150 FLPA:** Winifried Wisniewski (cla). **Still Pictures:** Norbert Wu (cb). **150-151 NHPA / Photoshot:** B Jones & M Shimlock. **151 Ecoscene:** Christine Osborne (bl). **NHPA / Photoshot:** Laurie Campbell (cb). **152 SeaPics.com:** Steven Kazlowski (bc). **152-153 Getty Images:** Duncan Murrell. **153 Bruce Coleman Ltd:** Pacific Stock (bc). **Coral Planet Photography:** Zafer Kizilkaya (ca). **Science Photo Library:** B & C Alexander (tc); Simon Fraser (br). **154 Dr. Mike Musyl.** (br). **Science Photo Library:** European Space Agency / NOAA (c). **SeaPics.com:** Mako Hirose (bl). **154-155 Science Photo Library:** Douglas Faulkner; Dr. Mike Musyl (bc). **155 Dr. Mike Musyl.** (bl). **156-157 Science Photo Library:** Bernhard Edmater. **157 Science Photo Library:** Martin Bond (br); NASA (ca). **158 Chris Gomersall Photography:** (bl). **Photolibrary:** (ca). **Still Pictures:** Thomas Raupach (bc). **158-159 SeaPics.com:** Doug Perrine. **159 NHPA / Photoshot:** Norbert Wu (clb). **160-161 SeaPics.com:** Richard Herrmann. **162-163 Alamy Images:** Juniors Bildarchiv / F304. **163 Corbis:** Frans Lanting (fcrb); Jenny E. Ross (crb). **164 Corbis:** Ariel Skelley (cl). **NHPA / Photoshot:** Martin Harvey (tr). **165 Alamy Images:** Steve Bloom Images (ca). **Corbis:** Joe McDonald (tr). **NHPA / Photoshot:** (tc); James Warwick (cra). **Photolibrary:** Mike Powles (tl). **166 Alamy Images:** Royal Geographical Society / Martha Holmes (c). **167 Alamy Images:** ImageState / Mike Hill (b); Malie Rich-Griffith (c). **Ardea:** Jean-Paul Ferrero (cr); Pat Morris (tr). **FLPA:** S. Maslowski (tl). **NHPA / Photoshot:** Daniel Heuclin (cr). **168 Ardea:** Chris Harvey (c). **Getty Images:** National Geographic / Skip Brown (tr). **169 FLPA:** Minden Pictures / Mitsuaki Iwago (br); Eddie Schuiling (ca). **Photolibrary:** Kathie Atkinson (cr). **170 Getty Images:** Taxi (r). **Photolibrary:** Alan Root (bl). **171 FLPA:** Minden / M. Iwago (br); Mark Newman (tr). **Photolibrary:** Clive Bromhall (cr). **172 naturepl.com:** John Downer Productions (c). **Photolibrary:** David Haring (tr). **173 Corbis:** Kevin Schafer (br); Clem Haagner / Gallo Images (c). **SuperStock:** Mirko Stelzner (tr). **174 Alamy Images:** Steve Bloom Images (bl). **Corbis:** Renee Lynn (br). **Getty Images:** Tim Davis (tl); Manaj Shah (tr, b). **175 Alamy Images:** D. Robert Franz / ImageState (br). **naturepl.com:** Bruce Davidson (c); Anup Shah (bl). **176 Getty Images:** G.K. & Vikki Hart (b). **National Geographic Stock:** Chris Johns (tl). **naturepl.com:** Jeff Rotman (r). **177 FLPA:** Minden Pictures / Frans Lanting (br). **naturepl.com:** Anup Shah (cr). **SuperStock:** (tr). **178 Alamy Images:** Steve Bloom Images (c). **Getty Images:** Mitch Reardon (tr). **179 Alamy Images:** Pictures Colour Library (br). **Corbis:** Yann Arthus-Bertrand (tl, tc, tr). **Photolibrary:** (cr). **180 Getty Images:** Anup Shah (bl); National Geographic / Beverly Joubert (br); Art Wolfe (tr). **181 Getty Images:** Daniel J. Cox (tr); Kevin Schafer (c). **182 Alamy Images:** Bryan & Cherry Alexander Photography (tr). **NHPA / Photoshot:** Nigel J Dennis (b). **183 Photolibrary:** Patti Murray / AA (tr). **SeaPics.com:** Doug Perrine (tl). **184 Ardea:** Pascal Goetgheluck (b). **Corbis:** W. Perry Conway (l); D. Robert & Lorri Franz (tr). **185 Corbis:** Tom Brakefield (br). **FLPA:** Frans Lanting (tr). **naturepl.com:** Brian Lightfoot (tc). **186 Bruce Coleman Ltd:** Johnny Johnson (bl). **Corbis:** Rose Hartman (c). **187 Ardea:** Ian Beames (tl). **Getty Images:** National Geographic / Bates Littlehales (cr). **NHPA / Photoshot:** Kevin Schafer (tr); Manfred Danegger (br). **188 Corbis:** Paul A. Souders (tr). **Getty Images:** Joseph Van Os (c). **189 NHPA / Photoshot:** Anthony Bannister (bl); Steve Robinson. **Photolibrary:** David Cayless (c); Herbert Schwind / OKAPIA (bc). **SeaPics.com:** (tc). **190 Corbis:** Tom Brakefield (c). **191 Ardea:** Nick Gordon (cr); Clem Haagner (tl). **FLPA:** Minden Pictures / Frans lanting (br). **naturepl.com:** John Downer (tr); Mark Payne-Gill (cl). **192 Bruce Coleman Ltd:** Kim Taylor (tl). **Getty Images:** Thea Allats (r). **Photolibrary:** Waina Cheng (bl). **193 naturepl.com:** Dietmar Nill (tr). **Photolibrary:** (cl). **194 Bruce Coleman Ltd:** Jim Watt (bl). **Corbis:** T. Allofs (r); H. Heintges (br). **195 Bruce Coleman Ltd:** Johnny Johnson (br). **naturepl.com:** Wendy Darke (tr). **196 Ardea:** Francois Gohier (c). **SeaPics.com:** Phillip Colla (tr). **197 Alamy Images:** Steve Bloom Images (cl). **Ardea:** D. Parer & E. Parer-Cook (tr). **Bruce Coleman Ltd:** Rinie Van Meurs (br). **NHPA / Photoshot:** David & Irene Myers (cr). **198 Alamy Images:** Jan Tove Johansson / ImageState (r). **FLPA:** Silvestris fotoservice (cl). **Photolibrary:** Kathie Atkinson (bl). **199 Ardea:** M. W. Gillam (tl). **Bruce Coleman Ltd:** (bl). **Corbis:** Martin Harvey / Gallo Images (bc). **Getty Images:** Daniel J. Cox (tr). **Photolibrary:** Steve Turner (br). **200 Alamy Images:** Bryan & Cherry Alexander Photography (c). **Photolibrary:** Mike Price / SAL (bl). **201 Alamy Images:** Worldwide Picture Library (c). **Ardea:** Masahiro Iijina (br); Wolshead / Ben Osborne (tr). **204-205 Corbis:** Danny Lehman. **205 Photolibrary:** Daniel Cox (crb). **206 Science Photo Library:** Jim Amos (l). **206-207 Ardea:** Brian Bevan. **207 Alamy Images:** Steve Bloom Images (ca). **Ardea:** Jack A. Bailey (cra); Roberto Bunge (tc); John Daniels (br). **Ardea:** Eric Dragesco (cra); Ingrid van den Berg (tr); Andrey Zvoznikov (tl). **FLPA:** Frans Lanting / Minden Pictures (ca). **NHPA / Photoshot:** Jean-Louis Le Moigne (bl). **208 Alamy Images:** Dennis Kunkel / Phototake Inc (c). **208-209 Ardea:** Brian Bevan. **209 Ardea:** Francois Gohier (br); P. Green (bl); M. Watson (ca). **NHPA / Photoshot:** Steve Dalton (t). **210 Alamy Images:** Jan Baks (t). **Ardea:** E. Mickleburgh (cl). **210-211 Corbis:** Krahmer. **211 Alamy Images:** Christopher Gomersall (c). **Ardea:** John Daniels (br); R. T. Smith (tl). **NHPA / Photoshot:** Manfred Danegger (cla); Alan Williams (ca). **212 naturepl.com:** Jeff Foott (br). **NHPA / Photoshot:** Stephen Calton (bl); Kevin Schafer (tr); Eric Soder (tl). **212-213 Corbis:** Scott Tysick. **213 Ardea:** J.S. Dunning (bl). **Photolibrary:** Robert Tyrrell (t). **214 Ardea:** John Cancalosi (cla). **Getty Images:** Taxi / Benelux Press (bl). **214-215 naturepl.com:** Klaus Nigge. **215 Ardea:** John Daniels (br). **Corbis:** D. Robert & Lorri Franz (fcr); Kennan Ward (fbr). **216 FLPA:** David Hoskings (tl). **NHPA / Photoshot:** Nigel J. Dennis (tr). **216-217 Photolibrary. 217 Corbis:** Joe Macdonald (tr). **FLPA:** Mark Newman (br); R. Tidman (tl). **naturepl.com:** Angelo Gandolfi (cb); David Tipling (c). **218 FLPA:** Minden Pictures. **NHPA / Photoshot:** Andy Rouse (bl). **219 FLPA:** Neil Bowman (tr); Minden Pictures (cr); Silvestris (cl). **NHPA / Photoshot:** Bill Coster (bl, clb, crb). **Photolibrary:** Miriam Austerman (br). **220 Corbis:** Kevin Schafer (c). **naturepl.com:** Barrie Britton (tl). **Photolibrary:** William Gray (bl). **220-221 Alamy Images:** Sami Sarkis. **221 Corbis:** Peter Johnson (tr); Joe Macdonald (cra); D. Robert & Lorri Franz (cla). **FLPA:** David Hoskings (tl). **naturepl.com:** Pete Oxford (br). **222 naturepl.com:** Thomas D. Mangelsen (t). **222-223 Corbis:** Greg Stott. **223 Alamy Images:** John Pickles (tl). **Getty Images:** John Biustina (c). **naturepl.com:** Tony Heald (tr); Tom Vezo (cr). **Photolibrary:** Richard & Julia Kemp / SAL (br). **224 Ardea:** M. Watson (br). **naturepl.com:** Bernard Castelein (tl); Bengt Lundberg (bl). **NHPA / Photoshot:** Roger Tidman (c). **224-225 naturepl.com:** Dave Watts. **225 naturepl.com:** Hanne & Jens Eriksen (bl). **NHPA / Photoshot:** G.I. Bernard (br); Laurie Campbell (tl). **226 Ardea:** John Can calosi (cr). **FLPA:** Neil Bowman (cl). **naturepl.com:** George McCarthy (tl); Mike Wilkes (bl). **226-227 Getty Images:** Gail Shumway. **227 FLPA:** Gerard Laci (br). **naturepl.com:** Jim Clare (tr). **228 Alamy Images:** Mike Lane (br). **Ardea:** J.B & S Bottomley (cr). **Bruce Coleman Ltd:** Jorg & Petra Wegner (cl). **Corbis:** Rauschenbach (bl). **naturepl.com:** Neil Lukas (tl); Ashok Jain (cra). **NHPA / Photoshot:** Haroldo Palo Jr (bc). **228-229 Corbis:** T. Allofs. **229 Ardea:** J. Cancalosi (cr); Kenneth W. Fink (br). **NHPA / Photoshot:** Dave Watts (tr). **230 Ardea:** D. Parer & E.Parer-Cook (bl). **Bruce Coleman Inc:** Norman Tomalin (c). **naturepl.com:** Staffan Widstrand (tl). **230-231 naturepl.com:** Tom Vezo. **231 Bruce Coleman Ltd:** Tero Niemi (c). **naturepl.com:** Hanne & Jens Eriksen (br); Phil Savoie (tr). **232 Ardea:** (bl). **DK Images:** Natural History Museum (tl). **232-233 Heather Angel / Natural Visions. 233 Ardea:** Jean-Paul Ferrero (tl); Chris Harvey (cr). **naturepl.com:** John Cancalosi (cl); Andrew Cooper (c); William Osborn (tr); Pete Oxford (br). **234 DK Images:** Natural History Museum (fclb, clb, bc, br, crb). **FLPA:** Tui De Roy / Minden Pictures (crb); Frans Lanting / Minden Pictures (bl). **235 Alamy Images:** Steve Bloom Images (cl); Hans Beste (cr). **Ardea:** Hans & Judy Beste (c); B.L. Sage (tr). **Corbis:** Steve Kaufman (tl). **DK Images:** Natural History Museum (cra); Jerry Young (br). **236 Auscape:** (clb). **Corbis:** H. Reinhard (bl). **FLPA:** David Hoskings (br); P. Perry (t). **237 FLPA:** A R Hamblin (cl). **Getty Images:** Benelux Press. **238 Ardea:** John De Meester (c). **Photolibrary:** Roland Mayr. **239 Alamy Images:** Mike Lane (c). **Ardea:** Chris Knights (bl). **Corbis:** Tim Fitzharris (br). **naturepl.com:** Nick Gordon (tl). **NHPA / Photoshot:** Stephen Dalton (tr). **Photolibrary:** Colin Milkins (cl). **240 Ardea:** Chris Knights (c). **FLPA:** William S. Clark (bl); FotoNatura Stock (t). **240-241 NHPA / Photoshot:** eric Soder. **241 Bruce Coleman Ltd:** Christer Fredriksson (tr). **FLPA:** Richard Brooks (cr). **naturepl.com:** David Kjaer (cl); Brian Lightfoot (br). **NHPA / Photoshot:** Manfred Danegger (tl). **242 FLPA:** S & D & K Maslowski (br). **242-243 Getty Images:** John Warden. **243 Corbis:** W. Wisniewski (bl). **FLPA:** D Kinzler (br). **OSF:** Peter Hawkey / SAL (tr). **244 Natural Visions:** (tr). **244-245 naturepl.com:** Tony Heald. **245 FLPA:** Tui De Roy / Minden Pictures (tr). **Photolibrary:** Robin Bush (cr); Daniel Cox (br). **246 Ardea:** John Cancelossi (l). **National Geographic Stock:** Beverly Joubert. **247 Ardea:** Kenneth W. Fink (cra). **Corbis:** Greg Stott (bc). **FLPA:** F De Noover / Foto Natura Stock (tr). **Getty Images:** Andy Caulfield (tl). **naturepl.com:** John Downer (cl). **Photolibrary:** Alan Root / SAL (tc). **248-249 Getty Images:** Joseph Van Os.

Jacket images: *Front:* **Corbis:** Kevin Schafer tl; Bill Varie clb. **Getty Images:** Stone / Paul Chesley fcrb; Taxi / Paul & Lindamarie Ambrose ftl; Visuals Unlimited / Joe McDonald br. **Thomas Marent:** fcra. **Masterfile:** Scott Tysick fclb. **naturepl.com:** Bernard Castelein tr; Pete Oxford fcla. **Science Photo Library:** David A. Hardy, Futures: 5 Years In Space (background). *Back:* **Alamy Images:** Blickwinkel / Frischknecht tr. **Corbis:** Theo Allofs tc; Gary Bell clb; Frans Lanting fcla; Micha Pawlitzki cb. **DK Images:** Jamie Marshall (background). **naturepl.com:** Aflo tl; Georgette Douwma br; Tom Vezo fcra. *Spine:* **Corbis:** Frans Lanting b. **Science Photo Library:** David A. Hardy, Futures: 5 Years In Space t (background).

All other images © Dorling Kindersley
For further information see: **www.dkimages.com**

Come on an eye-opening **journey** to explore the incredible **natural world**.

Along the way, meet some of **Earth's** fascinating **mammals** and **birds**, experience the **planet's** most extreme **weather**, explore its deep **oceans**, and witness the extraordinary power of **volcanoes**.

Amazing action photographs capture the drama and huge variety of life on our Earth, from the familiar to the bizarre.

Content previously published in *DK Guides*: *Birds, Mammal, Oceans, Savage Earth,* and *Weather.*

DK

Discover more at
www.dk.com

£12.99

ISBN 978-1-40534-909-3
9 781405 349093